A Research Agenda for Lived Experience and Disability Policy

Elgar Research Agendas outline the future of research in a given area. Leading scholars are given the space to explore their subject in provocative ways, and map out the potential directions of travel. They are relevant but also visionary.

Forward-looking and innovative, Elgar Research Agendas are an essential resource for PhD students, scholars and anybody who wants to be at the forefront of research.

For a full list of Edward Elgar published titles, including the titles in this series, visit our website at www.e-elgar.com.

A Research Agenda for Lived Experience and Disability Policy

Edited by

JENNIFER SMITH-MERRY

Professor of Health and Social Policy, Australian Research Council Industry Laureate Fellow, Centre for Disability Research and Policy, The University of Sydney, Australia

DAMIAN MELLIFONT

Lecturer, Centre for Disability Research and Policy, The University of Sydney, Australia

Elgar Research Agendas

Edward Elgar
PUBLISHING

Cheltenham, UK · Northampton, MA, USA

Published by

Edward Elgar Publishing Limited
The Lypiatts
15 Lansdown Road
Cheltenham
Glos GL50 2JA
UK

Edward Elgar Publishing, Inc.
William Pratt House
9 Dewey Court
Northampton
Massachusetts 01060
USA

Authorised representative in the EU for GPSR queries only: Easy Access System Europe – Mustamäe tee 50, 10621 Tallinn, Estonia, gpsr.requests@easproject.com

A catalogue record for this book is available from the British Library

Library of Congress Control Number: 2026932102

This book is available electronically in the Elgaronline
Sociology, Social Policy and Education subject collection
https://doi.org/10.4337/9781035332403

MIX
Paper | Supporting responsible forestry
FSC® C013604

ISBN 978 1 0353 3239 7 (cased)
ISBN 978 1 0353 3240 3 (eBook)
ISBN 978 1 0494 0354 0 (ePub)
Printed and bound by CPI Group (UK) Ltd, Croydon, CR0 4YY

I dedicate this work to Professor Richard Freeman who has been a mentor to me and many scholars. He gave me the space early in my career to think critically about the ways that different types of knowledge give rise to different policy outcomes.
Jennifer Smith-Merry

I dedicate this work to the memory of Dr Ray Cash who provided me with many years of kind and compassionate psychiatric care.
Damian Mellifont

Contents

List of contributors

Zia Ullah Akhunzada has recently completed his PhD in Social Welfare from The Chinese University of Hong Kong. Prior to commencing his PhD, he worked as a social work lecturer at the Kohat University of Science and Technology, Pakistan.

Matilda Alexander is a leader and human rights lawyer with over 20 years of experience including at Queensland Advocacy for Inclusion, Prisoners' Legal Service and LGBTI Legal Service. She has won multiple awards for her work with disadvantaged communities and holds an enduring passion for justice and human rights. She taught prison law at Griffith University and has previously worked at the Queensland Human Rights Commission and Legal Aid Queensland. She is currently CEO of Queensland Advocacy for Inclusion and Patron of the LGBTI Legal Service. She has been selected three times as a delegate to the United Nations Conference of State Parties to the Convention on the Rights of Persons with Disabilities in New York and is appointed to the Independent Ministerial Advisory Council, Legal Aid Queensland Board, Queensland Disability Advisory Council, LGBTIQ+ Roundtable and the National Strategy Advisory Group.

Farman Ali has recently completed his PhD in Social Welfare from The Chinese University of Hong Kong. Prior to commencing his PhD, he worked as an Assistant Professor at the University of Malakand, Pakistan.

Galuh Fitri Amalia Susilo is a researcher and policy analyst specialising in inclusive policy, government relations and social justice. She is currently pursuing a Master of Public Policy with a specialisation in political economy at the University of Sydney, for which she has been awarded a prestigious, fully-funded, LPDP Scholarship from Indonesia's Ministry of Finance. Her research focuses on gender equality and governance frameworks that promote equitable outcomes. Amalia's latest research explores inclusive economic policy in Indonesia, with a focus on microfinance and its impact on the empowerment of marginalised communities, highlighting the role of grassroots participation in shaping inclusive policies. Her previous work includes policy research on multi-level governance, sister city cooperation and environmental justice. She has collaborated with government agencies and international organisations to support inclusive development initiatives. She is committed to advancing research that informs inclusive policy making and strengthens participatory governance, ensuring that marginalised voices remain central to policy discourse.

Muhammad Karim Amrullah is a doctoral student of law at the Faculty of Law of Universitas Gadjah Mada, funded by Indonesia's Ministry of Finance. He graduated with his law bachelor's degree in 2016 and law master's degree in 2018. During his time as a student he was Secretary (2013–2014) and Chairman (2015) of the Student Activity Unit of Different Ability Care. Since 2022 Karim has been a civil servant lecturer (assistant professor) in the Civics and Law Education Department, Faculty of Social Science, Law and Politics at Yogyakarta State University. He is also a Member of the Faculty Representative for the Disability Center in the university where he works. As well as lecturing, Karim is a Coordinator of the Advocacy and Consultation Division at the Difapedia Foundation and Head of the Education Department at Rumah Disabilitas. Karim was born with syndactyly hand and scoliosis, making him passionate about disability inclusion.

Jodie Bailie is a Senior Research Fellow based in a rural area, holding dual appointments with The University of Sydney's University Centre for Rural Health and the Centre for Disability Research and Policy. Her research is driven by a strong commitment to health equity, with a focus on strengthening the quality of health care for people with disability, Aboriginal and Torres Strait Islander communities and rural populations.

Alix Beckett is currently pursuing a Graduate Diploma of Indigenous Health Promotion at The University of Sydney, and is a proud Wiradjuri woman from central New South Wales and a CDRP affiliate. She is passionately dedicated to research development for Indigenous individuals and communities. With lived experience as a person with single-sided deafness (SSD), her work surrounds the support for Indigenous voices and perspectives within disability research, ensuring that Indigenous people with disabilities are recognised. She is an advocate for culturally informed approaches, striving to create equitable support systems for Indigenous communities in metro and rural/remote Australia.

Jemma Chao is a Wiradjuri woman from Dubbo Western New South Wales, Australia, with a rich cultural heritage that includes family roots in Europe. As an experienced Strategic Planner, Event and Project Management, and Research Assistant, she brings a wealth of expertise to her work. Jemma is particularly skilled in collaborating with Aboriginal communities, focusing on initiatives related to health, disability, workforce and education. In her previous roles, Jemma has played a crucial part in advancing health research that supports the workforce and education of Aboriginal and Torres Strait Islander communities. Her commitment to fostering positive outcomes through strategic planning and community engagement underscores her dedication to improving services and initiatives for her people.

Elroy Dearn completed their PhD in 2022 after 20 years of systemic advocacy in government and non-government organisations. Their PhD explored the experience of choice and control for people with psychosocial disabilities living in institutions over the first 18 months of the National Disability Insurance Scheme. Elroy has held senior policy and research positions in local and state government and at the Victorian Office of the Public Advocate. Focal areas for their research and advocacy include homelessness, institutionalisation, psychosocial disability, and human rights. Elroy is working as a research fellow at RMIT University and Summer Foundation on research relating to pathways out of private supported boarding houses and the experience of young people living in residential aged care.

Gisselle Gallego is a Senior Lecturer at the School of Medicine at the University of Notre Dame Australia and a Senior Research Officer at the Centre for Disability Studies. She is a clinician, medical educator, inclusive researcher and disability advocate. She advocates for systemic changes in health care education and practice. Her research and teaching focus on the experiences of people from culturally and linguistically diverse backgrounds and people with disability, as well as the intersection of these.

John Gilroy is a Yuin man from the NSW South Coast and is a Professor of Indigenous Health and Disability, specialising primarily in disability studies. John has worked in disability and ageing research and community development with Aboriginal communities, government and non-government stakeholders for most of his life. He was the first person to create Indigenous research methodologies in disability research. John is passionate about Aboriginal owned and driven research as means to influence policy. John has led many research projects in urban and rural/remote Aboriginal and Torres Strait Islander communities.

Jennifer Kent is an Associate Professor in Urbanism at the University of Sydney School of Architecture, Design and Planning. Jennifer's research interests are at the intersections between urban planning, transport and human health. She specialises in combining quantitative and qualitative data with understandings from policy science to explore day-to-day mobility, with an explicit mandate to record and theorise shifts away from private car use towards more sustainable transport modes in car-oriented cities. Issues examined to date include parenting and private car use, companion animals and transport, the links between cities and loneliness, and the interpretation of health evidence into planning and transport policy.

Mandy Lau is a social worker holding a PhD in Social Welfare, with a specialisation in health care and disability research. Mandy effectively synthesizes research evidence into clinical practices, underscoring the importance of quality of life for individuals with disabilities.

Miguel Loyola is a Lecturer in the Business School at the University of Western Australia. With a rich international background, his expertise lies in bridging the gap between behavioural sciences, transport policy, and sustainability. Originally from Ecuador, Miguel began his academic journey in engineering, expanding his global perspective through studies in transport planning in Israel and research that culminated in a PhD in Australia, where he focused on the implementation of sustainable transport policies. His professional experience spans both industry and government sectors, where he has led projects on road safety, electric vehicles, active transport, disabled transport, and the socio-economic impacts on disadvantaged groups. Miguel is dedicated to creating more inclusive and sustainable transport systems that address the needs of diverse communities worldwide.

Rachelle A. Martin is a Senior Lecturer at the University of Otago in New Zealand where she undertakes disability and rehabilitation research and teaches and supervises people studying rehabilitation at a post-graduate level. With over 20 years of clinical experience working as a neurorehabilitation physiotherapist, Rachelle is passionate about ensuring that people who experience disability or live with the enduring consequences of health conditions can lead the lives they aspire to. She collaborates with others within participatory research and co-design projects, listening with curiosity to the ways that people want to engage with health services and meaningfully participate in the activities and life roles that matter most to them.

Damian Mellifont is a neurodivergent researcher who leads and contributes to studies that advance the economic and social inclusion of people with disability. Damian is a Postdoctoral Fellow and Lecturer at the University of Sydney and member of the Centre for Disability Research and Policy (CDRP) Leadership Group, having been an active member of the centre over the last 10 years, with extensive prior experience in government policy. Damian strongly advocates for the disability inclusion mantra of 'Nothing About Us Without Us' to be consistently applied to research about disability. Damian's lived experience-led and co-designed studies cover a range of topics including supporting the recruitment, retainment and advancement of employees with disability, redressing ableism the workplace and beyond, encouraging disability inclusive disaster risk reduction, and supporting a greater representation of people with disability in leadership roles. Damian is also Editor of the Disability Studies Collection at Lived Places Publishing.

Kevin P. Morgan, born Ronald Robert Joynson/Proulx, is a 1960s Scoop survivor who has been legally blind since birth and was adopted by an Irish family on the West Coast of Canada. He is of Oji-Cree and French descent, with his ancestral roots found in the Red River in Manitoba and Chippewa of North Dakota. For over 25 years, Kevin has worked for one of the largest federal government organisations in Canada. He has an MA in Leadership Studies with senior management roles and is a special advisor in Indigenous cultural knowledge, leadership, mentoring and dialogue/engagement within the public service.

Lexi Nahwegiizhic, whose traditional name is Giizhigokwe, Little Sky Woman, is a two-spirit, Ojibwe woman living with several neurodiverse medical conditions, including ADHD and dyslexia. She comes from Sheguiandah First Nation in Ontario. She is an inspirational leader and keynote speaker frequently called upon for her wisdom in Indigenous teachings and mental health. She strives to empower people to become prouder, and more resilient. Her background is in neuroscience, where she uses her gift for teaching and to serve as a translator between science and business realities.

Dinesh Palipana is a doctor, lawyer and researcher in spinal cord injury. He works in the emergency department at the Gold Coast University Hospital. He is a Senior

Lecturer at Griffith University and Assistant Professor at Bond University, and was a senior advisor to the Disability Royal Commission. Dinesh has a spinal cord injury with quadriplegia and was the 2021 Queensland Australian of the Year. His biography, *Stronger*, explores the journey of a person with an acquired disability.

Claire Quilliam is a Senior Research Fellow with the Department of Rural Health, The University of Melbourne, based in Shepparton, Australia. Claire is autistic. Claire holds a PhD in Social Work and Social Policy. Her research focuses on ways to improve access to good quality health and human services for rural people, especially for rural disabled people. Claire's current area of work focuses on developing sustainable and place-based rural health and human service workforce approaches.

Téa Rundback is a proud neurodivergent, disabled woman who is a disability activist, business owner, consultant, speaker, emcee and academic writer. She holds a Bachelor of Commerce with Distinction, majoring in Human Resource Management, and is a trained psychosocial recovery coach. Her work focuses on disability employment, invisible disabilities and neurodivergence, integrating lived experience with research and organisational practice to advance inclusive systems and workplaces. Since writing this chapter in 2024, she attained her goal of securing employment in January 2026 as Disability & Inclusion Partner at Australia's leading not-for-profit employment services provider.

Sam Sam is an Assistant Director at the Australian Government Department of Health and Aged Care and a board member of People With Disability Australia. They hold a Master of Science in Epidemiology from the University of Melbourne.

Jennifer Smith-Merry is Professor of Health and Social Policy and Australian Research Council Industry Laureate Fellow (2024–2029) in the University of Sydney School of Health Sciences. Jen was Director of the Centre for Disability Research and Policy (2018–2024), a multi-disciplinary centre whose mission is to make life better for people with disability by translating research to policy and practice. Her research focuses on disability and mental health policy, particularly in relation to the National Disability Insurance Scheme. Jen works closely with people with lived experience of disability and has a strong interest in critical theoretical approaches to policy analysis.

Elder Annie Smith St-Georges is a traditional Algonquin Elder from Kitigan Zibi. As a teacher and social worker, Elder Annie led sharing circles and has spoken on accessibility, disability, trauma and suicide to provide knowledge on the impact of colonial education. Annie has been featured in many documentaries most notably in *KWEKÀNAMAD* (The Wind is Changing) regarding her son's suicide due to cultural abuse.

Sze Hwee Jace Tay is an autistic genderfluid graduate student of communication studies at Wee Kim Wee School of Communication and Information, Nanyang Technological University. Their main area of interest is disability history and the disability movement, with a particular focus on neurodiversity and neurodivergence. He is currently conducting research into the impact of digitalisation on neurodivergent students and employees. She is also working to advocate for disability and neurodivergent rights in Singapore, as well as highlighting disabled perspectives within Singaporean history.

Neil Turton-Lane is a consumer/survivor based in Melbourne, Australia, dedicated to supporting social change and human rights gains for marginalised peoples. Over the past 20 years, Neil has worked as an advocate, peer practitioner and community development worker across mental health and disability sectors. Currently, Neil is employed as the Lived and Living Experience Workforce Change and Development Lead at Better Health Network.

Muhammad Novsyaroni Umar was born with a physical disability of both hands, making him a disability scholar with a lived experience. Funded by Indonesia's Ministry of Finance, he is currently a PhD candidate in Media and Communications at the University of Sydney. His PhD research addresses Indonesia's digital disability activism and involved 70 participants across diverse-led organisations with different types of disabilities. He is an experienced public relations and communications professional with a focus on diversity and inclusion. He was also a Media Assistant Trainee with the United Nations (UN) HABITAT in 2016. In 2022, United People Global awarded him a Certified Sustainability Leader for intersecting disability with the UN Sustainable Development Goal (SDG) 4 through inclusive education for human sustainability. Umar's research expertise also covers digital disability policy in relation to digital inequalities. He has been providing disability policy making recommendations for local universities and regional governments in Indonesia.

Sarah Veli-Gold is an Aboriginal researcher and physiotherapist proudly connected to the Gomeroi Community in Northern NSW. After graduating from the University of Sydney in 2017, Sarah worked for several years as an acute care physiotherapist at St Vincent's Public Hospital. She has since returned to the university sector to help strengthen the cultural capabilities of future physiotherapy graduates, to promote culturally safe health care services. She is currently enrolled in a PhD working with community to explore the lived experiences of mob living with traumatic brain injury and co-design in research.

Susan Wadsworth found herself drawn to looking at ways to gain better outcomes for herself and her community after acquiring a spinal cord injury (T6 complete paraplegic) nine years ago. She realised that there was a vast, educated, highly motivated yet largely underutilised talent pool in the disabled community and that solutions to access issues would be found by involving and asking those with lived experience of disability. It became her goal to be part of improving access for all New Zealanders, particularly around kāinga (housing) and how it can impact a disabled person's overall well-being, knowing that if access is improved for a person who needs it, it improves access for anyone who uses it. Susan has worked as a public servant for nearly 20 years and has good knowledge of funding streams available in Aotearoa, New Zealand. Susan lives independently, with her two pugs for company and great comic relief.

Luke Wakely is an Academic Team Leader and Associate Professor at the University of Newcastle Department of Rural Health. Luke is ADHD and autistic. His research aims to improve outcomes for people with a disability in rural areas, particularly for children and their families. He is passionate about redressing inequity for rural communities. Luke has worked his entire career in rural Australia and currently works and resides in the rural town of Tamworth, NSW. Luke is an APA titled paediatric physiotherapist and holds a PhD, a Masters in Health Science (Paediatric Physiotherapy) and a Bachelor of Applied Science (Physiotherapy).

John T. Ward is a Métis and Non-Status Indian from the Algonquin territory of Kitchisibi. His specialisation is Indigenous wholistic knowledge, ethics, disabilities, learning disabilities and dyslexia among Indigenous people in Canada. He also works as a HR advisor in disability and Indigenous knowledge in the Government of Canada.

Daryl W. J. Yang is a Singapore-qualified lawyer who previously served as Honorary Secretary of the Disabled People's Association Singapore. He has worked with both Singaporean and international civil society organisations to advocate for queer, feminist and disability justice. A Fulbright scholar, Daryl obtained his LLM from Berkeley Law, where he specialised in disability and discrimination law. His research interests include comparative constitutional and equality law, socio-legal studies and international human rights. Daryl's writing has been published in peer-reviewed edited volumes and journals, including *International Journal of Disability and Social Justice*, *International Journal of Discrimination* and *Law and Feminist Legal Studies*.

Kuansong Victor Zhuang is Assistant Professor in Disability Communication at the Wee Kim Wee School of Communication and Information, Nanyang Technological University. He was a Chevening scholar at the University of Leeds in 2013/2014, a 2022/2023 Princeton University Fung Global Fellow and a visiting fellow at the University of Sydney in 2023/2024. His research lies at the intersections of communications, media and cultural studies, and disability studies, especially as it pertains to inclusion and the workings of technology. He hopes to use his research to contribute to current debates about how inclusion happens both in Singapore and around the world.

List of abbreviations

Abbreviation	Term
ACC	Accident Compensation Corporation (New Zealand)
ADA	Americans with Disabilities Act
ADHD	Attention deficit hyperactivity disorder
AMA	Australian Medical Association
CPT	Co-production team
CRA	Canada Revenue Agency
CRPD	Convention on the Rights of Persons with Disabilities
DEN	Disability employment network
DPI	World Congress of Disabled People's International
DPA	Disabled People's Association
DPO	Disabled People's Organisation
DRIP	Declaration of the Rights of Indigenous Peoples
DSP	Disability Support Pension
EIRTW	Early Intervention and Return to Work
EM	Enabling Masterplan
GEDSI	Gender Equality, Disability, and Social Inclusion
HR	Human resources
IFED	Indigenous Federal Employees with disAbilities
KCII	Knowledge Circle for Indigenous Inclusion
LGBTQIA+	Lesbian, gay, bisexual, transgender, queer, intersex, asexual, plus
MAiD	Medical assistance in dying
MDANZ	Medical Deans of Australia and New Zealand
MMAT	Mixed Methods Assessment Tool
NDIS	National Disability Insurance Scheme
NGO	Non-governmental organisation
NMP	Nominated Member of Parliament
NSW	New South Wales

Abbreviation	**Term**
PAP	People's Action Party (Singapore)
PRISMA	Preferred Reporting Items for Systematic Reviews and Meta-Analyses
QAI	Queensland Advocacy for Inclusion
QDN	Queenslanders with Disability Network
QPI	Queensland Parliamentary Inquiry
RDD	Radical disability disclosure
RTO	Return to office
SAM	Safeguards, assessments, methodology
TCWF	Tripartite Committee on Workplace Fairness (Singapore)
TTSS	Taxi Transport Subsidy Scheme (Australia)
UN	United Nations
UNCRPD	United Nations Convention on the Rights of Persons with Disabilities
UK	United Kingdom
USA	United States of America
WHO	World Health Organization

1 Introduction: Lived experience and policy making

Jennifer Smith-Merry and Damian Mellifont

1.1 Introduction

This book focuses on lived experience of disability and the way the knowledge from lived experience does and can (or should) impact the way that policy is designed. In reading the chapters in this book there are some fundamental concepts that we need to tease apart for you before we start. The most important of which is probably the answer to the question: What do we mean by lived experience?

1.1.1 Base concepts: What is lived experience?

Lived experience. We all have it. By its literal definition it is something that we have through living it (rather than getting second-hand through a book such as this) and it is something that is experienced (rather than learned). Every lived experience will be different even when it is the same experience because we all perceive our realities slightly differently.

The editors of this book, and the authors of this chapter – Damian and Jen – have a great deal in common. We both grew up in the same city, we both love see-through Swatch watches and we both have an academic interest in policy – we are clearly two very cool people. We have these lived experiences in common but we both come to our understanding of policy and what it can and should be from different experiences, which leads us to have different sets of expertise. Jen has no lived experience of disability and Damian has lived experience of disability. This shapes our academic interests, and our analysis of policy problems and their solutions. It is the lived *expertise* that comes from lived experience and the perspective it provides on policy, and on academic consideration of policy, that we are interested in within this volume.

1.1.2 Academic consideration of lived experience

Academic consideration of lived experience has focused on a few separate areas – the shape of lived experience knowledge and how it is used, and the content and value of the knowledge produced by lived experience.

1.1.3 Embedding lived experience knowledge in policy design

First to the second point, which is probably more the practical one that is covered in this book: What is (or should be) valuable about lived experience to policy makers?

Inclusion of lived experience is viewed as a solution to the 'democratic deficit', which occurs when people who are subject to policy have little involvement, or are sometimes actively excluded, in policy making (Speed & Reeves, 2025). The result of this is that policy can only be made with the perspective of already dominant players, such as the state.

Some groups are more prone to this exclusion than others because of the historical marginalisation, or demonisation, of their voices, for example in the case of welfare recipients (Speed & Reeves, 2025). People with disability have a history of being marginalised in relation to society, often being institutionalised as a result of their disability or lacking the same rights as other people to access education, employment and health care. This has meant that they have not had the same social or economic resources through which to access the means of policy participation. For this reason, it is important that volumes such as this highlight how we can reverse this lack of participation by prioritising disability experiences.

The disability community is well-attuned to the problems of policy developed *without* lived experience. Public transport that doesn't include disability means that people cannot access buses or train stations, and lack of inclusion in education policy has meant that people with disability have not been accommodated within education or have been segregated in education streams that do not allow progression to higher forms of education. These are a small number of examples of a much broader exclusion that results in entrenched marginalisation, which further excludes people with disability from having their needs met by policy.

There have therefore been strong calls for greater involvement in policy making from people with disability, including the creation of dedicated strategies to ensure involvement (e.g. Löve et al., 2017; Meltzer et al., 2021). The specific benefits of including lived experience vary by policy area but the broad benefits are universal. In relation to climate change Abbott and Wilson (2015, p. 223) describe the following benefits:

- "Exposes the politics and power relations at play in public policy making to those whose lived experiences are being institutionalised.
- Generates a space for joint learning and broader, deeper knowledge alongside the inputs from science.
- Exposes the dominant frames within which climate change debates are constructed.
- Provides a peg for voicing other pressing social issues that could lead to a polycentric framing."

These points are generally applicable by removing the phrase 'climate change', for example by replacing it with the phrase 'disability policy' or 'drug policy'. Integrating lived experience into policy making offers a range of benefits that enhance the relevance, effectiveness and legitimacy of public policy (Olsen et al., 2025). Individuals with first-hand experience provide unique insights into how policies impact real lives, revealing gaps, unintended consequences, and opportunities for reform that traditional data may overlook. Lived experience contributions diversify the evidence base, bringing emotional, contextual and qualitative knowledge into decision-making (Sartor, 2023). Including lived experience also fosters trust and engagement, particularly among communities historically marginalised or excluded from policy processes, or where there is existing mistrust between policy and the community.

Given its many benefits, then, why is lived experience frequently ignored or deprioritised in policy making? Firstly, as discussed further below, lived experience is often an embodied form of knowledge that must usually be translated into language to transmit it to others. Where policy makers do not have their own lived experience it is difficult for them to understand people's experiences and take up the knowledge through policy. Secondly, lived experience does not yet 'fit' with the mechanisms of traditional policy making, which requires special effort for it to be inserted into policy design cycles. Olsen et al. (2025) write that it is 'uncomfortable and time-consuming' and that meaningful engagement is difficult, despite its importance. The knowledge from lived experience, which is largely qualitative in nature and based in narrative (Clifton, 2025), is also deprioritised in relation to the 'quantitative certainty' provided by statistics. As Abbott and Wilson (2015) write, "so much would be lost if we tried to turn [lived experiences] into numbers". As we have written about elsewhere (Smith-Merry, 2020), lived experience is frequently deprioritised in favour of the 'hard evidence' validated through 'evidence hierarchies' that prioritise highly structured forms of evidence such as systematic reviews. Despite this, there is a growing imperative to include lived experience in policy making and policy makers continue to struggle to do this in ways that are non-tokenistic and useful, giving rise to multiple government efforts to understand lived experience inclusion in policy (e.g. Frawley, 2020; Multicultural NSW, 2023).

1.1.4 Lived experience knowledge

Now to the more tricky and theoretical points: What is the shape of knowledge produced by lived experience and what makes some lived experience more valuable?

When one of us (Jen) first started writing about lived experience the term used was 'experiential knowledge' (Smith-Merry, 2012, 2014). This term came about because of empirical work focused on mental health policy consultations that brought to light the ways in which knowledge from experiences of people with mental ill-health and practitioners emerged and dominated during public consultation events but slipped away again when policy documents were put together and government documents and written forms of authority dominated. What this showed was that what we now call 'lived experience' is an embodied form of knowledge that is held by individuals implicitly as a basis of their experience. That experience must then be formalised through language or action to be transmitted to others. It is therefore a very special form of knowledge that differs substantially from other forms of knowledge used in policy making.

McIntosh and Wright (2019) have drawn attention to the slipperiness of the term and its usage in the context of social policy, concerned that while the term appears to have utility for policy scholars, its methodological and theoretical conceptualisation are still evolving. This doesn't mean that the idea should be not be used, but that in its academic and professional practice and through ongoing discourse around its meaning, these dimensions become more firm (Clifton, 2025, forthcoming; McIntosh & Wright, 2019). This volume, which engages with lived experience and policy from very broad and, at times, disparate perspectives, is part of this process of 'firming up' the meaning of lived experience. As a *research agenda* it also takes forward the concept into future research and practice. These chapters do not 'solve' lived experience but provide jumping off points for the next steps in research.

1.1.5 Concerns and conflicts

As highlighted above in our discussion of 'experiential knowledge' there are a range of different terms frequently used to refer to what we are calling 'lived experience' in this volume. Other terms include 'consumer knowledge', 'living experience', 'expert by experience' and 'embodied experience' (Clifton, 2025; Frawley, 2020; Voronka, 2016).

Lived experience as a term is not universally used or loved (Casey, 2023; McIntosh & Wright, 2019; Voronka, 2016), with some for example critiquing it as being meaningless or confusing or applying to everyone (who doesn't have lived experience and what is its opposite – deceased experience?). Other critiques are that the term 'lived experience' can homogenise disability experiences, which can be risky because, as Voronka (2016, p. 190) argues in relation to mental illness, the use of this phrase can result in "... undercutting our various differences by effacing interlocking oppressions and the different ways we experience madness, conflating our conceptual and ideological standpoints as universally shared, and reifying mental illness". On the other hand a focus on the individual experience in 'lived experience' may overshadow the collective experience of disability which may also be important in non-Western cultures (Haang'andu, 2018; Howell et al., 2019).

Recent work has delineated lived experience from 'lived expertise'. Clifton et al. (2025) point out the limitations of lived experience as a subjugated form of knowledge in relation to the 'expert' knowledge of 'professionals'. They prefer to use the term 'lived expertise' arguing that to differentiate "... disability lived experience from disability lived expertise makes the knowledge, values and skills of disabled people explicit" (Clifton, 2025). Similar to this thinking, recent practices have also delineated *Lived Experience* from *lived experience*, arguing that 'large L, large E' (capitalised) Lived Experience roles represent professionalised forms of lived experience – in other words, lived expertise – which should be prioritised in the way that policies and services are designed (National Mental Health Commission, 2023). Predominantly used in relation to the mental health sector, such roles are characterised by: (1) professional recognition: validating lived experience as a form of expertise, not just anecdotal insight; providing for the development of lived experience career pathways, including leadership roles; (2) ethical and reflective practice: 'Lived Experience' roles require boundaries, supervision, and trauma-informed approaches, emphasising using lived experience *with intention*, not just sharing personal stories; (3) systemic influence: these roles are designed to influence policy, service design, and cultural change – not just provide peer support. The way that different contours of lived experience can be applied through lived expertise in different settings, and the hierarchies of knowledge that are created *within* lived expertise, are all areas that need to be further teased out (Moran, 2024; Voronka, 2016).

Some concerns related to including lived experience are the unequal power differentials between some lived experience voices. Some groups of people with disability may experience marginalisation *within* disability communities because of the nature of their disability, which may create more barriers to inclusion (Moran, 2024). For example, people who are non-verbal may be excluded because of inaccessible communication, people with mental illness may be excluded because of stigma around the trustworthiness of their opinions or their ability to fully consent, so to people with intellectual disability, because of both the inaccessibility of communication and concerns about their ability to consent. People with disability who experience other intersectional advantages, such as those that come with education and belonging to a socially dominant gender or race, may also have their voice elevated above other groups. This is an important consideration because under the United Nations Convention on the Rights of Persons with Disability all rights should be equal – particular groups of people with disability don't have more right to participate in society than others. Under this convention people with disability have the right to participate in policy making and their involvement must be facilitated (Frawley, 2020).

1.1.6 Policy worlds

Policies, narrowly considered, are documents that are used to provide definition and structure to a government's approach to directing resources and action in a defined area. Policies, in reality, are much broader than that as they are the documentary culmination of the broader processes that sit behind them and the implementation processes that sit in front of them. Policies are made through the back and forth of knowledge transfer and translation through meeting (through public and bureaucratic structured and unstructured processes) and writing (both formal and informal) (Freeman & Sturdy, 2014). Meetings and writing are not disembodied processes, and the knowledge produced in each encounter will be reflected in the way that the policy is shaped and what it finally includes. It will be also shaped by other non-human actors such as laws and other policies. This is messy business. Added to this messiness is the unpredictability of the implementation context, which also shapes how a policy is enacted. Each policy is interpreted by different people acting within different contexts, with different personal and organisational drivers impacting how a policy is taken up (Yanow, 1996, 1999).

1.1.7 This volume: Policy worlds and lived experiences

This volume brings together policy worlds and lived experiences to explore the different ways that lived experiences are included, or otherwise, in policy. The chapters are deliberately diverse and consider a very broad range of contexts. They bring together different aspects of lived experience, with different cultural contexts, into different policy settings. The aim of this discord is to enable you as the reader to understand both the specificities of policy making contexts and the universal opportunities and challenges to policy making that come from centring lived experience.

Our chapters include perspectives from Singapore, Australia, Canada, New Zealand, Indonesia and Pakistan – all very different contexts for policy making but yet sharing some important similarities, including all reflecting histories of colonisation. While governments in many of these countries have embraced, at least on paper, the concept of lived exclusion in policy, others are yet to act on the promise of lived expertise.

The volume opens with chapters that deliberately explore disability policy in three very different contexts: Pakistan, Singapore and rural Australia. The following chapters consider how lived experience is currently being considered in relation to specific policies across the very different contexts of the neighbouring countries of Australia, Indonesia and Singapore. These chapters show that while governments may prioritise lived experience, prioritisation can be difficult in reality without structured processes of inclusion and a genuine willingness to take on learnings from lived experience

The final five chapters together ask what changes when we place lived experience at the heart of our thinking. These chapters are challenging because they force us to think about the absences from policy of critical lived experience voices, the way that policy has reinforced or failed to address the legacies of colonial practices, the challenges of lived experience coming up against structured bureaucratic thinking, and the necessity to take on difficult topics to really consider the diversity of lived experience.

References

Abbott, D., & Wilson, G. (2015). Institutionalising lived experience in the public policy process. In *The Lived Experience of Climate Change: Knowledge, Science and Public Action* (pp. 223–253). Springer.

Casey, P. J. (2023). Lived experience: Defined and critiqued. *Critical Horizons*, *24*(3), 282–297.

Clifton, S., Cooper, E., Bourke, J., Connor, S., Denton, S., Dominish, B., Gibellini, C., Gilroy, J., Hallahan, L., Jessep, S., Katterl, S., Mellifont, D., Farrant, F. Q., O'Brien, B., Watharow, A., & Wynn., R. (2025). Disability lived experience and expertise: Recognising the expert contributions of people with disability. *Evidence & Policy.*

Frawley, P. (2020). *Lived Experience of People with Disabilities.* Australian Institute of Family Studies. https://aifs.gov.au/resources/short-articles/lived-experience-people-disabilities

Freeman, R., & Sturdy, S. (2014). Introduction: Knowledge in policy – embodied, inscribed, enacted. In *Knowledge in Policy* (pp. 1–18). Policy Press.

Haang'andu, P. (2018). Transnationalizing disability policy in embedded cultural-cognitive worldviews: The case of sub-Saharan Africa. *Disability and the Global South*, *5*(1), 1292–1314.

Howell, C., Lorenzo, T., & Sompeta-Gcaza, S. (2019). Reimagining personal and collective experiences of disability in Africa. *Disability and the Global South*, *6*(2), 1719–1735.

Löve, L., Traustadóttir, R., Quinn, G., & Rice, J. (2017). The inclusion of the lived experience of disability in policymaking. *Laws*, *6*(4), 33.

McIntosh, I., & Wright, S. (2019). Exploring what the notion of 'lived experience' offers for social policy analysis. *Journal of Social Policy*, *48*(3), 449–467.

Meltzer, A., Dickinson, H., Malbon, E., & Carey, G. (2021). Why is lived experience important for market stewardship? A proposed framework for why and how lived experience should be included in stewarding disability markets. *Evidence & Policy*, *17*(2), 335–347.

Moran, R. J. (2024). Towards a scholarship of critical lived experience engagement: Big feelings, big stories, big learning. In *Disrupting the Academy with Lived Experience-Led Knowledge* (pp. 36–50). Policy Press.

Multicultural NSW. (2023). *Lived Experience Literature and Practice Review: Approaches to Embed the Voice of Refugee Lived Experience in Decision-making*. New South Wales Government. https://multicultural.nsw.gov.au/wp-content/uploads/2025/01/Lived-Experience-Literature-and-Practice-Review-2024.pdf

National Mental Health Commission. (2023). *National Lived Experience (Peer) Workforce Development Guidelines*. National Mental Health Commission. https://www.mentalhealthcommission.gov.au/lived-experience/lived-experience-workforces/peer-experience-workforce-guidelines/national-lived-experience-%28peer%29-workforce-develop

Olsen, M., de Pinho Campos, K., & Fones, G. (2025). Meaningful engagement with people with lived experience: Challenging, messy, and more vital than ever. *BMJ*, *390*, r1138. https://doi.org/10.1136/bmj.r1138

Sartor, C. (2023). Mental health and lived experience: The value of lived experience expertise in global mental health. *Global Mental Health (Camb)*, *10*, e38. https://doi.org/10.1017/gmh.2023.24

Smith-Merry, J. (2012). Experiential knowledge in action: Consulting practitioners for policy change. *Policy and Society*, *31*(2), 131–143.

Smith-Merry, J. (2014). Seeing knowledge in mental health in Scotland. In *Knowledge in Policy* (pp. 21–42). Policy Press.

Smith-Merry, J. (2020). Evidence-based policy, knowledge from experience and validity. *Evidence & Policy*, *16*(2), 305–316.

Speed, E., & Reeves, A. (2025). Why is lived experience absent from social security policymaking? *Journal of Social Policy*, *54*(1), 22–37.

Voronka, J. (2016). The politics of 'people with lived experience'. Experiential authority and the risks of strategic essentialism. *Philosophy, Psychiatry, & Psychology*, *23*(3), 189–201.

Yanow, D. (1996). *How Does a Policy Mean? Interpreting Policy and Organizational Actions*. Georgetown University Press.

Yanow, D. (1999). *Conducting Interpretive Policy Analysis*. Sage Publications.

2 Centring disabled voices: Inclusion of lived experiences in policy

Sze Hwee Jace Tay and Kuansong Victor Zhuang

2.1 Introduction

In a commentary written for *Today* in 2019, Cassandra Chiu (2019) lamented the dismal state of affairs with regards to disabled representation in organizations that served disabled people. Spotlighting various organizations, Chiu noted how their boards and management councils did not have majority disabled representation. As she succinctly puts it, disabled people do not need others to speak for them, but rather, "what [they] hope for is a voice of our own". Chiu's commentary is prescient – she became president of the disabled-led Disabled People's Association Singapore in 2023, one of the few disabled-majority-led organizations in Singapore. There are two others – the Singapore Association of the Visually Handicapped, and Handicaps' Welfare Association – but these are a rarity in the Singapore landscape. Instead, as Chiu points out, disabled people's voices are mediated through others, family members or non-disabled board members/professionals.

Chiu's call turns our attention to a key issue which we attempt to address in this chapter – disabled voice. What does it mean to do disabled voice, and to highlight disabled voices in not only policymaking, but also research and crucially throughout every segment of society?

What we describe as disabled voice is not new. Beginning from the 1970s, the disability rights movement put forth a call for their voices to be recognized. When first formed in Singapore in 1981, Disabled People's International, the first disability-led international organization, adopted the slogan, a voice of our own (Zhuang, 2010). As James Charlton (1998) explains, disabled activists globally adopted "nothing about us without us" from the 1990s. These slogans signified the concerted call for disabled people's voice and self-representation, a demand to be heard over the influence of marginalizing institutions, agencies and society at large. It was a call for recognition, that disabled people should have their own voice to speak and to write their own stories; to be involved in determining the circumstances of their own life.

Chiu's demand for disabled voice is also seen and heard in other global locations. The extensive call for disabled people's participation in Australia's Disability Royal Commission in 2019 was a significant platform for disabled people's voices to be heard in government policy (Ellis, 2024). Similarly, New Zealand disability policy has made government collaboration with Disabled People's Organizations a priority since 2013 (Office for Disability Issues, 2016). Notably, incorporating disabled people's voices also sees a focus on disabled leadership in these cases. Internationally, the United Nations Convention on the Rights of People with Disabilities is a key demonstration of an international agreement centring disabled people's voices – the parallel reporting process, for instance, calls for disabled people's organizations to be involved and to give feedback on state parties' progress towards achieving the obligations of the convention (Harpur, 2012).

Yet despite the global regime of disability rights present in the United Nations Convention on the Rights of Persons with Disabilities, there are still problems and issues involved in centring disabled people's voices across different national contexts. This is especially so as, despite the proclaimed universality of rights, how it is implemented, understood and localized is very much context dependent (Brennan, 2020; Cogburn and Reuter, 2017; Degener and Quinn, 2002).

This brings us to the crux of our chapter – disabled voice. By disabled voice, as is clear in our introduction, we spotlight the importance of ensuring disabled people's self-representation across different domains – from policy, to research, as well as across various aspects of society and culture. However, as will be clear in our chapter, what is understood by disabled voice (even when there is effort made to include disabled people's voice) can still be circumscribed by conditionality and power dynamics that constrict the degrees towards which they can influence mainstream non-disabled narratives and policies that impact disabled people. Our focus on disabled voice spotlights the importance of lived experience and articulating it, especially for disability policy. In other words, how can policy be responsive to disabled voice and provide opportunities for lived experiences to lead, rather than be led. We note, more crucially, the importance of a politics of concession that provides new possibilities for disabled voice. Disabled voice in this sense operates not as something to be ignored or seen as a token, but as a series of negotiations to enact change under constrained political conditions.

This chapter consists of four main sections. First, we situate our discussion of and theorization of disabled voice amidst larger scholarship within disability studies, interspersed with our own personal reflections on how we have attempted to do disabled voice in our previous research. Next, we will introduce the Singapore context as a case study for the conditions in which disabled voice is permitted to influence policy, and the ways in which it limits the power of that voice. Finally, we propose how for researchers and policymakers a clearer understanding of disabled voice can be an impetus for greater participation, power and understanding, the translation of voice to societal change.

Our choice of Singapore as a site for discussing our theorization of disabled voice is crucial for two key reasons. Beyond being a context that both authors are familiar with, the Singapore policy context is unique as it has signed and ratified the United Nations Convention on the Rights of Persons with Disabilities and embraced disability inclusion as policy, but has chosen not to pass any disability rights legislation (Zhuang, 2016). Amidst the demonstrated efforts made by the state towards disabled inclusion in policy, we ask: How can disabled people's call for self-representation be embraced, given its centrality to inclusion as highlighted in the Convention (Lawson, 2006)? Crucially, we believe the Singapore context offers key lessons for a global audience, especially in understanding the workings of policymakers towards disability inclusion and disabled people's self-representation. The intersection of this investigation thus offers a perspective on both the progress made and limitations present in current incorporations of disabled voice.

2.2 Disabled voice in academia and research

We open first of all, with a focus on disabled voice in academia, where there have been various critiques of disabling structures within institutions of higher education that are hostile and alienating to disabled scholars. As Margaret Price points out, disabled academics and their abilities to thrive in academia are further inhibited by the ways in which accessibility is being addressed (Price, 2024). Writing about the centrality of oral communication and presentation, Jason Olsen and others (2020) highlight how some disabled academics are seen as less credible simply because they choose not to or cannot present their works in these normative ways. And, as Anon Ymous and others critique, disabled scholars are often expected to be productive amidst an unwillingness to support their needs (Ymous et al., 2020). Disabled voice in the academe is thus mediated by notions of productivity linked to the normate, especially pertinent given how neoliberal standards of academic productivity pervade universities.

A particular inclination as a result of these pressures is a need to pass – to hide one's disability and to present oneself as capable and non-disabled. Academics and students alike have expressed experiences of a desire to avoid the appearance of 'needing help', or fear that when they do disclose their disability that they will be subjected to judgement by their peers or colleagues (Lourens, 2021; Barkas, Armstrong and Bishop, 2022). The presence of such fears demonstrates a need for more open institutional support for disability. But more crucially, this highlights how disabled voice in the academe is being limited by institutional expectations of performance. The case of the disabled academic's voice offers a segue into crucial issues we want to highlight in disabled voice more broadly. That is to say: What does it mean to incorporate disabled voice in research and policy?

This question around what mediates disabled voice highlights crucial problems in disability research. Recent research methodologies involving disabled people have been keenly aware of the past violence and mistreatment that unethical practices have subjected disabled people to (Arstein-Kerslake et al., 2020); however, underlying ableist assumptions have not been entirely addressed. Of particular note are the conditions under which disabled people are permitted to participate in research. As Marty Heath highlights in a conference presentation, designations of disabled people as a 'vulnerable population' have been critiqued as infantilizing disabled people by marking them as separate from the general population (Heath, 2024). As Heath goes on to explain, ethical board requirements often judge mental capacity for the ability to consent to research, something which is frequently denied to a large proportion of disabled people, ensuring that only the most non-disabled of disabled people have a voice in research participation. While researchers can attempt to create more accessible and inclusive research designs, the institutional limitations create bureaucratic barriers that limit the kinds of disabled voices that participate in scholarship.

There is, of course, growing attempts at incorporating disabled people's voices across research and policy. One notable aspect where this is being done is through the adoption of participatory action research, where the subject populations – in this case, disabled people – are empowered to act and to do research that benefits their lives and communities (Hammel et al., 2008; Balcazar et al., 1998). As Kristy Liddiard and others (Liddiard, Whitney, et al., 2019; Liddiard, Runswick-Cole, et al. 2019) highlight, co-production with disabled people offers key insights and exciting opportunities to rethink how we produce, disseminate and write research. There is a significant emergence of academic works, books and art centring the disabled experience and making use of the insights of disabled researchers and co-collaborators. The production of these works situates the disabled experience in local and communal contexts, highlighting the uniqueness and creativity of the disabled experience (Zhuang, Wong and Goodley, 2023; Rapp and Ginsburg, 2024). A particular highlight of these experience-based works are the intersectional experiences of disability alongside issues such as reproductive health, socioeconomic class and race, where collaboration lends credence to experience, and experience lends nuance to these intersectional issues. The United Nations Convention on the Rights of Persons with Disabilities, as we discuss above, also has built-in mechanisms for ensuring disabled people's voices are heard, particularly with the parallel reporting process, a form of co-production.

Yet, we caution that even as researchers are aligned with the principles of disability studies and the disability rights movement the ways in which disabled voice come to emerge can be problematic and mediated. As researchers, both Jace and Victor have interviewed disabled people as part of oral history projects. Reflecting on their experiences doing oral history, Jace recalls how they worked to continuously consult with neurodivergent interviewees about their experiences, and went over their contributions to ensure they were not misrepresented. However, as the researcher, Jace felt he still retained power over how their voices are represented, even as the interviewees had the opportunity to correct their own representations. Victor also interviewed disabled people on their experiences in advocacy in the 1980s in Singapore. These interviews for Victor come to be subsumed within a broader historical activism of change in the project.

Crucially, these disabled voices come to be mediated by academic writing and narrative. As Jace reflects, the experiences that were recounted to her highlighted tangible frustration from experiences with Singapore's education and employment systems. They especially resonated with the stories of bullying and social isolation. However, he wonders, how he can condense such acute pain into objective academic conclusions? Similarly, the stories Victor records in speaking to disabled activists told of hope and aspirations. How do we tell and write of these lived experiences within academic writing, which has its rules and structures as well as quirks and idiosyncrasies? And while historical writing allows for disabled people's voices to partly emerge, especially when told in their own voice, these are always partial. More importantly, can the same be said for other disciplines in the social sciences, where an overall demand for academic objectivity directly conflicts with the realities of the stories being told? To try and capture emotion – anger, pain, sadness and victory – into the story of the critical academic narrative is a delicate work requiring significant consideration. Can academic narratives capture that which was lived and properly represent disabled voice?

2.3 The politics of concession: Voice and the case of Singapore

If the incorporation of disabled voice in research and academe is already fraught with difficulties, then the same could be said about disability policy. As the anecdote we highlight at the start of this chapter notes, Cassandra Chiu's lament of the lack of disabled peoples' leadership in Singapore must be situated within the larger policy context in Singapore, where the state has been keen to foster disability inclusion, but without a focus on disability rights legislation (Yang et al., 2023). Consequently, there is also a perverse reliance on medicalization and independence (Zhuang, 2016; Tay, 2023c). And, as we pointed out earlier, while other national contexts, like Australia and New Zealand, as well as international instruments such as the Convention on the Rights of Persons with Disabilities, have well-established mechanisms for disabled leadership and participation, the Singapore case offers an opportunity to understand the issues at stake with regards to disabled voice.

Central to our analysis in this section is the Enabling Masterplan – a roadmap that charts the directions Singapore should take to achieve an inclusive society. First initiated in 2007, it is now in its fourth edition from 2022–2030 and places great emphasis on ensuring that disabled people are capable of leading productive and independent lives (Ministry of Social and Family Development 2021, 2016). Throughout the four Masterplans to date, disabled people were widely consulted, as part of focus group discussions and the solicitation of feedback. Disabled voice is thus present and incorporated as part of policy. However, as Cassandra Chiu's commentary spotlights, disabled leadership is also conspicuously absent within the Masterplans. Among the various chairs that have helmed the four Enabling Masterplans to date, none has identified publicly as having a disability. And while disabled people may form and constitute part of the steering/executive committee, there is no commitment towards ensuring a disabled majority in terms of its composition. Neither is there an overt discourse in society that highlights this as a major problem.

In this context, we introduce an important term – what we have highlighted as a politics of concession. There are instances of tension and negotiation that occur where disability rights activism brushes against dominant structures and institutions that demarcate conditions for inclusion. Mask requirements and restrictions during the COVID-19 pandemic is one such example, where laws requiring wearing masks caused tension with people with invisible disabilities that would impair their ability to wear a mask. In most places, this necessitated a concession by some disabled people of their mobility freedoms to meet pandemic restrictions (Pendo, Gatter and Mohapatra, 2020). Another instance of this tension occurs in the negotiation of the right to work, and policies enabling work for disabled people. Such policies provide an avenue of inclusion for disabled people capable of productive work, but at the same time they exclude disabled people incapable of such work (Blattner, 2021). The process of disabled advocacy thus comes into conflict and tension with wider social needs and norms – necessitating that one side make concessions for inclusion. Rather than see orientation to disabled voice – specifically, disability rights and its politics as a zero-sum game – we instead posit this within a larger strategic focus. Can we allow disabled voice to be diluted to allow for the pursuit of the greater good? In the context of change, especially a change that is not guided by disability rights legislation, can we take a staged approach towards achieving disabled people's emancipation in society?

In the Singapore context, we note specifically how disabled people have navigated the operations of inclusion – in embracing productive notions of citizenship across the arts (Zhuang, 2021) as well as in arguments about accessibility. We note, for instance, how, despite the emergence of the language of disability rights in Singapore in the 1980s, the ways in which advocacy was carried out and changes made in the domain of physical accessibility almost always fell back on pragmatic reasons such as disabled people's productivity and economic contribution (Zhuang, 2020). In particular, we note how by embracing Singaporean notions of meritocracy, disabled people were thus able to put forth a position to advocate for change, in the end culminating in the passing of the Code on Accessibility in the Built Environment in the 1990s. Similarly, we note that while disabled people have advocated for inclusion from the 1980s onwards, and the formation of the Advisory Council on Opportunities for the Disabled in 1988 was a key milestone, it was not until the first Enabling Masterplan of 2007 that there have been more concrete moves made towards a policy of inclusion (Zhuang, 2016).

Crucially, we note how disabled voice comes to be mediated by concession as a means for change. In Jace's own letters to the *Straits Times*, a mainstream newspaper, the term 'entrenched ableism' was removed from their initial submission, alongside downplaying the extent of institutional issues and discrimination (Tay 2023a, 2023b). Jace recalls being frustrated with the removal of these terms in their letters, but conceded to the changes being made so that they would get their letters and opinions published. In other words, disabled voice comes to also be mediated by what is seen as acceptable or not.

We note of course that change may be slower and incremental as a result of having to concede to such constraints. This observation is not new; disabled advocates like Eric Chen have publicly expressed frustration with the slow rate of change in Singapore, and the misrepresentation or dilution of their ideas (read: voice) by non-disabled people (Chen, 2021). Appealing to statist (and non-disabled) assumptions and narratives about disability is in some ways a tactical necessity for some disability advocates. For advocates operating within systems that may not be geared towards disability rights, these concessions are necessary to ensure that their perspectives and suggestions – disabled voice – are not dismissed outright and can be heard.

However, these concessions by definition exist in an unequal power balance when it comes to the representation of disabled perspectives. To return to our example of the Enabling Masterplans, the crux of the matter is perhaps this: Should the focus be on ensuring disabled voice and leadership, or to ensure that the focus on inclusion stays its course, especially when the former encounters institutional resistance? In the context of Singapore, overt advocacy tends to be frowned upon, as many others have documented in the case of other marginalized groups and activism, such as with LGBTQIA+ groups, migrant workers and also across socioeconomic class (Chua, 2014; Lyons and Yee, 2009; Kaur and Yuan, 2017). Disabled activists thus have to tread the line between active resistance and change. Yet, we have to ask if concession is really the way to allow a voice to be heard. How can we move past that to enable change?

2.4 Centring disabled voice?

We conclude by highlighting our agreement with Cassandra Chiu on the importance of disabled voice and leadership, not only in policy but also within academia and research. More importantly, while concession may allow space for disabled voice to emerge, our stance is that it is not enough.

Advocacy for disabled voice has demonstrated the necessity of its acknowledgement, and the pressure on institutions to heed it. Yet, it is clear that there are methodological limitations that limit and constrain disabled voice, stemming from assumptions about who can speak, and who is entitled to voice, among other pressing issues. In response to these limitations, we propose something other than simply listening to disabled voices – a dialogue of disability. Our use of the term dialogue builds on a longer tradition within communication that highlights the importance of dialogue to allow for differing perspectives – it is also in difference that allows for new perspectives and change even as tension is rife (Anderson, Baxter and Cissna, 2004; Baxter, 2006). The process of dialogue is one that is continuous, and subject to review; a back and forth that should involve disabled people at all levels of development. Crucially, who is permitted to speak should not be limited to those who can express themselves verbally. The process of dialogue can and should include all manner of expression, be it non-verbal, creative and more. The full breadth of disabled experience is broad, and more than just the oral can be incorporated. As Victor's recent edited volume on disability studies highlights (Zhuang, Wong and Goodley, 2023), academic publication can also be reimagined to allow for a variety of ways in which ideas and research can be presented – from pictures, to interviews, and to short papers spotlighting personal experience. There is also a need to recognize and set aside the assumptions implicit in the selection method that limits who is capable of expressing voice.

If we are to create a full dialogue of disability, we must move beyond just listening, or just consulting, to a consideration of the full force of disabled lived experience, and all the pain, love and creativity it entails. Only then can society appreciate the lives that are presented and represented in pen and policy.

References

Anderson, Rob, Leslie A. Baxter and Kenneth N. Cissna (Eds.). 2004. *Dialogue: Theorizing Difference in Communication Studies*. London: Sage.

Arstein-Kerslake, Anna, Yvette Maker, Eilionóir Flynn, Olympia Ward, Ruby Bell and Theresia Degener. 2020. Introducing a human rights-based disability research methodology. *Human Rights Law Review*, *20*(3), 412–432. https://doi.org/10.1093/hrlr/ngaa021

Balcazar, Fabricio E., Christopher B. Keys, Daniel L. Kaplan and Yolanda Suarez-Balcazar. 1998. Participatory action research and people with disabilities: Principles and challenges. *Canadian Journal of Rehabilitation*, *12*, 105–112.

Barkas, Linda Anne, Paul-Alan Armstrong and Garry Bishop. 2022. Is inclusion still an illusion in higher education? Exploring the curriculum through the student voice. *International Journal of Inclusive Education*, *26*(11), 1125–1140.

Baxter, Leslie A. 2006. Communication as dialogue. In *Communication as …: Perspectives on Theory*, edited by Gregory J. Shepherd, Jeffrey St. John and Ted Striphas, 101–109. London: Sage.

Blattner, Charlotte E. 2021. Right to work or refusal to work: Disability rights at a crossroads. *Disability & Society*, *36*(9), 1375–1398.

Brennan, Ciara Siobhan. 2020. Disability rights during the pandemic: A global report on findings of the COVID-19 Disability Rights Monitor, edited by Steven Allen, Rachel Arnold, Ines Bulic Cojocariu, Dragna Ciric Milovanovic, Sándor Gurbai, Angélique Hardy, Melanie Kawano-Chiu, Natasa Kokic, Innocentia Mgijima-Konopi, Eric Rosenthal, and Elham Youssefian. COVID-19 Disability Rights Monitor (COVID-19 DRM). https://anrows.intersearch.com.au/anrowsjspui/bitstream/1/20742/1/Disability-Rights-During-the-Pandemic-report-web.pdf

Charlton, James. 1998. *Nothing About Us Without Us*. Berkeley: University of California Press.

Chen, Eric. 2021. Situation of Singapore in 2021. https://masterplan.iautistic.com/action/situation-of-singapore-in-2021/

Chiu, Cassandra. 2019. When organisations representing people with disabilities in Singapore are not inclusive. *Today*, 27 March 2019. https://www.todayonline.com/commentary/when-persons-disabilities-singapore-are-left-out-bodies-representing-them

Chua, Lynette J. 2014. *Mobilizing Gay Singapore: Rights and Resistance in an Authoritarian State*. Singapore: NUS Press.

Cogburn, Derrick L. and Tina Kempin Reuter, eds. 2017. *Making Disability Rights Real in Southeast Asia: Implementing the UN Convention on the Rights of Persons with Disabilities in ASEAN*. Lanham, MD: Lexington Books/Fortress Academic.

Degener, Theresia and Gerard Quinn. 2002. A survey of international, comparative and regional disability law reform. In *Disability Rights Law and Policy: International and*

National Perspectives, edited by Mary Lou Breslin and Silvia Yee, 3–125. Amsterdam: Brill Nijhoff.

Ellis, Katie. 2024. Australia's Disability Royal Commission: Media Advocacy and Social Change. ICA 2024, Gold Coast, Australia.

Hammel, Joy, Susan Magasi, Allen Heinemann, Gale Whiteneck, Jennifer Bogner and Evelyn Rodriguez. 2008. What does participation mean? An insider perspective from people with disabilities. *Disability and Rehabilitation, 30*(19), 1445–1460.

Harpur, Paul. 2012. Embracing the new disability rights paradigm: The importance of the Convention on the Rights of Persons with Disabilities. *Disability & Society, 27*(1), 1–14. https://doi.org/10.1080/09687599.2012.631794

Heath, Marty. 2024. Rejecting the Label of 'Vulnerable Subjects': How Rethinking Ethical Guidelines for Research with Participants with Physical Disabilities Can Lead to Better Research. ICA 2024, Gold Coast, Australia.

Kaur, Parveen and Yeo Si Yuan. 2017. Inhuman punishment and human rights activism in the little red dot. In *A History of Human Rights Society in Singapore*, 36–53. Routledge.

Lawson, Anna. 2006. The United Nations Convention on the Rights of Persons with Disabilities: New era or false dawn. *Syracuse Journal of International Law and Commerce, 34*(2), 563–619.

Liddiard, Kirsty, Katherine Runswick-Cole, Dan Goodley, Sally Whitney, Emma Vogelmann and Lucy Watts. 2019. 'I was Excited by the Idea of a Project that Focuses on those Unasked Questions' Co-Producing Disability Research with Disabled Young People. *Children & Society, 33*(2), 154–167.

Liddiard, Kirsty, Sally Whitney, Katy Evans, Lucy Watts, Emma Vogelmann, Ruth Spurr, Carrie Aimes, Katherine Runswick-Cole and Dan Goodley. 2019. Working the edges of posthuman disability studies: Theorising with disabled young people with life-limiting impairments. *Sociology of Health & Illness, 41*(8), 1473–1487.

Lourens, Heidi. 2021. Supercripping the academy: The difference narrative of a disabled academic. *Disability & Society, 36*(8), 1205–1220. https://doi.org/10.1080/09687599.2020.1794798

Lyons, Lenore and Yeong Chong Yee. 2009. Migrant rights in Singapore: Political claims and strategies in human rights struggles in Singapore. *Critical Asian Studies, 41*(4), 575–604. https://doi.org/10.1080/14672710903328047

Ministry of Social and Family Development. 2016. Third Enabling Masterplan (EMP3) 2017–2021. Edited by Ministry of Social and Family Development: Ministry of Social and Family Development.

Ministry of Social and Family Development. 2021. Enabling Master Plan 2030. Ministry of Social and Family Development.

Office for Disability Issues. 2016. New Zealand Disability Strategy 2016–2026 Office for Disability Issues. https://www.disabilitysupport.govt.nz/disabled-people/resources-for-people-new-to-the-disability-community/new-zealand-disability-strategy-2016-2026

Olsen, Jason, Miro Griffiths, Armineh Soorenian and Rebecca Porter. 2020. Reporting from the margins: Disabled academics reflections on higher education. *Scandinavian Journal of Disability Research, 22*(1), 265–274.

Pendo, Elizabeth, Robert Gatter and Seema Mohapatra. 2020. Resolving tensions between disability rights law and COVID-19 mask policies. *Maryland Law Review Online, 80*, 1.

Price, Margaret. 2024. *Crip spacetime: Access, Failure, and Accountability in Academic Life.* Durham, NC: Duke University Press.

Rapp, Rayna and Faye Ginsburg. 2024. *Disability Worlds.* Durham, NC: Duke University Press.

Tay, Sze Hwee Jace. 2023a. Forum: Do more to ensure protection in specific areas for people with autism. *The Straits Times.* https://www.straitstimes.com/opinion/forum/forum-do-more-to-ensure-protection-in-specific-areas-for-people-with-autism

Tay, Sze Hwee Jace. 2023b. Forum: Have bigger role for neurodivergent people in shaping social compact. *The Straits Times*. https://www.straitstimes.com/opinion/forum/forum-have-bigger-role-for-neurodivergent-people-in-shaping-social-compact

Tay, Sze Hwee Jace. 2023c. 'The game was rigged from the start': Singapore's neoliberal meritocracy and the neurodivergent experience. In *Not Without Us: Perspectives on Disability and Inclusion in Singapore*, edited by Kuansong Victor Zhuang, Meng Ee Wong and Dan Goodley, 371–392. Singapore: Ethos.

Yang, Daryl, Kuansong Victor Zhuang, Gerard Goggin and Meng Ee Wong. 2023. From enabling access to enabling rights: Singapore's practical approach to disability policy. In *Elgar Handbook on Disability Policy*, edited by Sally Robinson and Karen Fisher, 151–165. Cheltenham: Edward Elgar Publishing.

Ymous, Anon, Katta Spiel, Os Keyes, Rua M Williams, Judith Good, Eva Hornecker, and Cynthia L Bennett. 2020. 'I am just terrified of my future': Epistemic violence in disability related technology research. Extended Abstracts of the 2020 CHI Conference on Human Factors in Computing Systems.

Zhuang, Kuansong Victor. 2010. Enabling the Singapore story: Writing a history of disability. In *Monograph 42: Studies in Malaysian & Singapore History: Mubin Sheppard Memorial Essays*, edited by Bruce Lockhart and Tse Siang Lim, 37–71. Kuala Lumpur: Malaysian Branch of the Royal Asiatic Society.

Zhuang, Kuansong Victor. 2016. Inclusion in Singapore: A social model analysis of disability policy. *Disability & Society*, *31*(5), 622–640. https://doi.org/10.1080/09687599.2016.1197821

Zhuang, Kuansong Victor. 2020. At the margins of society: Disability rights and inclusion in 1980s Singapore. *Disability and the Global South*, *7*(1), 1813–1829. https://disabilitygloba lsouth.files.wordpress.com/2020/05/07_01_02.pdf

Zhuang, Kuansong Victor. 2021. The included: Disability-led arts within inclusion in Singapore. *Journal of Literary & Cultural Disability Studies*, *15*(4), 471–487. https://doi.org/10.3828/jlcds.2021.36

Zhuang, Kuansong Victor, Meng Ee Wong and Dan Goodley (Eds.). 2023. *Not Without Us: Perspectives on Disability and Inclusion in Singapore*. Singapore: Ethos.

3 Re-imagining policymaking with rural people with disability in Australia

Claire Quilliam, Luke Wakely and Jodie Bailie

3.1 Introduction

People with disability who reside in regional, rural, and remote communities (rural herein) deserve to lead good quality and healthy lives, with access to appropriate and timely healthcare and other services. However, in Australia and internationally, people with disability in rural communities continue to experience a poorer quality of life despite a myriad of policies and interventions aiming to prevent this (Department of Social Services, 2021; World Health Organization, 2022). Two intersecting inequities underpin this experience for rural people with disability in Australia. First, people from metropolitan areas have greater access to a range of healthcare and other services compared to rural people (Australian Institute of Health and Welfare, 2024b). Second, people with disability are more likely to experience chronic ill-health than people without disability (Australian Institute of Health and Welfare, 2024a). These contexts, experiences, and the associated inequities have a considerable negative impact on quality of life for people with disability residing in rural areas (Grabowska et al., 2021). Article 25 of the United Nations Convention of the Rights of Persons with Disabilities (2007) states that "persons with disabilities have the right to the enjoyment of the highest attainable standard of health without discrimination on the basis of disability" and that Stated Parties shall provide "health services needed by persons with disability … as close as possible to people's own communities, including in rural areas". Given that Australia is a signatory to the Convention, significant work is required to ensure that rural people with disability in Australia can access the healthcare they require in a timely and appropriate manner.

Place and context are critical policy aspects when considering policy as a *process* of making, implementing, experiencing, enforcing, and practising policies, law, and procedures (Fisher & Robinson, 2023). How people with disability experience policy will differ according to place and context. The rise in co-design in policymaking reflects the growing awareness of context and the recognition that policy must accurately identify problems in context to effectively address them (Blomkamp, 2018). To varying extents, people with disability, their families, service providers, and other community members are involved in the making of policy that impacts the lives of people with disability in Australia (Quilliam et al., 2022). This process has seen substantial leaps forward in disability policy and access to services for many people with disability in Australia, although there is significant room for improvement to ensure that all Australians with disability benefit to the same extent (Smith-Merry, 2024). Literature has explored the lived experiences of people with disability who reside in rural areas of Australia in different places and contexts (Bird et al., 2024; Prowse et al., 2022; Wakely et al., 2023). Despite this, we feel that policymaking efforts in Australia have often fallen short of achieving authentic engagement with rural people with disability. Subsequently, disability policies continue to poorly reflect the lives of rural people with disability (Quilliam et al., 2022; Quilliam et al., 2025). The lack of positive movement towards health equity and quality of life for rural Australians with disability, alongside ongoing policymaking, tells us one thing: it is time for Australian policy stakeholders to reimagine how policies are made with rural people with disability.

In this chapter, we start by introducing the Australian rural context, describe the complexity and uniqueness of rural people and communities, and highlight particularly rural community experiences. Second, we review studies that explore the lived experience of Australian rural people with disability. Third, we argue that historically, and currently, approaches to policymaking in Australia have resulted in policies that have not fully accounted for rural ways of doing and being, and the experiences of rural people with disability. Fourth, we describe a new way forward for policymaking with rural people with disability. We argue that policymaking impacting rural people with disability needs to be rurally grounded and led by rural people with disability. Last, we describe research required to improve policymaking for rural people with disability.

3.2 The Australian rural context, people, and communities

Approximately 7 million people – one-third of the Australian population – reside in rural Australia (Australian Institute of Health and Welfare, 2024b). People in rural areas of Australia experience impairment associated with disability at higher rates than those in metropolitan communities (Australian Institute of Health and Welfare, 2024b). Thus, including rural people with disability in policymaking is essential.

A key characteristic of rural areas in Australia is that they are heterogeneous (Liaw & Kilpatrick, 2008). The simplest way of defining rural is to consider it to encompass areas outside of major cities (Australian Institute of Health and Welfare, 2024b). However, this is an overly simplistic approach. There have been multiple attempts to classify rural areas by population size, town size, and geographical remoteness in respect to service access and market sufficiency (Versace et al., 2021). While each classification iteration builds on the previous, remaining health equity issues highlight concepts beyond market sufficiency, including consumer preference and cultural safety (Kuipers et al., 2022). The heterogeneity of rural areas also means that solutions to inequitable service access for people with disability need to be driven from a local level (Nordberg, 2021).

One way of framing *rural* when considering disability policy is to consider rural as a culture, or a way of life. Framing rural in this manner then encourages one to consider the question: What is the nature of this culture or way of life? Considering rural in this manner subsequently privileges the knowledge of those who understand this way of life; those with lived experience. This framing also flips thinking on what has been termed *geographical narcissism*, defined as a subtle, often unconscious devaluation of rural knowledge and a belief that metropolitan reality is definitive or superior to rural realities (Fors, 2018). It is a human tendency to consider one's own worldview to be central and definitive (Winther, 2014). It is a natural bias for those in urban areas to consider that their ways of being and doing, their culture, is the definitive one. Subsequently, this thinking has a tendency to devalue other social constructions of reality (such as rural). Considering rural as a culture or way of life also shifts from thinking of rural being simply about geography or access to resources, which are crucial elements in rural contexts, yet reductive when considering the *complexity* of rural communities.

Disability can be framed similarly as having a cultural, lived experience element. Drawing on the relational model of disability and understanding that disability is a situational or contextual phenomenon, people with disability are disabled when they and their environment are mismatched (Goodley, 2016). The augmented complexities presented by residing in a rural area is an important environmental characteristic to consider when thinking about the lives of people with disability. Australia's vast and relatively sparse population density means that geographical distance is often a considerable barrier to access to support and services for people with a disability (Australian Institute of Health and Welfare, 2024b). In Australia, rural communities are generally underserved in terms of disability services and support (Productivity Commission, 2017). Financial incentives and market-driven initiatives through the National Disability Insurance Scheme (NDIS) have been largely unsuccessful in rural contexts (Bailie et al., 2024; Gilroy et al., 2023; Wakely et al., 2023). It is challenging to implement a programme of this nature with significant shortages in the rural disability workforce (Kuipers et al., 2022; Wakely et al., 2023). Some initiatives, such as those implemented via the Rural Health Multidisciplinary Training programme, are working towards redressing rural workforce inequity (Department of Health and Aged Care, 2024). Yet, these initiatives generally focus on training health professionals, rather than the multidimensional nature of disability support.

Due to their smaller population density, rural communities are generally close-knit in nature, and community members often have dual relationships with other community members (Crowden, 2010). This can have both positive and negative effects on the lives of rural people (Quilliam et al., 2023), including for people with disability. People within rural communities are often more aware of the needs of people with disability and can serendipitously provide support (Wakely et al., 2023). However, this also means disability might be more visible and subsequently 'othered' in rural areas (Wakely, 2018; Wakely et al., 2018; Wakely et al., 2010). Dual relationships can add complexity to rural support and services, for example, maintaining confidentiality, seeking health for sensitive issues, and defining of professional roles may be more difficult (Endacott et al., 2006; Szumer & Arnold, 2023).

3.3 Lived experience of Australian rural people with disability

People in rural communities are sensitive and vigilant to metrocentric policy development (Beach et al., 2019). Rural residency is a key equity area that needs to be sensitively accounted for in policymaking, although this is only one complexity to consider. While many people in rural areas thrive, those who do not usually have multiple intersectional barriers to overcome (Ellem et al., 2019). Current disability policy in Australia is often insensitive to the needs of the very people with disability it impacts (Frawley, 2020). Disability policymaking that is insensitive to heterogeneity, of which rural is an excellent example, is also likely to poorly consider other minority experiences including those who are less educated, those of low socioeconomic backgrounds, or those from culturally diverse backgrounds (Ellem et al., 2019). Given the higher proportion of Aboriginal and Torres Strait Islander people residing in rural and remote areas, disability policymaking that is insensitive to those in rural communities is unlikely to be culturally sensitive (Bird et al., 2024; Gilroy et al., 2018; Gilroy et al., 2023). This means that many rural people with disability are hit with a *double (or triple) whammy* of disability policy not reflecting their lived experience and, in turn, creating further barriers to achieving health equity and living a good life. This disconnection between policy and rural experiences is reflected in the poor utilisation of the personal budgets eligible individuals receive as part of NDIS plans in rural areas compared to metropolitan areas (Commonwealth of Australia, 2023a; Disney et al., 2021). The disconnection between policy and rural experiences is also reflected by the minimal attention of the rural lived experiences of disability in the research literature. The literature tends to be narrow in focus, situated in particular rural areas, and poorly applied to international contexts.

Lived experience accounts from rural people with disability in rural areas emphasise that they experience a lack of understanding from others about their circumstances, on two fronts. First, as noted previously, close-knit rural communities providing support to members with disability when needed can highlight differences associated with disability and create additional rural-specific stressors for people with disability (Ellem et al., 2019; Wakely, 2018). Second, misunderstandings from those outside rural areas, who do not understand the rural context, impact rural people with disability (Wakely, 2018; Wakely et al., 2018). This is particularly true in the lived experience accounts about the impact of the NDIS on rural people (Dintino et al., 2019; Prowse et al., 2022; Wakely et al., 2023). Consistently, study participants have lamented not being able to explain their specific needs related to the context of where they live and work. This lack of empathetic understanding of those distributing NDIS funding has meant delays or disapproval of requested services and equipment that participants deem essential and necessary (Dintino et al., 2019; Loadsman & Donelly, 2021; Wakely et al., 2023). Rural people with disability have reported that the policy governing the funding and services they require limits access to services and their potential as human beings (Collings et al., 2019). They argue that access to support for basic activities of daily living is often provided, but often not the support to enable community participation and contribution to life beyond this (Bird et al., 2024; Wakely et al., 2023).

One other key area identified by the lived experience of rural people with disability that needs considering is the development of non-disability-specific policy. For example, in policy related to climate change (Bailie et al., 2022), disaster management (Bailie et al., 2022), and population health (Zhang & Chand, 2023) that impact rural communities, the voice of rural people with disability is often absent, despite these policies potentially having a profound impact on them (Bailie et al., 2022; Zhang & Chand, 2023).

3.4 Approaches to disability policymaking

The literature describing the experiences of rural people with disability and the inequities in service access suggests that we need to reflect on disability policymaking approaches. Blomkamp's (2018) public policy co-design thinking provided a lens through which to view how disability policymaking in Australia has fared in including the voices of rural people with disability when shaping policy problems and solutions. Blomkamp (2018) offers three components of policy co-design: a *process* that is iterative in design and geared toward innovation, *principles* that promote participatory practices and acknowledge lived experience and associated expertise, and *practical tools* that enable participation and testing of ideas. Blomkamp (2018) notes the importance of involving key stakeholders in the design process, where key problems are defined. In the following section, we review key Australian disability policy documents and the inclusion of rural content, including rural voices and rural systems, through Blomkamp's policy co-design thinking.

3.4.1 Historical disability policymaking approaches

The turn of the century resulted in a significant shift in disability policy in Australia. The United Nations CRPD triggered national reflection on how people with disability in Australia were fairing at a time when some (but not all) institutions had or were closing and community-based housing was expanding (Wiesel & Bigby, 2015). The aim of this service delivery shift was to include people with disability in day-to-day community life. However, it became apparent that more was needed to ensure that people with disability were meaningfully included in the community and not segregated in education, employment, health, recreation, and other aspects of life (National People with Disabilities and Carer Council, 2009).

The *Shut Out* report (National People with Disabilities and Carer Council, 2009) was a foundational piece in Australian disability policymaking that informed the development of the nation's first National Disability Strategy. The report drew on consultations with people with disability, family members and carers, service providers, advocacy and lobby groups, business representatives, National People with

Disabilities and Carer Council members, and government officials. The report used these consultations to define the current problems faced by people with disability and their strengths in navigating an under-resourced and fragmented disability service provision system. In the report, the terms 'regional', 'rural', 'remote', and 'non-metropolitan' were used 28 times collectively, although many times these terms were often mentioned in combination (e.g., 'rural and remote', p. 56). Consultations occurred in 40 non-metropolitan communities, although limited consultations were held in Tasmania, Western Australia, the Northern Territory, and Queensland. The quotes included in the report are rich and informative, illustrating Blomkamp's (2018) concept of *principles*. However, it is difficult to determine if the quotes were from rural or metropolitan-based participants and to what extent the rural participants defined key problems. It is worth pointing out that this is a considerable problem in the literature. Studies and reports may include both rural and urban people or stakeholders in their data collection, but often do not report outcomes separately. This means that rural/urban differences are often impossible to deduce (Bailie et al., 2024). Finally, the Chair of the National People with Disabilities and Carer Council (who oversaw government advice on the development and implementation of the National Disability Strategy) only attended consultations in capital cities (National People with Disabilities and Carer Council, 2009, p. vi). While the voices of rural people with disability would have been heard by other key policymakers, we wonder to what extent the lack of exposure to rural communities, rural people with disability, and rural ways of doing and being might have shaped the Chair's thinking around the definition of key problems and solutions to address these.

Following the *Shut Out* report, the Council of Australian Governments (2011) released the *National Disability Strategy 2010–2020*. This Strategy was the first of its kind because it represented Commonwealth-State/Territory government agreement to improving the lives of people with disability in Australia. Drawing on the findings of the *Shut Out* report, the Council of Australian Governments described six policy and outcome areas:

1. Inclusive and accessible communities.
2. Rights protection, justice and legislation.
3. Economic security.
4. Personal and community support.
5. Learning and skills, and
6. Health and well-being.

The Strategy highlights "the diversity of experiences of people with disability" (p. 14), including that of living in a rural area, as underpinning the outcome areas (Council of Australian Governments, 2011). However, the terms 'regional', 'rural', 'remote', and 'non-metropolitan' were rarely used in the Strategy, with only six meaningful mentions in total, and a number of these being mentioned in combination. The term 'regional' was not mentioned, and the term 'rural' was mentioned twice.

On reflection, the Strategy adopted a rather *placeless* approach and presented policy directions that did not differ according to ways of doing and being in rural communities and metropolitan cities. For example, in the health and well-being policy and outcome area, there is a commitment to ensuring "people with disability attain [the] highest possible health and wellbeing outcomes throughout their lives" (p. 59) and a policy direction tasked with building the capability of existing healthcare professionals to meet the healthcare needs of people with disability, but no acknowledgement that rural people with disability face difficulties accessing healthcare to begin with (Australian Institute of Health and Welfare, 2024b). This policy direction assumes that rural people with disability have access to health professionals and healthcare and does not acknowledge geographic features within this discussion. An approach underpinned by rural thinking may have resulted in efforts to expand the rural health workforce and representation of people with lived experience in this workforce, in addition to capability-building strategies with the existing workforce. Such metro-centric policy solutions illustrate that the rural voices included in the *Shut Out* report may not have optimally shaped policymakers' understanding of the key problems, or that the *principle* of embedding lived experience, as noted by Blomkamp (2018), did not translate from the *Shut Out* report to the Strategy. This suggests that additional policymaking systems may be required to retain rural thinking in the transition from problem definition to solution identification, when developing national policy of relevance to both metropolitan and rural people with disability.

3.4.2 Recent disability policymaking approaches

A recent example of disability policymaking, the work to design *Australia's Disability Strategy 2021–2031*, illustrates an explicit focus on involving key stakeholders. As noted by Quilliam et al. (2022), this process involved an extensive two-stage consultation method that sought particular stakeholder perspectives (The Social Deck, 2021). However, the Victorian Council of Social Service (2020) suggested that the timing of the position paper release prevented people with disability from shaping its focus. Further, face-to-face engagements were predominantly held in metropolitan areas, with online options being the main option for rural people with disability to participate – with the exception of consultations with Aboriginal and Torres Strait Islander communities and six in-person community workshops in non-metropolitan settings (Quilliam et al., 2022). Adopting rural ways of doing and being in this process would have involved acknowledging the importance of relationality in rural settings (Quilliam et al., 2023) and policymakers valuing time with rural people with disability in different rural contexts. These policymaking limitations suggest that it is as important to adopt *practical tools* at the early stages of policymaking as it is to involve people with relevant lived experience, as noted by Blomkamp (2018).

Another recent policymaking example is described in the *Alternative Commissioning for Remote and First Nations Communities* report (Commonwealth of Australia, 2023a). Roughly one decade after the commencement of the NDIS roll out, the government acknowledged that the marketised approach taken under this scheme (individuals use their budgets to purchase services on an open disability market), with minimal market stewardship, had largely failed to support service access for many people with disability, particularly in remote communities (Commonwealth of Australia, 2023a). This report, which considers alternatives to an open market approach where this is failing, is a step in the right direction in acknowledging the need for different policy solutions for access to services for rural people with disability. However, the *Alternative Commissioning* report offered only minor details around the *process* taken to co-design its content. The report drew on past reviews, inquiries, and ongoing market trials to shape alternative commissioning approaches going forward, for example, the Productivity Commission (2017) National Disability Insurance Scheme (NDIS) Costs report, and the Thin Market Trials (Ernst and Young Australia, 2019), which describes outcomes from a small range of implemented market activities. Many policy problems are defined in the Alternative Commissioning report (Commonwealth of Australia, 2023a). But, while the report suggests that policymakers will pilot alternative commissioning with communities (p. 4), it is difficult to know who contributed to the identification of policy problems initially. This means that the government risks designing solutions that are not suitable for implementation in rural contexts. Points of concern we have identified surrounding the definition of policy problems and solutions in the report include: the conflation of the service needs of diverse Aboriginal and Torres Strait Islander communities with the service needs of people living in rural and remote communities; assignment of alternative commissioning approaches to remote or very remote communities (MM6–7) and not regional and rural communities (MM 3–5) when the percentage of participants underclaiming in regional and remote areas is similar – 31% and 32% respectively (Commonwealth of Australia, 2023a, p. 37); and the marketised framing of service provision in rural communities, especially the use of the term 'contestable market' (p. 11), when it is not uncommon for rural services to collaboratively support service access (Ramsden et al., 2021).

As indicated by Blomkamp (2018), the initial policymaking *process* requires appropriate input to adequately define problems and identify solutions. Including people with disability from a variety of regional, rural, remote, and very remote communities from the beginning of the Alternative Commissioning work may have resulted in the identification of relevant policy problems and suitable solutions for a range of rural contexts.

3.4.3 Summary of approaches to policymaking

Reviewing key disability policy documents has illustrated that Australian disability policymaking has historically been, and is currently, shaped by metropolitan ways of doing and being. These policies tend to better suit the lives of metropolitan-based people with disability as a result. In saying this, metropolitan-based people with disability do not always fare well from these policies (Wiesel & Bigby, 2015). However, the lived experiences of rural people with disability illustrate that rural people continue to navigate a system that is not made for their existence. The consequences of designing and implementing metrocentric national policies for rural people are clearly far from intentional, and yet these consequences point to a common flaw in policymaking – that relevant voices are not shaping thinking at key times in the process. Rural people with disability must co-design policies that impact them, from the very start of problem definition and throughout the entire policymaking process.

3.5 A new way of policymaking with rural people with disability in Australia

We need a bold new way of policymaking with rural people with disability: where co-design is not just structured into aspects of disability policymaking, but where rural people with disability actively lead problem definition and shape solutions in policymaking over time, so that implemented strategies of all kinds reflect rural ways of doing and being. For this to occur in Australia, we need new *voice* and *action* structures, where lived experience of rural people with disability directly guides the policymaking process. Distributed rural proofing, described by Nordberg (2021), offers a structural model for achieving this. Distributed rural proofing identifies the role of local actors, local networks, and extra-local networks in defining policy problems and solutions that build on local strengths. We now describe the three structures and how they could shape rural Australian disability policymaking.

3.5.1 Local actors (or localisability policymakers)

Local actors could be people with disability located in different regional, rural, and remote communities. To borrow from Lipsky (2010), these actors could be considered a kind of *street-level* bureaucrat, or what we could call a *local disability policymaker*. Local disability policymakers could be embedded in local government councils, community, or advocacy organisations. In addition to lived experience, local disability policymakers would have deep contextual knowledge of the community and its inherent resoufces, strengths, and areas to strengthen to ensure people with disability in the community can access services in a timely and suitable manner.

3.5.2 Local networks

Local disability policymakers could be embedded in local rural networks that meet regularly to discuss local issues regarding the inclusion of people with disability in the community. These networks would comprise people with disability, their families and carers, service providers, and rural researchers. These networks could be involved in contextually based co-designed research to inform local action. Given that all levels of government are responsible for ensuring rural people with disability live included lives in their communities (Commonwealth of Australia, 2023b), state and territory governments could fund local networks and ensure they are well-equipped to support local problem definition, solution identification, and implementation. Elements of the participatory citizenship approach used in a regional Tasmanian community could be adopted in the local network structure (Ramcharan et al., 2020).

3.5.3 Extra-local networks

Local disability policymakers could also be part of a national disability policymaker network. Through this extra-local network, local disability policymakers would share local strengths, defined problems, and solutions to consider in national policymaking. Extra-local networks would also inform non-disability-specific policy development (including health, education, transport, construction, etc.) to ensure rural ways of *doing and being* informed all aspects of policymaking impacting the lives of rural people with disability. Given its national relevance to policymaking, this extra-local network could be funded by and sit within a Commonwealth Government Department. Additional extra-local networks could be developed to support jurisdictional policy development or by rurality, to share policy problems and solutions.

3.5.4 Benefits of active rural disability policymaking

Adoption of an active and inclusive rural disability policymaking model would allow for quick and thorough communication between people with disability living in regional, rural, and remote communities and government bureaucrats from all portfolios. It would ensure rural ways of doing and being are not forgotten to metrocentric policymaking ways. It would prevent the adoption of a superficial model of rural proofing, where junior policymakers are tasked with tick-box style activities to complete, rather than involving key decision-makers in rural thinking (Shortall & Alston, 2016). By adopting a distributed model of rural proofing into disability policymaking, pressure on governments to demonstrate intensive consultation processes may be relieved. This may consequently reduce the cost of conducting extensive reviews before updating national policies and strategies.

3.6 Future research

Like any other aspect impacting the lives of rural people with disability, policymaking approaches require research and evaluation. Evidence is required to understand how rural proofing concepts can and should be applied in Australia (Shortall & Alston, 2016). Critical to informing policymaking approaches is rigorous, comprehensive data about the rural disability population and the supporting workforce (Bailie et al., 2024; Smith-Merry, 2024). Then, an active rural disability policymaking model can be piloted prior to its long-term adoption. Piloting such a model would require the development of partnerships with local, state/territory, and commonwealth governments to ensure the adequate development and evaluation of the implementation of the three structures (local actor, local networks, and extra-local networks) and their connecting features. It would require rural researchers with disability to lead the pilot's design and implementation. Within this lived-experience-led research programme, case studies could be undertaken to understand the long-term impact of local disability policymakers, local networks, and extra-local networks on the lives of people with disability in rural communities. Longitudinal policy data should be captured and analysed to determine the extent to which national policies in all portfolios incorporate rural ways of doing and being, including in problem definition and solution identification.

3.7 Conclusion

In this chapter, we have described the Australian rural context, people, and communities and the impacts of these characteristics on rural ways of doing and being. We discussed the lived experience of rural people with disability in accessing services they require to live good quality lives and reviewed approaches to policymaking that have largely resulted in rural people with disability navigating poorly suited service systems. The concept of rural proofing was then used to describe an active and inclusive model of policymaking that enables rural people with disability to identify community strengths, define problems, and translate these into solutions at a local and national level. Finally, we have described the research activities required to evaluate such a policymaking model and understand its impact on the lives of rural Australian people with disability.

References

Australian Institute of Health and Welfare. (2024a). *People with Disability in Australia*. Australian Government. https://www.aihw.gov.au/reports/disability/people-with-disability-in-australia/data

Australian Institute of Health and Welfare. (2024b). *Rural and Remote Health*. Australian Government. https://www.aihw.gov.au/reports/rural-remote-australians/rural-and-remote-health

Bailie, J., Disney, G., Quilliam, C., & Kavanagh, A. M. (2024). The NDIS at ten years: Designing an equitable scheme for the next decade. *The Medical Journal of Australia*, *220*(1), 54. https://doi.org/10.5694/mja2.52173

Bailie, J., Matthews, V., Bailie, R., Villeneuve, M., & Longman, J. (2022). Exposure to risk and experiences of river flooding for people with disability and carers in rural Australia: A cross-sectional survey. *BMJ Open*, *12*(8), e056210. https://doi.org/10.1136/bmjopen-2021-056210

Beach, D., Johansson, M., Öhrn, E., Rönnlund, M., & Per-Åke, R. (2019). Rurality and education relations: Metro-centricity and local values in rural communities and rural schools. *European Educational Research Journal*, *18*(1), 19–33. https://doi.org/10.1177/1474904118780420

Bird, K., Bohanna, I., McDonald, M., Wapau, H., Blanco, L., Cullen, J., McLucas, J., Forbes, S., Vievers, A., Wason, A., Strivens, E., & Barker, R. (2024). A good life for people living with disability: The story from Far North Queensland. *Disability & Rehabilitation*, *46*(9), 1787–1795. https://doi.org/10.1080/09638288.2023.2205172

Blomkamp, E. (2018). The promise of co-design for public policy. *Australian Journal of Public Administration*, *77*(4), 729–743. https://doi.org/10.1111/1467-8500.12310

Collings, S., Dew, A., & Dowse, L. (2019). 'They need to be able to have walked in our shoes': What people with intellectual disability say about National Disability Insurance Scheme planning. *Journal of Intellectual and Developmental Disability*, *44*(1), 1–12. https://doi.org/10.3109/13668250.2017.1287887

Commonwealth of Australia. (2023a). *Alternative Commissioning for Remote and First Nations Communities*. Australian Government. https://www.ndisreview.gov.au/resources/paper/improving-access-supports-remote-and-first-nations-communities

Commonwealth of Australia. (2023b). *Working Together to Deliver the NDIS: Independent Review into the National Disability Insurance Scheme: Final Report*. Commonwealth of Australia. https://www.ndisreview.gov.au/resources/reports/working-together-deliver-ndis

Council of Australian Governments. (2011). *National Disability Strategy 2010–2020*. Commonwealth of Australia. https://www.health.gov.au/resources/publications/national-disability-strategy-2010-2020

Crowden, A. (2010). Virtue ethics and rural professional healthcare roles. *Rural Society, 20*, 64–75. https://doi.org/10.5172/rsj.20.1.64

Department of Health and Aged Care. (2024). *Rural Health Multidisciplinary Training (RHMT) Program*. Australian Government. https://www.health.gov.au/our-work/rhmt

Department of Social Services. (2021). *Australia's Disability Strategy 2021–2031*. Commonwealth of Australia. https://www.disabilitygateway.gov.au/document/3106

Dintino, R., Wakely, L., Wolfgang, R., Wakely, K. M., & Little, A. (2019). Powerless facing the wave of change: The lived experience of providing services in rural areas under the National Disability Insurance Scheme. *Rural & Remote Health, 19*(3), 5337. https://doi.org/10.22605/RRH5337

Disney, G., Yang, Y., Summers, P., Gupta, A., Byars, S., Bonyhady, B., & Kavanagh, A. (2021). *NDIS Utilisation Project: Describing, Understanding and Explaining Inequalities in Plan Utilisation*. https://apo.org.au/sites/default/files/resource-files/2021-10/apo-nid314668.pdf

Ellem, K., Baidawi, S., Dowse, L., & Smith, L. (2019). Services to young people with complex support needs in rural and regional Australia: Beyond a metro-centric response. *Children & Youth Services Review, 99*, 97–106. https://doi.org/10.1016/j.childyouth.2019.01.033

Endacott, R., Wood, A., Judd, F., Hulbert, C., Thomas, B., & Grigg, M. (2006). Impact and management of dual relationships in metropolitan, regional and rural mental health practice. *Australian and New Zealand Journal of Psychiatry, 40*(11–12), 987–994. https://doi.org/10.1080/j.1440-1614.2006.01922.x

Ernst and Young Australia. (2019). *NDIS Thin Markets Project – Discussion Paper to Inform Consultation*. Department of Social Services. https://engage.dss.gov.au/wp-content/uploads/2019/04/Thin-Markets-Project-Discussion-Paper-2019-04-05.pdf

Fisher, K. R. & Robinson, S. (2023). Introduction to disability policy through a human rights lens. In S. Robinson & K. Fisher (Eds.), *Research Handbook on Disability Policy*. Edward Elgar Publishing. https://doi.org/10.4337/9781800373655.00006

Fors, M. (2018). Geographical narcissism in psychotherapy: Countermapping urban assumptions about power, space, and time. *Psychoanalytic Psychology, 35*(4), 446–453. https://doi.org/10.1037/pap0000179

Frawley, P. (2020). *Lived Experience of People with Disabilities*. Australian Institue of Family Studies. https://aifs.gov.au/resources/short-articles/lived-experience-people-disabilities

Gilroy, J., Dew, A., Lincoln, M., Ryall, L., Jensen, H., Taylor, K., Barton, R., McRae, K., & Flood, V. (2018). Indigenous persons with disability in remote Australia: Research methodology and Indigenous community control. *Disability & Society, 33*(7), 1025–1045. https://doi.org/10.1080/09687599.2018.1478802

Gilroy, J., Veli-Gold, S., Wright, W., Dew, A., Jensen, H., Bulkeley, K., & Lincoln, M. (2023). Disability workforce and the NDIS planning process in regional, rural and remote regions of Australia: Scoping review. *The Australian Journal of Rural Health, 31*(5), 839–854. https://doi.org/10.1111/ajr.13020

Goodley, D. (2016). *Disability Studies: An Interdisciplinary Introduction* (2nd edn). Sage Publications.

Grabowska, I., Antczak, R., Zwierzchowski, J., & Panek, T. (2021). Individual quality of life and the environment – towards a concept of livable areas for persons with disabilities in Poland. *BMC Public Health, 21*(1), 740. https://doi.org/10.1186/s12889-021-10797-7

Kuipers, P., Lakhani, A., & Jensen, H. (2022). Responding to the 'thin' markets of rural and remote disability services. Quantitative and spatial analysis is part of the picture. *Rural and Remote Health, 22*(2), 7011. https://doi.org/10.22605/RRH7011

Liaw, S.-T. & Kilpatrick, S. (eds). (2008). *A Textbook of Australian Rural Health*. Australian Rural Health Education Network.

Lipsky, M. (2010). *Street Level Bureaucracy: Dilemmas of the Individual in Public Services* (2nd edn). Russell Sage Foundation.

Loadsman, J. J. & Donelly, M. (2021). Exploring the wellbeing of Australian families engaging with the National Disability Insurance Scheme in rural and regional areas. *Disability & Society, 36*(9), 1449–1468. https://doi.org/10.1080/09687599.2020.1804327

National People with Disabilities and Carer Council. (2009). *Shut Out: The Experience of People with Disabilities and Their Families in Australia*. https://www.ourcommunity.com.au/files/shut_out.pdf

Nordberg, K. (2021). Distributed rural proofing – An essential tool for the future of rural development? *Sociologia Ruralis, 61*(1), 141–162. https://doi.org/10.1111/soru.12316

Productivity Commission. (2017). *National Disability Insurance Scheme (NDIS) Costs*. Australian Government. https://www.pc.gov.au/inquiries-and-research/ndis-costs/report/

Prowse, A., Wolfgang, R., Little, A., Wakely, K., & Wakely, L. (2022). Lived experience of parents and carers of people receiving services in rural areas under the National Disability Insurance Scheme. *The Australian Journal of Rural Health, 30*(2), 208–217. https://doi.org/10.1111/ajr.12837

Quilliam, C., Glenister, K., Ervin, K., & Weller-Newton, J. (2023). Revisiting rural healthcare access through Held's ethics of care. *Social Theory & Health, 21*, 178–193. https://doi.org/10.1057/s41285-022-00181-9

Quilliam, C., O'Shea, A., Holgate, N., & Alston, L. (2022). Starting with us: Imagining relational, co-designed policy approaches to improve healthcare access for rural people with disability. *The Australian Journal of Rural Health, 30*(6), 809–815. https://doi.org/10.1111/ajr.12891

Quilliam, C., Wakely, L., French, L., Ellis, N., McNeil, R., Fallon, T., Kersten, M., Bagley, K., Spong, J., Doney, R., Stubb, C., Devitt, A., & McKinstry, C. (2025). Placing rural in the National Disability Insurance Scheme Review. *Australia Journal of Social Issues, 60*, 1077–1083. https://doi.org/10.1002/ajs4.70024

Ramcharan, P., David, C., & Marx, K. (2020). You are here! Negotiating liminality in place in the context of the National Disability Insurance Scheme. *Qualitative Social Work, 19*(3), 359–379. https://doi.org/10.1177/1473325020915775

Ramsden, R., Davies, S., Colbran, R., Haigh, A., Connors, M., Nott, S., Lowe, E., Edwards, M., Clegg, R., Bagnulo, S., & Pit, S. (2021). Collaborative care: Primary health workforce and service delivery in Western New South Wales: A case study. The *Australian Journal of Rural Health, 29*(5), 768–778. https://doi.org/10.1111/ajr.12796

Shortall, S. & Alston, M. (2016). To rural proof or not to rural proof: A comparative analysis. *Politics and Policy, 44*(2), 35–55. https://doi.org/10.1111/polp.12144

Smith-Merry, J. (2024). The NDIS at ten years: Designing an equitable scheme for the next decade. *The Medical Journal of Australia, 220*, 55. https://doi.org/10.5694/mja2.52174

Szumer, R. T. O. & Arnold, M. (2023). The ethics of overlapping relationships in rural and remote healthcare. A narrative review. *Journal of Bioethical Inquiry, 20*(2), 181–190. https://doi.org/10.1007/s11673-023-10243-w

The Social Deck. (2021). *A New National Disability Strategy – Stage 2 Report on Targeted Workshops*. The Department of Social Services. https://www.health.gov.au/resources/publications/a-new-national-disability-strategy-stage-2-consultation-summary-report-of-targeted-workshops

United Nations. (2007). *Convention on the Rights of Persons with Disabilities (CRPD)*. https://social.desa.un.org/issues/disability/crpd/convention-on-the-rights-of-persons-with-disabilities-crpd

Versace, V. L., Skinner, T. C., Bourke, L., Harvey, P., & Barnett, T. (2021). National analysis of the Modified Monash Model, population distribution and a socio-economic index to inform rural health workforce planning. *The Australian Journal of Rural Health, 29*(5), 801–810. https://doi.org/10.1111/ajr.12805

Victorian Council of Social Service. (2020). *Advancing an Accessible and Inclusive Australia*. https://vcoss.org.au/disability-aging-carers/2020/11/advancing-australia/

Wakely, L. (2018). *The Lived Experience of Parenting a Premature Infant in a Rural Area* [PhD thesis, The University of Newcastle]. Newcastle, Australia. https://hdl.handle.net/1959.13/1355384

Wakely, L., Green, E., Little, A., Fisher, K., Wakely, K., Currie, K., & Wolfgang, R. (2023). The lived experience of receiving services as a National Disability Insurance Scheme participant in a rural area: Challenges of choice and control. *The Australian Journal of Rural Health, 31*(4), 648–658. https://doi.org/10.1111/ajr.13000

Wakely, L., Langham, J., Johnston, C., & Rae, K. (2018). Physical activity of rurally residing children with a disability: A survey of parents and carers. *Disability and Health Journal, 11*(1), 31–35. https://doi.org/10.1016/j.dhjo.2017.05.002

Wakely, L., Rae, K., & Cooper, R. (2010). Stoic survival: The journey of parenting a premature infant in the bush. *Rural and Remote Health, 10*(1475), 1–10. http://www.rrh.org.au/publishedarticles/article_print_1475.pdf

Wiesel, I. & Bigby, C. (2015). Movement on shifting sands: Deinstitutionalisation and people with intellectual disability in Australia, 1974–2014. *Urban Policy and Research, 33*(2), 178–194. https://doi.org/10.1080/08111146.2014.980902

Winther, R. G. (2014). World Navels. *Cartouche, 89*, 15–21. http://www.rgwinther.com/Winther2014World_Navels.pdf

World Health Organization. (2022). *Global Report on Health Equity for Persons with Disabilities*. https://www.who.int/publications/i/item/9789240063600

Zhang, Y. & Chand, S. (2023). Impact of COVID-19 on utilisation of funds by people with disabilities: Lessons drawn from the Australian National Disability Insurance Scheme. *International Journal of Health Policy & Management, 12*, 7663. https://doi.org/10.34172/ijhpm.2023.7663

4 Navigating disability in times of conflict: The case of disability policies in Pakistan

Farman Ali, Zia Ullah Akhunzada and Mandy Lau

4.1 Introduction

More than one billion people in the world experience some form of disability, and the majority of disabled people live in developing countries (WHO & World Bank, 2011). Disability studies and research scholarship have been dominated by the global North, leaving the unique issues of disabled people in the South (including Pakistan) under-theorised in a way that constitutes 'scholarly colonialism' (Meekosha, 2008, p. 2). Gender roles, religion, history, colonisation, war, economy, and geopolitics all play a part in shaping a unique disability experience in the global South in ways that North-based academic theorisation fails to adequately address. It may mean that disability experience in the developing world differs from that in the centre, and therefore, the Northern theorisation may not necessarily represent the voices of disabled people in the periphery. Pakistan, with its political and economic instabilities, is home to a large number of disabled people due to climate crises, war conflicts, chronic diseases, earthquakes, and risky workplaces, among other reasons. The exact number of disabled people in Pakistan is vague; however, estimates put the figure close to 31 million (British Council, 2019; Rathore & Mansoor, 2019).

Though disabled people face multifaceted issues across the globe, those living in the war zone of Pakistan's peripheries experience unique problems due to the confluence of gender, disability, war, religion, culture, and geopolitics. Also, Pakistan has some unique features that differentiate it from other countries in both the global South and North. For instance, Pakistan has suffered the loss of around US$18 billion over the past decade due to earthquakes and floods, and the country is considered one of the most disaster-prone regions in South Asia (World Bank, 2017; as cited in United Nations Office for Disaster Risk Reduction & Asian Disaster Preparedness Centre, 2019). Natural calamities have affected a large number of people, including disabled people. Furthermore, poverty in Pakistan is widespread and on the rise (Bhatti, Haq, Javed, & Shirazi, 1999). Natural disasters further increase vulnerability, create cycles of poverty (United Nations Office for Disaster Risk Reduction & Asian Disaster Preparedness Centre, 2019), and cause a high prevalence of impairment from injuries sustained by the victims. Pakistan has also been facing militancy and terrorist attacks since 9/11, resulting in many civilians and armed personnel becoming victims and sustaining serious injuries (Raja, 2013; Rathore, New, & Iftikhar, 2011). Due to economic crises, the Pakistan government has taken austerity measures (Mumtaz, 2019), resulting in developmental cuts that affect the welfare sector (Dawn, 2020). This situation could affect the meagre resources available to disabled people. Furthermore, high inflation in the country makes it difficult for people to meet their nutritional needs. Among these, the most affected are those who live in rural areas, which are the major reservoirs of poverty in Pakistan (Chaudhry, Malik, & Ashraf, 2006). Moreover, vector-borne diseases such as dengue and malaria cause around 1 million fatalities globally each year, and survivors of these infections endure lasting debilitation and physical and visual impairments (WHO, 2014). These diseases are widespread in Pakistan (Nieto, Khan, Ullah, & Teglas, 2012). Other diseases, including tuberculosis, diabetes, and hepatitis are also widespread in many parts of the country (WHO, 2018). These medical conditions have serious implications for disability prevalence.

Given these challenges, which lead to increased risk of disability, it is important to critically analyse the issues facing disabled people in light of Pakistan's disability policies. The involvement of disabled people is important in decision-making, policies, and disability services that affect them directly or indirectly (Meltzer, Dickinson, Malbon, & Carey, 2021; Mellifont, Smith-Merry, & Bulkeley, 2023; Löve, Traustadóttir, Quinn, & Rice, 2017). However, it is arguably true that developing countries in the global South are failing to formulate policies based on lived realities, and Pakistan is no exception. Multiple factors may impede this process, prompting scrutiny of the ways in which these policies fail to meaningfully include disabled people in various facets of life.

Research reported in this chapter arises from larger Master of Philosophy and Doctor of Philosophy projects on disability, masculinity, and war in Pashtun-majority areas of Pakistan. Pashtun, Pakhtun, and Pathan are different names for the Pashtu-speaking ethnic population that resides on both sides of the border between Afghanistan and Pakistan. The study is an attempt to critically analyse disability policies and understand how these policies reflect or exclude the voices and lived experiences of Pashtun men with acquired physical disabilities, navigating injuries, and disabilities in war-affected regions. Pashtun men are more prone to injuries and impairments due to tribal enmities, working in hazardous workplaces, and war conflicts in the Pashtun-majority areas. Therefore, the issue of impairment and how it is addressed in policy has significant repercussions for the Pashtun men and their families. We present policy issues and discuss how existing disability policies in Pakistan appear to be unresponsive and unable to solve the basic issues of Pashtun men with acquired disabilities in particular and disabled people in general.

4.2 Policy reforms in Pakistan

Though effective disability policies in Pakistan have largely been forgotten as part of the current national policy agenda, significant policy reforms include the *Disabled*

Persons Ordinance, 1981, the *National Policy for Persons with Disabilities, 2002*, the *National Plan of Action, 2006*, the *Special Citizen Act, 2008*, and the *Special Citizen Act, 2009*. There has also been the formulation of province-specific policies after the devolution of key subjects to provinces from the centre through the 18th constitutional amendments. Below is a brief overview of the legislative and policy framework in Pakistan.

The government of Pakistan promulgated the *Disabled Persons Ordinance* in 1981. The Ordinance is supposed to extend to the whole of Pakistan. Under the ordinance, a National Council for the development of disabled people has been established that focuses on policy formulation to improve employability and rehabilitation services. The task of medical assessment and identification of eligible individuals for the rehabilitation programmes has been assigned to the National Council. Moreover, the Ordinance guides the National Council to evaluate and coordinate the execution of policy under the patronage of the Ministry of Health and Social Welfare. Under the Ordinance, provincial governments are obligated to execute the policy formulated by the National Council and undertake appropriate measures regarding the employment, rehabilitation, and welfare of disabled people. The Ordinance also allocates a 1% employment quota (later increased to 2%) for disabled people. The quota system requires federal, provincial, and district departments to enforce quota percentages for government employees. In this regard, ministries/departments are required to allocate a 2% quota for disabled individuals proportional to the overall sectioned strength/posts. In the case of noncompliance, a bill presented in the National Assembly titled *Further to Amend the Disabled Persons (Employment and Rehabilitation) Ordinance 1981* stipulates that: "If any institution or department ignores the quota of two percent (2%) for disabled persons while giving advertisement for employment, then a serious action to be taken against them." In 1981, provincial governments amended the *Disabled Persons Ordinance*, according to the provincial needs and requirements. For example, the province of Punjab increased its employment quota from 2% to 3%. However, the modified versions of the *Disabled Persons Ordinance 1981* lack a sufficient penalty mechanism. Therefore, disabled candidates often legally challenge recruitment processes that fail to follow relevant legislation and policies.

Another key policy document is the *National Policy for Persons with Disabilities, 2002*, which charts out a comprehensive plan for the optimal development of disabled people in the country. After a long consultative process with all the stakeholders, the government of Pakistan developed its first national policy for persons with disabilities. The stakeholders involved in formulating the policy document included the federal ministries of health, labour and manpower, science and technology, housing and work, and relevant prominent non-governmental organisations (NGOs). It has a vision, strategies, and guiding principles that aim to develop and empower disabled people in the country. The aims and objectives in the policy document emphasise access to facilities for the mainstreaming of disabled people, their involvement in planning and implementation of programmes related to rehabilitation and education, ensuring their rights and equal opportunities, adequate formulation of a legislative framework for their rehabilitation and employment, use of modern technology, and the removal of financial and technical barriers in the implementation of disability programmes in the country. Given the broad scope of the *National Policy for Persons with Disabilities, 2002*, the government required another plan for its implementation. Therefore, in order to operationalise and translate the policy, the government of Pakistan formulated the *National Plan of Action* in 2006. The *National Plan of Action* includes both short-term goals (2006–2009) and long-term goals (2009–2025). The short-term goals include measures such as sample surveys in selected districts, prevention of disability, primary and secondary care, medical rehabilitation, promoting vocational training, employment provision, legislative support, and assistance from NGOs. The long-term goals focus primarily on creating a barrier-free environment for disabled people. The implementation strategy of the *National Plan of Action* targets 17 broad areas. This framework emphasises adopting an integrated approach through the involvement of all stakeholders, ranging from the centre to the district level, for the execution of short- and long-term goals. The *National Action Plan* also strategises developmental interventions for disabled people living in rural and remote areas. However, the task of service delivery in these areas has been assigned to non-governmental organisations.

Another important legislative move is the enactment of the *Special Citizen Act, 2008*. The government of Pakistan promulgated the *Special Citizen Act, 2008* in order to facilitate a barrier-free physical environment. The Act seeks to provide accessible public places, including the allocation of seats in public transport and improving footpath accessibility for visually disabled people and wheelchair users. Under this Act, the concerned authorities are bound to construct accessible buildings, especially educational institutions, hospitals, banks, shopping malls, police stations, airports and railway stations, bus stops, and other important public places. Furthermore, in order to assist disabled people in road crossing, traffic police were assigned the task of prioritising and facilitating their crossing.

A year later, the government of Pakistan promulgated the *Special Citizens (Right to Concession in Movement) Act, 2009*. This Act urges a concessional rate for persons with disabilities on both public and private transport, even if they work but are unable to pay standard fares. The Act in this regard implements a half-price fare for railways and other transport available in the country. These policy and legislative measures are the outcome of national and international disability activism and the international pressure of groups including the United Nations, its affiliated bodies, and local organisations within the country such as disabled peoples organisations (DPOs). Pakistan, however, is still lagging behind in providing basic facilities and is unable to fully address the needs of disabled people. While these policies and legislation are important measures, they are, by and large, not based on the lived experiences of disabled people.

4.3 Navigating the complexity of disability in war conflict

One of the most neglected areas of disability policy and legislative framework is the group of disabled people living in a war zone. The number of war-affected disabled people is underestimated, particularly in Pakistan, but also in the international context in general (Mitchell & Karr, 2015). Within Pakistan, some regions have been affected by militancy and the war against terror. One of these regions is Khyber Pakhtunkhwa, a province that borders Afghanistan. In war-affected regions of Khyber Pakhtunkhwa, citizens sustain serious injuries that cause impairments, as well as other complex challenges resulting from war-related conflict. In order to understand this, we conducted interviews with married men with physical disabilities and their immediate family members in Swat Valley, which is an administrative and war-affected district of the province of Khyber Pakhtunkhwa. The armed conflict in Swat can be linked to 9/11 and the security challenges that came after it. After United States forces attacked the hardline Taliban regime in the aftermath of 9/11, support for the then Taliban government surged in both Afghanistan and Pakistan. The Pakistani government backed the United States in its war on terror. This assistance sparked resentment among some hardline religious groups towards Pakistan's law enforcement institutions. With the passage of time, the global politics of this conflict spread to the periphery, including the border and remote regions of Khyber Pakhtunkhwa, particularly Swat, which is frequently impacted by natural disasters. Using violence and threats against the citizens, the militants (locals and foreign elements) steadily spread their ideology in Swat and gained an avid following. They demanded implementation of strict Sharia (Islamic) rules based on their own interpretations in Swat and its adjacent districts. However, regarding the war on terror in general, many Pakistani believe that this war is induced by foreign powers to extend their presence to secure multiple interests, rather than being initiated by the locals. But this is not a simple theory to explain the origins of war, as other factors must be considered while analysing war, its causes, and politics. Orakazai (2011) argues that the war conflict in Swat stemmed from cultural, historical, social, and religious aspects. These factors, it can be argued, resulted in militancy and war-related conflict after the 9/11 attacks. Regardless of the cause, disabled people are the victims who have paid a huge price.

Many of the Pashtun men sustained injuries and are still the victims of the attacks that occurred due to the instability around this militancy and war. During the injury and treatment phases, they are often in limbo on account of the serious nature of their injuries and lack of information about the medical process. The challenges of war are inextricably linked to other interconnected social, political, and economic issues. Disabled men navigate the issue in a very uncertain way, which affects their well-being. Their families also experienced enormous challenges amid the war. War injuries create a plethora of problems and complications for disabled men and their families. Being fathers, they need to navigate the challenges and hardships of their disability to also support their dependent children's future. Sustaining war-related injuries themselves is problematic due to security restrictions such as curfews and the banned militants' violent threats that delay the treatment of injured citizens. This is explained by one of the participants as:

> I got hit by a gunshot and a man behind me was also hit. The moment the military noticed me, they alerted all the military checkpoints to allow our car to pass. After that, we travelled the long way from Bisham to Peshawar, where I received medical care from the Red Cross Hospital. I underwent several procedures. (Zafar)

People who sustain injuries are often taken to a hospital by their family members, and if the injuries are severe, they may receive multiple surgeries. The injuries to their limbs and spinal cords affect them in myriad ways, further exacerbating their and their families' issues. It is always a challenging time for the injured to navigate their economic, physical, and psychological conditions, especially when they have to travel to big cities for treatment. This can be fraught with other complexities, as Qasim explains:

> You are aware that at the time, there was a military operation against extremists, and civilians were not permitted to travel. Two to three others accompanied him to the hospital, while I remained behind. He was treated at CMH for three months. (Qasim)

During war-related conflict, injured individuals encounter physical barriers such as roadblocks and uncertainty in local hospitals that are compounded as a difficult time because of concerns about the safety of their family members living in conflict zones. During intense fighting between militants and law enforcement agencies in the past, their families had to leave their homes and flee to neighbouring safe areas where they were generally supported by their relatives or friends. In addition, residents often heard the sound of gunfire, mortar shells, and bombings during the fight, and families were concerned and apprehensive about the situation, not knowing what to expect next.

Unfortunately, existing disability policies do not capture the voices of disabled people living in volatile regions. There is no plan for safety and protection during conflicts for disabled individuals in these policies. The post-conflict phase has also been underestimated, rendering the existing policies incomplete, ineffective, unresponsive, and exclusionary. Disabled people and their families are impacted by war-related conflict, both directly and indirectly. During the war, pregnant wives of disabled men encounter difficulties, for example evacuating from their homes to a safe zone may have a negative impact on the mothers and their babies' health because of fear and uncertainty. Also, providing regular check-ups for newborn babies may not be feasible in this situation. Therefore, the babies may be born weak or with health conditions. These are some of the harsh realities that disabled people and their families have to face in the peripheries of the world but that are not recognised within disability policies, which are written without the context of conflict and war in mind.

Married men who sustain injuries are often the sole providers of income for their families; and they often lose their income due to impairment in an inaccessible physical environment. In addition, the wounds cause physical pain, and their medical treatment continues with a lot of uncertainties. They do not know, for example, whether their physical injuries will fully recover without any functional limitations. They often encounter setbacks and confusion, which changes the way that they understand and cope with their disability. This is shown in Fayaz's comment below:

> During my treatment in Peshawar, my leg became blue and the doctor amputated it. They did their best, but the treatment was ineffective. It was excruciatingly painful. At the start, my body temperature increased significantly. Afterwards, they informed me that my leg was afflicted with cancer and required amputation. (Fayaz)

The medical professionals amputated the leg due to the possibility of complications from the injury spreading to other parts of the body. In situations like this, the initial surgery is often not a success, and subsequent surgeries are necessary. Their precarious health condition creates uncertainty among spouses, children, and parents, which leaves them completely reliant on professional medical advice from hospitals and dealing with the uncertainty that brings on a day to day basis. In Pakistan, disability is still understood through a medical lens and medical experts are the key source of information. In our study, men with physical disabilities were those who had suffered injuries in war, and medical health experts and their advice were crucial to both the participants and their families. Limb amputations can have negative effects on both disabled men and their families. After the amputation, they are confronted with mental health issues and are required to make constant visits to the doctor for treatment. As receiving counselling and psychotherapy sessions are not common among the residents of Swat, visiting a medical doctor such as a psychiatrist seems the only viable (but expensive) option. Fayaz spoke about this:

> Mentally, yes, I feel stressed. My concern about my treatment is causing me and my family to feel pressure. I go to the psychiatrist occasionally for check-ups, but life is not simple, I mean it's challenging. Although I'm not very old, my beard is getting whiter because I tend to focus too much on life's challenges. (Fayaz)

Amputation affects the emotional and mental health of disabled men and can expose them to a variety of ableism and disableism experienced not only due to their physical impairment at a personal level but also from societal expectations and resulting pressure. Significantly, apart from the 'rapid form' of structural disablism experienced by participants, there was limited discussion of another important dimension of the experience of disability, i.e., a form of disablism that affects individuals at a psycho-emotional level (Thomas, 2007). Psycho-emotional disableism (Thomas, 2007) centres on the experiences of exclusion and restrictions imposed by societal expectations and attitudes that might be essential to understand the problems faced by disabled people.

A problem that disabled men face stems from the masculine role expectations constituted by the ideology of Pashtun masculinity in the Pashtun gender order. Therefore, failing to meet the demand put forward by the gender milieu, disabled men are being restricted at a subjective level. The injury and impairment changes men's lives, and they are often worried for their children and families, who are dependent on them. Their impairment challenges the ableist capacity to work in an inaccessible able-bodied world and therefore it affects those who rely on them for schooling, family expenses, and public space responsibilities.

War injuries have repercussions for the men living in the peripheries where their disabilities intersect with remoteness, poverty, inaccessibility, gender, unemployment, and cultural situatedness of the corporeality. In addition, they are confronted with health issues and have a lot of difficulty in managing their routine life. As a result, family members who rely on these men are unable to support them, causing sadness and despair among all family members, as expressed by one participant:

> [I]t has affected a lot. Our family suffered and I now have no pocket money; the cost is too much; I get an infection due to catheter every three days, and they charge 300 rupees for each visit. It's incredibly challenging. (Noman)

Moreover, dislocation from their native villages during war is another challenge for disabled men and their families that they need to navigate on top of their impairment, poverty, fear, and inaccessibility. They face internal displacement with a myriad of challenges and are forced to leave their native areas by inflicting fear-spreading tactics from the actors involved in the war by making them 'internally displaced persons' (IDPs). When forced to leave their native places due to fear and violence, men with physical disabilities find it hard to relocate. Also, they and their families need to cope with the hot weather and food shortages. Uncertainties follow them from their communities to the displaced areas as well. Although camps have been established for IDPs, the facilities there are limited. In these camps, there is no specialist support for disability. Dislocation is yet another site of uncertainty, challenge, and suffering for men with physical disabilities and their families. They are forced to leave their homes and native areas and settle in tent camps provided by the government. Moreover, the plan of return to their village is challenging owing to the presence of used/unused explosive weapons left during the war.

4.4 Lived experiences and policy challenges

Existing polices, formulated to address the problems disabled people face in Pakistan, are not without gaps. These policies play an important role to assist disabled people in Pakistan in one way or other. They do not, however, reflect the voices of those living in the peripheries of the periphery, including those living in, or with the consequences of, conflict and war. The war-affected men whose experiences are highlighted here have not been discussed in any policy document, nor is it on the agenda for policy discussion. There is no recognition of the lived experiences of disabled men such as those described in this chapter.

War conflict has implications for disabled people in two ways. First, war-related conflict produces impairments in regions that often already have meagre resources to accelerate the social inclusion of persons with disability and promote a culture of inclusivity that helps them achieve their goals. The impairment production then has repercussions for men and their families where there are gender segregations and gendered divisions of labour that are strictly practiced in both private and public spheres. Men who are the head of the household confront challenging life experiences as a result of injuries and impairments, which affects everyone in the family. In Pashtun cultural and geographic settings, war conflict primarily affects men, resulting in injuries and impairments. This critical issue has not received attention in policymaking, leaving the crisis unresolved so far, and it is also an under-theorised area within disability scholarship.

In conflict zones in Pakistan, injured people are often not aware of their health problems, and as a result, they are unable to get information about the nature of their injuries nor prospective surgeries that could result in amputation. They also do not know how or who to consult for treatment of injuries incurred during the conflict. As a result, their health and disability makes them vulnerable for an extended period of time, and they may have complicated health conditions which necessitate ongoing medical evaluation that they cannot receive support for. This predicament has a financial impact on them and their families, prompting them to take loans to treat their complex injuries. In addition to the precarious health predicament they are in, the psychological burden of losing the functionality of a body part in an ableist cultural context exacerbates the impact of their injury on their daily lives. The war and absence of a mitigation plan as part of existing policy frameworks intensifies their perilous situation. Unfortunately, the policy discourse relating to disability in Pakistan does not prioritise the issue of men's injuries and impairments in conflict areas and the impact on their families.

Second, disabled men living in crisis zones suffer numerous challenges, but their stories are difficult to hear due to geopolitics, security issues, and poverty. Men who acquire disability as a result of injuries have complex and unpleasant corporeal realities that are intertwined with war, gender, politics, and poverty. Existing disability policy and legislative frameworks in Pakistan fail to address the challenges that disabled persons face in the country's conflict zones. This is not to say that these policies do not have a beneficial and reformative impact, but the existing policies do not include the voices of disabled people living in remote areas, whose lived reality presents a unique disability experience. In Pakistan, the rural physical environment and cultural differences are significant compared to urban environments. Similarly, conflict and disaster-prone remote and rural regions encounter perilous realities linked to climate change, war, culture, physical inaccessibility, rurality, and poverty. Disability at the intersection of these harsh realities manifests a complex corporeality, necessitating specialised policies and legislation.

Existing policies are therefore ineffective in addressing the obstacles that disabled individuals face in rural and remote areas. There are various flaws in current policies that impede the realisation of the rights and inclusion of disabled people and are therefore unable to transform the lives of disabled people. Firstly, it is arguably true that disability policies in Pakistan are not based on indigenous and local realities, but rather on the ideas and culture of the Northern disability movement, which might demonstrate a different disability embodiment, cultural approaches, and perspectives than the Southern corporeal realities of Pakistan's peripheries. Though following a universalist Northern discourse is instrumental at a more abstract level, it is difficult to explain and figure out the practical coping strategies that can be taken into regions like Swat and other conflict zones affected by war, climate change, and poverty.

Secondly, it also means that existing policies do not reflect the lived experiences of disabled people in the region and therefore are not successful in achieving the goal of promoting a diversified culture where everyone enjoys and exercises their rights. It is worth mentioning that without dedicated research such as that presented here the voices of these disabled men and the rest of the disabled community would go unheard owing to remoteness, security challenges, lack of research, and poverty, which hinder disabled people from educating themselves and knowing their rights. It has been 15 years since war devastated the area, and disabled people have experienced physical and psychological pain throughout this period.

Thirdly, exposure to violence in the conflict zone affects the emotional and psychological well-being of disabled men. Living in a war zone is a traumatic experience where the wounds are not only physical but also psychological, with long-term implications for disabled people. Unfortunately, there has been no systematic effort by the government and NGOs to examine the mental health of disabled people, which is serious negligence on the part of authorities and humanitarian agencies professing to protect and care for disabled people. Finally, there is no mechanism in place for the implementation of existing policies in conflict or post-conflict zones, therefore limiting their practical implications. For example, physical inaccessibility hinders disabled people's engagement in communal life, preventing them from leading a meaningful life.

This exclusion has an impact on their cultural capital, pushing them into a vicious cycle of dependency and poverty. The *Special Citizen Act, 2008* mandates an accessible plan for disabled individuals during the construction of public buildings. However, due to the absence of implementation mechanisms across all regions, the reach of this Act is limited. For example, an important issue is the lack of an evacuation strategy for disabled individuals in areas of conflict. During the forced displacement of people from Swat to a safer region, disabled individuals were traumatised because of the absence of an accessible evacuation plan during the war. Though Pakistan has implemented extensive strategies to tackle militancy in volatile regions, including Swat, no major attempts have been made in the policy framework to make evacuation easier and more accessible for disabled persons during wartime.

The situation in Swat indicates that Pakistan's disability policies lack the voices and lived experiences of disabled people from the conflict zone in the remote rural regions. These disabled people have been affected by war and natural catastrophes and, hence, are unable to address the broader issues of disability in the context of their lives, which are rooted in a matrix of poverty, conflict, geopolitics, gender, and ableism.

4.5 Conclusion

A sizeable number of disabled people live in Pakistan, but those living in the remote and war-affected regions go under the radar of policymakers, and therefore they do not have any say or representation in policy discourse. Structural and prioritising difficulties on the part of the government foster an atmosphere that fails to produce a rational policy outcome. The crux of the issue is that the creation of existing policies does not truly understand or reflect the lived experiences of disabled people, and the resulting policy is therefore unable to transform their lives. Though, like other developing South Asian countries, Pakistan has also made some progress in terms of disability policy and legislative framework, the practical implementation of these policies remains a dilemma for disabled people in the country. Disability at the intersection of culture, gender, geopolitics, rurality, poverty, and war necessitates policies that could address complex indigenous issues with effective implementation mechanisms designed for these specific contexts. Thus, policymakers and relevant authorities in Pakistan need to delve deeply into the problems disabled people face and revisit the existing policy and legislative framework. The empirical evidence of this study underscores the importance of including the voices of disabled individuals living in conflict-affected areas in policies and legislation. Building on the research presented in this chapter, there is a pressing need to conduct more research studies in these areas, which can serve as a crucial tool for addressing policy gaps in Pakistan.

References

Bhatti, M. A., Haq, R., Javed, T., & Shirazi, N. S. (1999). A sectoral analysis of poverty in Pakistan. *The Pakistan Development Review*, *38*(4), 859–872. https://doi.org/10.30541/v38i4IIpp.859-872

British Council. (2019). *Moving from the Margins – Mainstreaming Young Persons with Disabilities in Pakistan*. www.britishcouncil.pk/sites/default/files/mypd_2019.pdf

Chaudhry, I., Malik, S., & Ashraf, M. (2006). Rural poverty in Pakistan: Some related concepts, issues and empirical analysis. *Pakistan Economic and Social Review*, *44*(2), 259–276. http://www.jstor.org/stable/25825297

Dawn. (2020, 21 February). Development cuts. Editorial. *Dawn*. https://www.dawn.com/news/1535725

Löve, L., Traustadóttir, R., Quinn, G., & Rice, J. (2017). The inclusion of the lived experience of disability in policymaking. *Laws*, *6*(33), 1–16. https://doi.org/10.3390/laws6040033

Meekosha, H. (2008). *Contextualizing Disability: Developing Southern/Global Theory*. In 4th Biennial Disability Studies Conference (pp. 1–20). https://www.lancaster.ac.uk/fass/events/disabilityconference_archive/2008/papers/meekosha2008.doc

Mellifont, D., Smith-Merry, J., & Bulkeley, K. (2023). The employment of people with lived experience of disability in Australian disability services. *Social Policy & Administration*, *57*(5), 642–655. https://doi.org/10.1111/spol.12898

Meltzer, A., Dickinson, H., Malbon, E., & Carey, G. (2021). Why is lived experience important for market stewardship? A proposed framework for why and how lived experience should be included in stewarding disability markets. *Evidence & Policy*, *17*(2), 335–347. https://doi.org/10.1332/174426421X16142714946996

Mitchell, D. & Karr, V. (2015). *Crises, Conflict and Disability*. London: Routledge.

Mumtaz, H. (2019, 8 April). Austerity measures. *Dawn*. https://www.dawn.com/news/1474665
Nieto, N. C., Khan, K., Uhllah, G., & Teglas, M. B. (2012). The emergence and maintenance of vector-borne diseases in the Khyber Pakhtunkhwa province, and the federally administered tribal areas of Pakistan. *Frontiers in Physiology*, 3(250), 1–7. https://doi.org/10.3389/fphys.2012.00250
Orakzai, S. B. (2011). Conflict in the Swat Valley of Pakistan: Pakhtun culture and peacebuiliding theory-practice application. *Journal of Peacebuilding & Development*, 6(1), 35–48. https://doi.org/10.1080/15423166.2011.179868996709
Raja, M. (2013, 27 March). Pakistani victims: War on terror toll put at 49,000. *The Express Tribune*. https://tribune.com.pk/story/527016/pakistani-victims-war-on-terror-toll-put-at-49000
Rathore, F. A. & Mansoor, S. N. (2019). Disability rights and management in Pakistan: Time to face the bitter truth. *Journal of the College of Physicians and Surgeons Pakistan*, 29(12), 1131–1132. www.jcpsp.pk/archive/2019/Dec2019/01.pdf
Rathore, F. A., New, P. W., & Iftikhar, A. (2011). A report on disability and rehabilitation medicine in Pakistan: Past, present, and future directions. *Archives of Physical Medicine and Rehabilitation*, 92(1), 161–166. https://doi.org/10.1016/j.apmr.2010.10.004
Thomas, C. (2007). *Sociologies of Disability, Impairment, and Chronic Illness: Ideas in Disability Studies and Medical Sociology*. London: Palgrave.
United Nations Office for Disaster Risk Reduction & Asian Disaster Preparedness Centre. (2019). *Disaster Risk Reduction in Pakistan*, status report. https://reliefweb.int/sites/reliefweb.int/files/resources/68230_7pakistandrmstatusreport.pdf
World Health Organization. (2014). *A Global Brief on Vector-Borne Diseases*. Geneva World Health Organization. https://apps.who.int/iris/bitstream/handle/10665/111008/WHO_DCO_WHD_2014.1_eng.pdf?sequence=1
World Health Organization. (2018). *Model Disability Survey General Result District, Province, Baluchistan Pakistan*. https://cdn.who.int/media/docs/default-source/documents/disability/mds-report-pakistan-general-results.pdf?sfvrsn=11d36802_1&utm
World Health Organization & World Bank. (2011). *World Report on Disability*. Geneva: World Health Organization. https://iris.who.int/items/ff302fed-0072-4478-89eb-b1cb96b73c09

5 The multi-layered, multi-faceted importance of the lived experience in disability health policy

Dinesh Palipana and Gisselle Gallego

5.1 People with lived experience in health care decision-making

People with disability comprise approximately 16% of the global population, and experience health disparities and discrimination (World Health Organization, 2024). In Australia, approximately one in six people have a disability, being almost 20% of the population (Australian Institute of Health Welfare, 2024). The United Nations Convention on the Rights of Persons with Disabilities (UNCRPD) recognises that people with disability have the right to disability-specific health services, as well as the highest attainable standard of health and the same range, quality and standard of health care as others (United Nations, 2006).

While with support and information many people with disability can manage their own health needs (Nouri et al., 2021), evidence shows that these needs are often not met due to financial, access and attitudinal barriers (Robey et al., 2013; Satchidanand et al., 2012). According to the *World Health Report on Disability* (World Health Organization, 2011), people with disability are four times more likely to report being treated badly, more than twice as likely to find health care provider skills inadequate to meet their needs, and nearly three times more likely to report being denied care (World Health Organization, 2011). The report also described the importance of health providers being respectful, knowledgeable and supportive to people with disability (World Health Organization, 2011). This was also echoed by the Australian Royal Commission into Violence, Abuse, Neglect and Exploitation of People with Disability (Disability Royal Commission), which highlighted that people with disability face significant barriers to receiving adequate health care. Contributing factors highlighted were negative attitudes, inadequate training and lack of understanding amongst health care professionals regarding the health needs of people with disability (Australian Government, 2023).

Negative attitudes towards people with disability not only have an impact on health care but, as described by Green et al. (2022), have detrimental implications for policy design. Their research on policy action on social determinants of health (SDH) highlighted that policies that aim to address inequalities do not focus on upstream measures such as education, employment and transport. This occurs as a result of a pervasive focus on the biomedical model of disability, which results in a "narrow framing of disability" (p. 223) around the medical aspects of disability. Their research also highlighted the lack of involvement of people with lived experience in the policy process, which results in policies not meeting the needs of people with disability.

Research from the United States by Smith et al. (2020) described how people with lived experience consider that policymakers fail to prioritise and understand their viewpoints and needs in health policy. This exemplifies an ongoing failure to recognise and prioritise the lived experiences, expertise and self-identified needs of people with disabilities in health policy. This is despite the World Health Organization (WHO) Global Report on Health Equity for Persons with Disabilities highlighting the importance of including people with lived experience of disability in the health sector's decision-making processes (World Health Organization, 2022).

Martin et al. (2022) have described that "developing knowledge sharing practices that entrust and empower disabled people to articulate their concerns and recommendations will contribute to their voices being more meaningfully included in future health-related policy and programme development" (p. 2). Furthermore, as described in the preamble of the UNCRPD "Persons with disabilities should have the opportunity to be actively involved in decision making processes about policies and programs, including those directly concerning them" (United Nations, 2006). Their lived experience can provide a significant contribution to the delivery of quality health services both as health care workers and service users (Fitzpatrick & Barrett, 2023). Participatory methods and co-design for developing programmes and health policy that includes people with lived experience of disability can enhance the health and well-being of policy end users (Donetto et al., 2015; Martin et al., 2022). However, research is needed to explore the best methods to support inclusive health policy and programme decision-making where there is meaningful participation of people with lived experience.

5.2 People with lived experience in medical education and research

It has been proposed that one way to address the negative attitudes, discrimination and bias, particularly in the health care system, is to have a diverse health workforce. In the foreword of the 2007 British Medical Association (BMA) (2007) publication, 'Disability equality in the medical profession' (BMA Equal Opportunities Committee, 2007, p. viii), Sir Bert Massie CBE, Chairman, Disability Rights Commission and a person with lived experience stated: "By welcoming more disabled medical students, and by retaining more disabled doctors in employment, the profession will improve its outward facing service and better reflect modern society."

In order to provide high-quality, responsive, equitable health care, the health care workforce should reflect society. Promoting health equity therefore requires the diversification of the health care workforce (Dearnley et al., 2010). The lived experience of health care providers can play a key role in reducing health care inequities towards people with disabilities (Philip, Nagesh & Singh, 2024). However, students, trainees and doctors with disabilities are underrepresented in the health care sector, not only in Australia but around the world (British Medical Association, 2020; Gertsman et al., 2023; Meeks et al., 2021; Nouri et al., 2021). This lack of representation in health care professions has the potential to increase bias in health service delivery and its policy-making (Philip, Nagesh & Singh, 2024).

Australia and other countries have legislation to support the rights of people with disability to education and employment; yet segregation, inaccessible physical environments, lack of accommodations, inadequate support, social exclusion and ableism still persist, including in health care education and research (Fuentes et al., 2024). It is important to note that Australia does not have a federal human rights act (Gavshon, 2024). While there is state-based legislation, according to the Australian Human Rights Commission, "UN Treaty bodies have repeatedly concluded that core treaties have not been adequately incorporated into Australia's legal system. Many of Australia's commitments to human rights are confined to rhetoric without corresponding domestic protections" (Australian Human Rights Commission, 2022, p. 12). This means that rights-based assertions often do not follow through from rhetoric into policy and practice.

One of the reasons for a lack of policy and practice action is that decision-making is not tied to the realities of people's lived experiences. As described by the Policy Lab in the United Kingdom (UK), "lived experience is an important part of policymaking, because it helps us to root policy decisions in real life experiences, ensuring a diversity of perspectives are considered and allowing for new ideas to emerge" (Policy Lab, 2024, p. 1). The Policy Lab works collaboratively and openly across the UK government and beyond. It is a multidisciplinary team and for their 'Lived experience in policy making guide' they partnered with people with lived experience, policymakers and sector experts from across England. Students, trainees and doctors with lived experience not only have an "insider's view" of the patient experience (Fitzmaurice et al., 2021) but have had to overcome several barriers and challenges in their day-to-day life, including in relation to health services. Through relating these experiences they can challenge ableism and the negative assumptions of peers in training and practice (Fitzpatrick & Barrett, 2023; Shakespeare, Iezzoni, & Groce, 2009). However, as described by Stergiopoulos et al. (2023), even though the perspectives of medical students with lived experience as patients holds a unique perspective, this perspective has largely been unstudied. This is therefore an important area for future research in order to inform policy for health education.

Disability may occur at any point: before people are interested in medicine, during their studies, or during their professional career. Hence, barriers to a disability-inclusive medical education can occur at all points, starting from the information provided before admissions to a medical programme, admission decisions, learning facilities, education, assessments, clinical placements and employment (Fitzpatrick & Barrett, 2023). Admission to Australian medical schools is competitive, and completion of studies is highly demanding, as is subsequent specialist training. Navigating this experience as a student with a disability can prove challenging, with a variety of unique significant barriers arising (Medical Deans Australia and New Zealand, 2021). Effective inclusion of students with disabilities, therefore, requires identification of the obstacles that prevent participation at the medical school level and beyond, along with an understanding of feasible and practical ways in which they can be addressed.

In 2015, a guidance document on the inclusion of students with disability was released by the Medical Deans Australia and New Zealand (MDANZ), who are the peak body representing professional entry-level medical education, training and research in Australia and New Zealand (Medical Deans Australia and New Zealand, 2017). This non-mandatory set of guidelines provided a framework to guide medical schools and individuals as a starting point for discussion about the skills and tasks a medical student will need to be "successful and how they will best achieve these outcomes".

However, the guidance was not informed by the lived experience of students, trainees or doctors with disability. It used ableist language and resulted in creating a guideline that would actually discriminate against people with physical disability. Instead of an inclusive, strengths-based approach with a focus on what people can do, the guideline included rigid psychological and physical requirements for medical education applicants. For example, it stated that: "Medicine is a profession that requires manual dexterity, and possession of fine motor skills is fundamental in providing adequate clinical care" (Medical Deans Australia and New Zealand, 2017, p. 12). Rather than focusing on cognitive abilities, this requirement emphasised physical capabilities and sensorimotor skills. Another requirement stated that "Effective and efficient verbal communication, in English, is an essential requirement to provide safe delivery of care during medical training" (Medical Deans Australia and New Zealand, 2017, p. 9). While the patient-doctor interaction requires effective and efficient communication, this does not need to be "verbal" as communication can be facilitated by assistive technology and through the use of sign language interpreters (Stauffer et al., 2022). Furthermore, as highlighted by Palipana (2022): "The reductionism of medicine to simple procedures does not do it justice, because the practice of medicine is primarily an intellectual activity closely coupled with humanism." This highlights the importance of including students, trainees and doctors with lived experience in policymaking. Doing so will ensure that the conditions in which medical education takes place, as regulated through policy, are more able to support students with disability and enable a more diverse workforce that can work better with patients with disability.

In 2019, the guideline was reviewed with a new version released in 2021 (Medical Deans Australia and New Zealand, 2021). The renewed process utilised the voice of people with disability in its creation. The need to rethink policies and guidelines because they have been exclusionary towards people with disability is not unique to Australia. In India, despite ratifying the UNCRPD, and in 2016 passing a rights-based legislation, students with certain disabilities were discriminated against by the National Medical Council (Singh, 2019). This precipitated several High Court rulings that allowed students with certain disabilities to be granted medical admission. McKee et al. (2016) in the US argue that the focus should be on functional requirements that enable and empower learners with disabilities, rather than technical requirements (also known as inherent requirements). For example, functional requirements can take into account the use of assistive technology that can allow people with disability to complete key tasks (McKee et al., 2016). This is also illustrated by a landmark law case in Canada where a deaf doctor, who was dismissed from their residency and denied accommodation for American Sign Language, decided to sue and won the case (Gertsman et al., 2023). They are now practising, have won multiple awards and recognitions, and have become a champion for other doctors and patients.

5.3 Inclusive policies

It is important to provide guidance on how to effectively implement inclusion policies that aim to enable students with disability to equally access medical education and increase representation within the medical profession. In Australia doctors with lived experience have been advocating for inclusive medical education (Bernard et al., 2023; Fitzmaurice et al., 2021; Lane, 2022), but there is still a dearth of research on medical education and environments for people with disability to practice within. There is also a clear tension between the intent of policies and inclusion. For example, the Royal Australasian College of Physicians' policy statement on disability endorsed the UNCRPD but failed to acknowledge doctors with lived experience and did not include workplace recommendations for doctors with disability (Bernard et al., 2023). As highlighted by Philip et al. (2024), regulatory bodies do not have disability-inclusive guidelines to support the inclusion of learners with lived experience.

As previously discussed, doctors and trainees with lived experiences can bring unique approaches and perspectives to patient care, health services, health policy and programmes. Research by Bradfield et al. (2023), illustrated the importance of acknowledging the lived experience of doctors with psychosocial disability. The authors emphasise that failing to do this inadvertently perpetuates stigma and barriers to care, and fails to recognise the knowledge from lived experience and how this can be used to improve access to support and treatment.

Jarus et al. (2023) noted that there is a lack of research on existing medical education accommodation policies, and how the gaps in these policies impact medical students with lived experience of disability. The authors further advocated for longitudinal policy-focused research projects to understand the impact of these gaps (Jarus et al., 2023). While there is research in the US (Meeks et al., Jain, 2020), the UK (Murphy, Dowell & Smith, 2022) and Canada (Jarus et al., 2023), in Australia research on the lived experiences of students, doctors and trainees with disability is limited. The Australian Medical Association (AMA) has called for more research to be conducted on these lived experiences, including longitudinal studies (Australian Medical Association, 2023). This need is also highlighted in a systematic review about ableism within health care professions by Lindsay et al. (2023), in which the authors conclude that "there is a critical need for a more in-depth understanding of the lived experiences and impact of workplace ableism within the health care professions" (p. 15). Longitudinal studies can help us understand the impact of having people with lived experience of disability informing policy and practice. Policies and procedures from professional and statutory bodies that regulate health professionals should also include health professionals with lived experience (Walker et al., 2013). It is important that they facilitate inclusion and recognise the needs of people with disability.

5.4 Lived experience and the future research agenda: Experiences, gaps and priorities

A change of culture in medicine is needed. It is important to have a disability inclusive, equitable and accessible medical education, training and practice framework informed by lived experience researchers working in partnership with students and practitioners with disability and their allies. To date, some changes have occurred based on self-advocacy, rather than systemic advocacy, and have been driven by articulate, passionate people with lived experience. These individuals have been instrumental in making medicine more inclusive for students with disability (Bernard et al., 2023; Fitzmaurice et al., 2021; Howick et al., 2023; Lane, 2022; Palipana, 2019). As previously described, people with lived experience were involved in the MDANZ guidance on medical programme applicants and students with a disability, as well as informing the position statements by the AMA and the Australian Medical Students' Association calling for inclusion, fair selection and support, organisational support, flexibility and reasonable adjustments and research (Australian Medical Association, 2023; Australian Medical Students' Association, 2020). However, more work is needed. As described in a recent systematic review, ableism is still present both at the individual level (bias, stigma and negative attitudes) and institutional level (inaccessible and unsupportive work environments) (Lindsay et al., 2023).

Research has a significant role in supporting the inclusion of lived experience in health care education and delivery by addressing both barriers and enablers. As depicted by Philip et al. (2024), these can be summarised in the ABCDE mnemonic (see Figure 5.1).

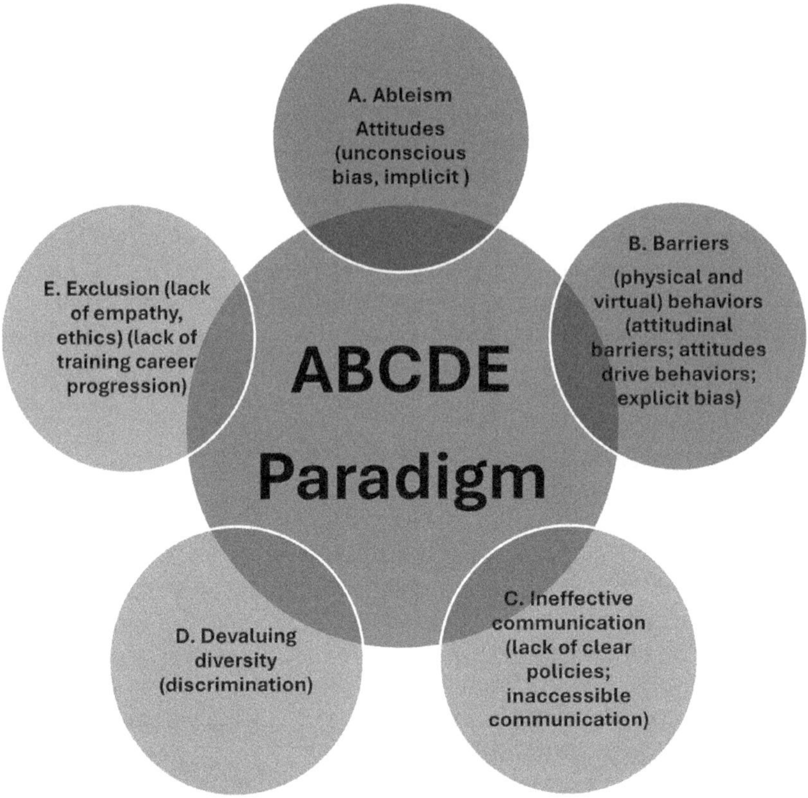

Source: Adapted from Philip, Nagesh & Singh (2024).

Figure 5.1 ABCDE Paradigm

Advocacy: research on systemic advocacy. To date, the onus has been on individuals to advocate for the profession (and their own self-advocacy) rather than making the education and work environments more inclusive.

Breaking barriers: there is no one-size-fits-all and there is diversity among people and the barriers they face in medical education and employment. One priority in Australia is to identify and explore these barriers and 'listen to the experiences of different groups'.

Communication – learner-centre pedagogy (LCP): research on the implementation of universal design by learning (UDL), having medical educators with lived experience and tackling the 'hidden/informal' curriculum.

Diverse capabilities: it is important that research concentrates on the misconceptions about disability and changing the perspective from people with diminished abilities to diverse competencies, and for disability to be seen as part of diversity. Organisational culture where the lived experience is seen as an expertise.

Empathy and empowerment: research on ethics, justice and autonomy. Best practice on lived experience researchers partnering with allies to co-design. Research that debunks the myths, such as the impact doctors with lived experience of disability have on patient safety.

Just as some advocate for rural-proofing of policies to take place, where policymakers consider during the design and implementation the impact policies will have in rural communities (Swindlehurst, 2005), we can advocate for policies to have 'disability-proofing' supported by lived experience-led research. In doing so, future research should focus on how the lived experiences of doctors, trainees and students can inform education and practice. Research is also needed on the development of models to support and develop sustainable and meaningful involvement of students and health professionals with lived experience of disability in research, practice and policy. As highlighted by Gupta et al. (2023), the impact of identity in professional spaces such as those of lived experience researchers who have a dual role as health care providers and patients is also an important area where future research is needed. And, finally, though it should go without saying that people with disability can perform as doctors (in the same way they have shown they can perform in every other profession) with appropriate adjustments and support, research evidence might be needed to prove the case to a recalcitrant medical profession.

5.5 Conclusion

> People with disability have valuable lived experience that cannot be taught and represent a powerful contribution to the delivery of quality health services both as service users and health workers. (Fitzpatrick & Barrett, 2023, p. 18)

Inclusive health services, policies and health workforce can benefit patients and improve patient outcomes. While allied health services have started to recognise the value of lived experience and incorporate it into the design and delivery of their work, the medical profession has not followed suit. It continues to rely on ableist assumptions that people with disability are incapable of being doctors. This ableism is so entrenched that it is unlikely to change without researchers, educators, policymakers and professional leaders demanding change.

Research and policy change needs to be backed up with clear implementation plans so that changes flow into all relevant areas. Policymakers, the medical profession and its organisational leaders will need to admit that their industry has been ableist and adjust its organisational policies to redress the situation. No change will occur unless universities adjust their entry requirements and work hard with students with disability to bring them into the profession. The university can be a place where educators and students with disability can work out together the adjustments and support that might be needed on the ground. There is still a gap between how lived experience research informs health education, health services and health and disability policy. It is important to increase lived experience research and demonstrate how it can be used to develop evidence-based approaches. Lived experience academics, researchers and allies can contribute to this shift. However, support, good practices and funding must prioritise this goal.

Note

In this chapter, we have chosen to use the terms 'people with disability' and 'people with lived experience of disability'. However, we acknowledge that this language may not be consistent with preferences among disability stakeholders across the globe.

References

Australian Government. (2023). *Royal Commission into Violence, Abuse, Neglect and Exploitation of People with Disability – Final Report.* https://disability.royalcommission.gov.au/publications/final-report

Australian Human Rights Commission. (2022). *A Human Rights Act for Australia* (position statement). https://humanrights.gov.au/human-rights-act-for-australia

Australian Institute of Health Welfare. (2024). *People with Disability in Australia.* https://www.aihw.gov.au/reports/disability/people-with-disability-in-australia

Australian Medical Association. (2023). *Supporting Doctors and Medical Students with Disability* (position statement). https://www.ama.com.au/sites/default/files/2023-08/AMA%20Position%20Statement%20-%20Supporting%20doctors%20and%20medical%20students%20with%20disability.pdf

Australian Medical Students' Association. (2020). *Policy Document Medical Students with Disabilities.* https://amsa.org.au/wp-content/uploads/2023/10/Medical-Students-with-Disabilities-2022.pdf

Bernard, S., Teasdale, N., O'Reilly-Hawes, J. & Palipana, D. (2023). Include us: Doctors with disability call the Royal Australasian College of Physicians to action. *Internal Medicine Journal*, *53*(6), 1091–1092. https://doi.org/10.1111/imj.16108

Bradfield, O. M., Spittal, M. J. & Bismark, M. M. (2023). 'I'm really glad that you're doing this research'. Qualitative research involving doctors with lived experience of mental health or substance use challenges in Australia and Aotearoa New Zealand. *International Journal of Qualitative Methods*, *22*, 16094069231182874. https://doi.org/10.1177/16094069231182874

BMA Equal Opportunities Committee; and British Medical Association. Science and Education Department. (2007). *Disability Equality in the Medical Profession.* London: Science and Education Dept., British Medical Association.

British Medical Association (BMA). (2020). *Disability in the Medical Profession. Survey Report 2020.* https://www.bma.org.uk/advice-and-support/equality-and-diversity-guidance/disability-equality-in-medicine/disability-in-the-medical-profession

Dearnley, C., Elliott, J., Hargreaves, J., Morris, S., Walker, L., Walker, S. & Arnold, C. (2010). Disabled people, effective practitioners: Enabling a health care workforce that better reflects society. *International Journal of Interdisciplinary Social Science*, *5*.

Donetto, S., Pierri, P., Tsianakas, V. & Robert, G. (2015). Experience-based co-design and healthcare improvement: Realizing participatory design in the public sector. *The Design Journal*, *18*(2), 227–248. https://doi.org/10.2752/175630615X14212498964312

Fitzmaurice, L., Donald, K., de Wet, C. & Palipana, D. (2021). Why we should and how we can increase medical school admissions for persons with disabilities. *The Medical Journal of Australia*, *215*(6), 249–251.e241. https://doi.org/10.5694/mja2.51238

Fitzpatrick, S. & Barrett, D. (2023). Disability inclusion in medical education: Towards a quality improvement approach. *Medical Education*, *57*(1), 17–20. https://doi.org/10.1111/medu.14952

Fuentes, K., Hsu, S., Patel, S. & Lindsay, S. (2024). More than just double discrimination: A scoping review of the experiences and impact of ableism and racism in employment. *Disability and Rehabilitation*, *46*(4), 650–671.

Gavshon, D. (2024). *Australia Needs a Human Rights Act*. https://www.hrw.org/news/2024/06/02/australia-needs-human-rights-act#:~:text=An%20Australian%20Human%20Rights%20Act,seek%20redress%20for%20rights%20violations

Gertsman, S., Dini, Y., Wilton, D. & Neilson, S. (2023). Tackling barriers in Canadian medical school admissions for students with disabilities. *CMAJ*, *195*(44), e1512–e1516. https://doi.org/10.1503/cmaj.230734

Green, C., Dickinson, H., Carey, G. & Joyce, A. (2022). Barriers to policy action on social determinants of health for people with disability in Australia. *Disability & Society*, *37*(2), 206–230. https://doi.org/10.1080/09687599.2020.1815523

Gupta, V., Eames, C., Golding, L., Greenhill, B., Qi, R., Allan, S., Bryant, A. & Fisher, P. (2023). Understanding the identity of lived experience researchers and providers: A conceptual framework and systematic narrative review. *Research Involvement and Engagement*, *9*(1), 26. https://doi.org/10.1186/s40900-023-00439-0

Howick, J., Palipana, D., Dambha-Miller, H. & Khunti, K. (2023). Turning diversity from a barrier to a facilitator of empathy in health care. *British Journal of General Practice*, *73*(726), 24–25.

Jarus, T., Liao, P., Battalova, A., Tikhonova, J., Das, S., Krejcik, V. & Mayer, Y. (2023). Policies as barriers for disabled medical learners: Exploratory study of learners' perspectives. *Disability & Society*, *38*(10), 1763–1778. https://doi.org/10.1080/09687599.2022.2041403

Lane, R. (2022). Dinesh Palipana: Clinician and leading disability rights advocate. *The Lancet (British edition)*, *400*(10355), 803–803. https://doi.org/10.1016/S0140-6736(22)01697-X

Lindsay, S., Fuentes, K., Ragunathan, S., Lamaj, L. & Dyson, J. (2023). Ableism within health care professions: A systematic review of the experiences and impact of discrimination against health care providers with disabilities. *Disability and Rehabilitation*, *45*(17), 2715–2731. https://doi.org/10.1080/09638288.2022.2107086

Martin, R. A., Baker, A. P., Smiler, K., Middleton, L., Hay-Smith, J., Kayes, N., Grace, C., Apiata, T. A. M., Nunnerley, J. L. & Brown, A. E. (2022). Flourishing together: Research protocol for developing methods to better include disabled people's knowledge in health policy development. *BMC Health Services Research*, *22*(1), 1252. https://doi.org/10.1186/s12913-022-08655-2

McKee, M., Case, B., Fausone, M., Zazove, P., Ouellette, A. & Fetters, M. D. (2016). Medical schools' willingness to accommodate medical students with sensory and physical disabilities: Ethical foundations of a functional challenge to 'organic' technical standards. *AMA Journal of Ethics*, *18*(10), 993–1002.

Medical Deans Australia and New Zealand. (2017). *Inherent Requirements for Studying Medicine in Australia and New Zealand*. https://medicaldeans.org.au/md/2020/12/Inherent-Requirements-FINAL-statement_July-2017.pdf

Medical Deans Australia and New Zealand. (2021). *Guidance on Medical Program Applicants and Students with a Disability*. https://medicaldeans.org.au/md/2021/04/Inclusive-Medical-Education-Guidance-on-medical-program-applicants-and-students-with-a-disability-Apr-2021-1.pdf

Meeks, L. M., Case, B., Joshi, H., Graves, L. & Harper, D. M. (2021). Prevalence, plans, and perceptions: Disability in family medicine residencies. *Family Medicine*, *53*(5), 338–346. https://doi.org/10.22454/FamMed.2021.616867

Meeks, L. M., Jain, N. R., & Elisa Laird, J. D. (Eds.). (2020). *Equal Access for Students with Disabilities: The Guide for Health Science and Professional Education*. Springer Publishing Company.

Murphy, M. J., Dowell, J. S. & Smith, D. T. (2022). Factors associated with declaration of disability in medical students and junior doctors, and the association of declared disability with academic performance: Observational study using data from the UK Medical Education Database, 2002–2018 (UKMED54). *BMJ Open*, *12*(4), e059179. https://doi.org/10.1136/bmjopen-2021-059179

Nouri, Z., Dill, M. J., Conrad, S. S., Moreland, C. J. & Meeks, L. M. (2021). Estimated prevalence of US physicians with disabilities. *JAMA Network Open*, *4*(3), e211254–e211254. https://doi.org/10.1001/jamanetworkopen.2021.1254

Office for Disability Issues. (2022). *Disability Toolkit for Policy*. https://www.whaikaha.govt.nz/resources/strategies-and-studies/guidelines/disability-toolkit-for-policy

Palipana, D. (2019). Turning disability into ability: How considered legal representation can reduce the effects of disability. *Precedent (Sydney, N.S.W.)*, *154*, 12–17. https://search.informit.org/doi/10.3316/ielapa.735989436078567

Palipana, D. (2022). The last word: Disability inclusion – why does it matter? *Medicus*, *62*(7), 56–56. https://search.informit.org/doi/10.3316/informit.695842644073797

Philip, S., Nagesh, S. & Singh, S. (2024). Knocking on access doors: Learners with disabilities in health professions. In *The Routledge International Handbook of Disability and Global Health* (pp. 431–445). Routledge.

Policy Lab. (2024). *Lived Experience in Policymaking Guide*. https://openpolicy.blog.gov.uk/wp-content/uploads/sites/35/2024/03/PL_Livedexperienceguide_v6-1.pdf

Robey, K. L., Minihan, P. M., Long-Bellil, L. M., Hahn, J. E., Reiss, J. G. & Eddey, G. E. (2013). Teaching health care students about disability within a cultural competency context. *Disability and Health Journal*, *6*(4), 271–279. https://doi.org/https://doi.org/10.1016/j.dhjo.2013.05.002

Satchidanand, N., Gunukula, S. K., Lam, W. Y., McGuigan, D., New, I., Symons, A. B., Withiam-Leitch, M. & Akl, E. A. (2012). Attitudes of healthcare students and professionals toward patients with physical disability: A systematic review. *American Journal of Physical Medicine & Rehabilitation*, *91*(6), 533–545. https://doi.org/10.1097/PHM.0b013e3182555ea4

Shakespeare, T., Iezzoni, L. I. & Groce, N. E. (2009). Disability and the training of health professionals. *The Lancet*, *374*(9704), 1815–1816. https://doi.org/https://doi.org/10.1016/S0140-6736(09)62050-X

Singh, S. (2019). Medical Council of India's new guidelines on admission of persons with specified disabilities: Unfair, discriminatory and unlawful. *Indian Journal of Medical Ethics*, *4*(1), 29–34.

Smith, S. D., Hall, J. P. & Kurth, N. K. (2020). Perspectives on health policy from people with disabilities. *Journal of Disability Policy Studies*, *32*(3), 224–232. https://doi.org/10.1177/1044207320956679

Stauffer, C., Case, B., Moreland, C. J. & Meeks, L. M. (2022). Technical standards from newly established medical schools: A review of disability inclusive practices. *Journal of Medical Education and Curricular Development*, *9*, 23821205211072763. https://doi.org/10.1177/23821205211072763

Stergiopoulos, E. & Martimianakis, M. A. T. (2023). What makes a 'good doctor'? A critical discourse analysis of perspectives from medical students with lived experience as patients. *Medical Humanities*, *49*(4), 613–622.

Swindlehurst, H. (2005). *Rural Proofing for Health: A Toolkit for Primary Care Organisations.* Institute of Rural Health.

United Nations. (2006). *Convention on the Rights of Persons with Disabilities and Optional Protocol.* https://www.un.org/disabilities/documents/convention/convoptprot-e.pdf

Walker, S., Dearnley, C., Hargreaves, J. & Walker, E. A. (2013). Risk, fitness to practice, and disabled health care students. *Journal of Psychological Issues in Organizational Culture,* 3(S1), 50–63.

World Health Organization. (2011). *World Report on Disability.* https://www.who.int/teams/noncommunicable-diseases/sensory-functions-disability-and-rehabilitation/world-report-on-disability

World Health Organization. (2022). *Global Report on Health Equity for Persons with Disabilities.* World Health Organization.

World Health Organization. (2024). *Disability.* World Health Organization. https://www.who.int/news-room/fact-sheets/detail/disability-and-health#:~:text=An%20estimated%201.3%20billion%20people,earlier%20than%20those%20without%20disabilities

6 The role of lived experience and the right to participate in the CRPD: The case of disability policymaking in technocratic Singapore

Daryl W. J. Yang

6.1 Introduction

In August 2014, Singapore welcomed its first wheelchair user in Parliament after lawyer Chia Yong Yong was appointed as a Nominated Member of Parliament (NMP) (Ng, 2014). The NMP scheme, first introduced in 1990, was intended to introduce alternative, non-partisan perspectives in the legislative chamber, particularly from those with special expertise and or from underrepresented sections of society (Rodan, 2009). Up to nine NMPs may be appointed by a Special Select Committee of Parliament to serve in each Parliament for a term of 2.5 years. NMPs can participate in parliamentary debates and vote on almost all parliamentary matters with some exceptions.[1] Since Chia stepped down in 2018 after serving for two terms, two other wheelchair users, Paralympian swimmer Yip Pin Xiu (2018–2020) and banking executive Ong Hua Han (2023–2025), have been appointed as NMPs.

Chia's 2014 appointment came one year after Singapore ratified the United Nations (UN) Convention on the Rights of Persons with Disabilities (CRPD) in July 2013. Adopted by the UN General Assembly in December 2006, the CRPD represents a paradigm shift from the individual model of disability to the human rights model of disability that prohibits the denial or restriction of human rights on the basis of a person's impairments (Degener, 2016). In the initial report submitted by Singapore to the Committee on the Rights of Persons with Disabilities (CRPD Committee), Chia's

1 In accordance with Article 39(2) of the Constitution of the Republic of Singapore, NMPs cannot vote on any motion pertaining to (a) a Bill to amend the Constitution; (b) a Supply Bill, Supplementary Supply Bill or Final Supply Bill; (c) a Money Bill as defined in Article 68; (d) a vote of no confidence in the Government; (e) removing the President from office under Article 22L; and (f) any question on which nominated Members are excluded by this Constitution from the number of Members required for an affirmative decision.

appointment was highlighted in the section on the right of disabled persons to participate in political and public life under Article 29 of the CRPD (Ministry of Social and Family Development, 2016, para. 358).

A key innovation of the CRPD is its emphasis on the meaningful participation of disabled people in its implementation and monitoring. This reflects the international disability movement's principle of self-representation, popularly expressed by the slogan "nothing about us without us" (Charlton, 2000). This principle animated the drafting of the CRPD itself, which was the first human rights treaty to involve non-state actors, particularly representative organisations of disabled people, in the negotiation process (Kanter, 2007, p. 308). In General Comment No. 7 (2018) on the participation of disabled people in the implementation and monitoring of the CRPD (GC7), the CRPD Committee affirmed that the right to participate is a "civil and political right and an obligation of immediate application, to be applied to decision-making, implementation and monitoring processes related to the Convention" (para. 28). According to the CRPD Committee, the participation of disabled people has a positive impact on decision-making processes because of their "lived experiences and knowledge of the rights to be implemented" (para. 9). Similarly, the 2016 report by the Special Rapporteur on the rights of persons with disabilities (SR Report) emphasised that disabled people bring "complementary and diverse perspectives [which] can make a significant contribution to policymaking and decision-making" (paras 25 and 27). These claims resonate with the abundance of scholarship that recognises the role of lived experience as a matter of sound policymaking, epistemic justice and respect for the dignity of disabled people (see for example, Lowe et al., 2023; Sartor, 2023; Robinson et al., 2021).

Yet, empirical research shows that the experiences of disabled people remain marginalised in decision-making process even when they are afforded a seat at the table (Petri et al., 2017; Radermacher et al., 2010). Drawing on Nancy Fraser's concept of participation parity to analyse the CRPD Committee's jurisprudence on the right to participate in GC7, this chapter argues that the CRPD as it currently stands may not sufficiently address and overcome what Fraser identified as the cultural barrier of misrecognition, which arises from "institutionalised value patterns that deny some people the status of full partners in interaction" (2013, p. 164). Using Singapore as a case study, it demonstrates how such cultural misrecognition arises from prevailing conceptions of citizen participation and disability. On one hand, the technocratic culture of governance in Singapore privileges the policy preferences of the ruling elite, as informed by the inputs of professionals and experts, over the subjective opinions and anecdotal experiences of citizens (Barr, 2020; Rodan & Jayasuriya, 2007). On the other hand, despite Singapore's ratification of the CRPD, the individual model of disability remains dominant and entrenches the conception of disabled people as objects and recipients of charity, medical treatment or social protection (Yang et al., 2023; K. Zhuang, 2016). Together, these factors contribute to the devaluation of the lived experiences of disabled people in decision-making processes and undermine the effectiveness of their participation and the intent behind the right to participate. This chapter thus fills a gap in the literature on the implementation of the CRPD's right to participate by attending to how broader conceptions of disability and policymaking influence the extent to which lived experiences are and can be incorporated in decision-making processes.

6.2 The right to participate in the CRPD

The concept of participation lies at the core of the CRPD. Article 1 of the CRPD defines 'persons with disabilities' as including those who have long-term physical, mental, intellectual or sensory impairments, "which in interaction with various barriers may *hinder their full and effective participation in society* on an equal basis with others" (emphasis added). This definition encapsulates the social model of disability, which recognises that disability is not the result of a person's own bodily impairments but the interaction of those impairments with social, institutional and physical barriers that limit their ability to participate in society (Degener, 2016, p. 3). The SR Report identifies three reasons why state parties should value participation by disabled people. First, it can lead to better decisions because disabled people "are best positioned to identify their own needs and the most suitable policies for meeting them" (para. 26). This would in turn result in greater efficiency, a more equitable use of resources and improved outcomes for disabled people and their communities. Second, participation can promote agency and empowerment by giving disabled people a sense of ownership and pride (paras 29 and 30). Finally, participation is identified as a "critical component of good governance and democracy" (para. 32).

In GC7, the CRPD Committee explained that the CRPD "recognises participation as both a general obligation and a cross-cutting issue" (para. 3). Notably, this obligation is enshrined in Articles 4(3) and 33(3) of the CRPD respectively. First, Article 4(3) requires state parties to closely consult with and actively involve persons with disabilities through their representative organisations in the development and implementation of legislation and policies to implement the CRPD, and in other decision-making processes concerning issues relating to persons with disabilities. Second, Article 33(3) requires civil society, particularly persons with disabilities and their representative organisations, to be involved in and participate fully in monitoring the implementation of the CRPD. In this regard, the term 'representative organisations' is also specifically defined to refer to organisations *of* disabled people that are "led, directed and governed by" disabled people themselves (para. 11). This contrasts with organisations *for* persons with disabilities, which provide services and/or advocate on behalf of disabled people, but which may prioritise their purpose as private entities over the rights of disabled people (para. 13).

The CRPD's emphasis on participation is reminiscent of Fraser's theory of justice, which focuses on the parity of participation. Specifically, Fraser conceives of justice as requiring social arrangements that allow all to participate as peers in social life, which demands the dismantling of institutionalised obstacles that prevent some from participation on par with others as full partners in social interactions (Fraser, 2013, p. 193). Such obstacles can come in three forms: economic maldistribution, cultural misrecognition, and political misrepresentation. Building on existing scholarship that has applied participation parity to the disability context (Mladenov, 2016; Knight, 2015; Danermark & Gellerstedt, 2004), the rest of this section examines how the recommendations set out in GC7 have focused on overcoming the obstacles posed by economic maldistribution and political misrepresentation, but not cultural misrecognition.

First, economic maldistribution refers to such economic dependence and inequality that undermine the independence and "voice" of disabled people (Fraser, 2013, p. 164). In this regard, GC7 expounds at length on the obligation of state parties to increase public resources available to disabled people and their representative organisations (paras 61–64) as well as to ensure that disabled people have access to reasonable accommodations in all decision-making processes (paras 45–46). In addition, state parties are required to ensure that these organisations are able to receive and access both national and foreign funding. The SR Report also addresses how the ability of representative organisations to access funding and resources is "integral and vital" to realising the effective participation of disabled people (para. 51).

Second, political misrepresentation refers to circumstances where "political boundaries and/or decision rules function to wrongly deny some people the possibility of participation on a par with others" (Fraser, 2013, p. 195). This can operate at two levels: first, ordinary-political misrepresentation relates to the merits of alternative systems of representation, such as first-past-the-post electoral systems and the use of quotas; second, misframing is concerned with how the community's boundaries are drawn, such as to "wrongly exclude some people from the chance to participate *at all* in its authorised contests over justice". Notably, without explicitly engaging with the charity model of disability, Fraser observes that misframing may result in a "political death" where those who suffer such misframing become "objects of charity or benevolence" (Fraser, 2013, p. 195).

The CRPD Committee addresses both forms of political misrepresentation in GC7. First, in respect of ordinary-political misrepresentation, GC7 calls on state parties to develop a legislative and policy framework that recognises the right to participation and involvement of representative organisations at all levels of authority and decision-making (para. 94(e)), establish permanent consultation mechanisms with representative organisations (para. 94(f)), and implement effective enforcement mechanisms with meaningful sanctions and remedies for violations of the right to participate (para. 94(m)). Second, in respect of misframing, GC7 calls for the repeal of all laws, including those denying legal capacity, that prevent disabled people from being closely consulted with and actively involved (para. 94(a)). The CRPD Committee also requires state parties to make existing consultation procedures in non-disability-specific areas of law accessible and inclusive of disabled people (para. 94(q)).

Finally, cultural misrecognition arises from "institutionalised value patterns that systematically depreciate some categories of people and the qualities associated with them" (Fraser, 2013, p. 164). For example, when heteronormativity is pervasively institutionalised in law, policy and social practices, queer people become a "despised sexuality" and suffer from "sexually specific forms of status subordination" (Fraser, 1999,

p. 75). In the context of disability, ableist misrecognition informed by the individual model of disability has resulted in the "systematic denial of respect and esteem to disabled people on the grounds of perceived bodily, psycho-emotional, or cognitive 'flaws'" (Mladenov, 2017, p. 109). As a result, the lived experiences of disabled people are viewed through the lens of tragedy or deficiency, and marginalised in favour of medical professionals and service providers (Calder, 2012, p. 108).

Troublingly, neither GC7 nor the SR Report addresses how such cultural misrecognition may arise in decision-making processes, even when disabled people are part of the decision-making process. Instead, all GC7 demands is that "public authorities should give due consideration and priority to the opinions of views of [representative] organisations" (para. 23) and give "due weight" to the views of disabled people, so that they are "not only heard as a mere formality or as a tokenistic approach to consultation" (para. 48). What suffices as due weight, consideration or priority is not clarified, nor does GC7 explain what would qualify as tokenism in the consultation process. There is also nothing in GC7 that addresses how entrenched cultural biases or stereotypes about disability may result in the disregard or dismissal of disabled people's views in decision-making processes.

In this regard, recent socio-legal scholarship highlights how the right to participate may be undermined when the perspectives of disabled people are not prioritised in decision-making processes and result in outcomes that are inconsistent with the interests of disabled people. For example, a Romanian study found that participation "does not translate into influence on policy formulation … [and] legitimises processes that [disability] organisations disagree with from a value perspective" (Safta-Zecheria et al., 2024, p. 164). Another study on the Kyrgyzstani disability movement also demonstrated how the participation of disabled people in the political process has a limited impact because policymakers "do not consider [them] as having valuable knowledge and perspectives" (Orozova et al., 2023, p. 247). Finally, research on the participation of persons with intellectual disabilities in Iceland revealed that while individuals with intellectual disabilities were consulted, their views were not meaningfully incorporated (Löve, 2023). Building on these insights, the next section turns to Singapore as a case study to examine how its political culture and the cultural dominance of the individual model of disability contribute to the marginalisation of the lived experiences of disabled people in the policymaking process.

6.3 The role of lived experiences in technocratic Singapore

While Singapore only ratified the CRPD in 2013, the country's relationship with the emergence of the international disability rights movement can be traced to 1981, when the inaugural World Congress of Disabled People's International (DPI) was held in the island city-state, and blind Singaporean Ron Chandran-Dudley was elected as DPI's first president (Zhuang, 2010, p. 68). Notwithstanding, Singapore has not fully embraced the CRPD's human rights model of disability policy and instead adopts an 'access-to-inclusion' approach that focuses on the provision of social welfare and public resources to promote the inclusion of disabled people but not necessarily their rights or autonomy (Yang et al., 2023).

That said, since the CRPD was ratified, the Singapore government has taken active steps to increase the representation and participation of disabled people at various levels of governance. First, as noted in the introduction, there have been three NMPs who are wheelchair users who have served or are serving in Parliament. Second, Chia was invited to serve as a consultant and non-governmental representative from the disability sector on the state delegation to the first periodic review before the CRPD Committee. Third, the Singapore government has increasingly involved and consulted with disabled people in the development of the Enabling Masterplan 2017–2021 (EM3) and the Enabling Masterplan 2030 (EM4), which are five-year policy roadmaps that guide Singapore's journey towards a more inclusive society.

However, increased representation does not necessarily translate into favourable policy outcomes for disabled people. Instead, representatives must also be willing and able to influence the policymaking processes. On the former requirement of willingness, political science scholarship distinguishes between descriptive representation and substantive representation, where a representative from a particular social group may not necessarily advocate for or advance the interests of that group (Reher, 2022; Chaney, 2015). The rest of this section focuses on the latter requirement: the (in)ability of disabled people to influence the policymaking process in Singapore even after they have been offered a seat at the table. Specifically, this can be attributed to the marginalisation of the lived experiences of disabled people under Singapore's political culture of technocratic pragmatism. Such marginalisation is exacerbated by Singapore's "pervasive reliance on the individual model of disability" (Zhuang, 2016, p. 634), which conceives of disabled people as passive recipients of social welfare, medical care and charity rather than rights-holding subjects equal to their non-disabled peers.

An island city-state in Southeast Asia, Singapore is widely admired as an 'economic miracle' for its rapid industrialisation and economic growth (Khan, 1997). Its success is often credited to the ruling People's Action Party (PAP), whose technocratic ideology conceives of good governance as "the application of impartial reasoning and disciplinary expertise to questions that would normally be considered political" (Barr, 2020, p. 55). This underpins, on one hand, the PAP's pragmatic approach to policymaking that eschews "generalising and universalising intentions of high theory and theorising in general" (Tan, 2012, p. 75) and, on the other hand, its technocratic disinterest in public opinion based on the belief that ordinary citizens lack sufficient knowledge and understanding to make "meaningful decisions about issues that can affect the fate of the country" (Leong, 2000, p. 445).

Singapore's pragmatic approach to policymaking has forestalled its embrace of the human rights model of disability policy as envisioned in the CRPD. Instead, disability policymaking in Singapore is not founded on the notion of rights but on a pragmatic set of considerations, such as economic cost and cost-efficiency balanced against the inclusion of disabled people in different spheres of society (Yang et al., 2023, p. 153). As a result, the state's focus on the investment of resources to foster disability inclusion rather than the realisation of the right of disabled people to full and effective participation "runs the risk of perpetuating and reinforcing the individual model of disability and the treatment of disabled people as objects of charity and welfare" (Yang et al., 2023, p. 154). Applying Fraser's framework of participation parity, Singapore's culture of technocratic governance and the individual model of disability thus combine to entrench the subordinate status of disabled people and the marginalisation of their lived experiences in the policymaking process.

While growing affluence and a more educated population have pushed the PAP government towards a more consultative mode of governance in recent years, this has arguably evolved in ways that bolster rather than threaten its power. Specifically, novel administrative mechanisms have increasingly been established to offer citizens an avenue for feedback, consultation and participation to bolster the PAP's political rule by administrative means (Rodan & Jayasuriya, 2007). In this regard, Singapore's consultative ideology of participation "emphasise[s] the problem-solving utility of incorporating stakeholders, interests and/or expertise into public policy processes to ensure the most effective functioning of economic, social, or political governance" (Rodan, 2018, p. 30). As a result, the technocratic elite retains control over the decision-making process because those consulted lack any democratic authority to represent others (Rodan, 2018, p. 31) and the inputs of ordinary citizens remain as "only one input among many rather than an essential ingredient in considering policy alternatives" (Leong, 2000, p. 445).

The Enabling Masterplan is an example of such administrative mechanisms deployed in the disability context. As noted earlier, disabled people have increasingly been included and involved in both the steering committee and consultation exercises with each successive report. Yet, disabled people represent only one among other stakeholders, which include caregivers, service providers, government bodies and the private sector. Using EM4 as an example, the operation of Singapore's technocratic model of policymaking can be gleaned from various aspects of the report. On one hand, while the report purports to "prioritise involving persons with disabilities, caregivers, and disability sector professionals, to ensure that their views, especially those of persons with disabilities, form the core" of EM4 (Enabling Masterplan Steering Committee, 2022, p. 32), disabled people were outnumbered as a matter of representation and made up the *minority* among those consulted. Only 64 of the more than 300 individuals consulted were disabled people, compared with 112 family members or caregivers of disabled people and 164 disability sector professionals, comprising social workers, allied health professionals and senior leaders of service organisations.

On the other hand, EM4 was co-chaired by the senior parliamentary secretary of the Ministry of Social and Family Development and the Ministry of Culture, Community and Youth, and the vice chairperson of the Singapore Business Federation. Neither of these individuals identifies as disabled; instead, they represent the public and private sectors respectively. In this regard, it is notable that the executive summary of EM4 spotlights quotes by top policymakers from various government ministries rather than disabled people; the first time that disabled people themselves are heard in the form of direct quotes appears only at page 30.

How different would policy outcomes be if Singapore's approach to policymaking centred the lived experiences of disabled people? Here, one can compare how EM4 addresses the un(der)-employment of disabled people and two reports on workplace discrimination published by the Disabled People Association (DPA), the only cross-disability representative organisation that advocates for the rights of disabled people in Singapore. The first report is a 2018 qualitative study to understand the types of 'unfair treatment' faced by disabled people at the workplace (Disabled People's Association & Institute of Policy Studies, 2018) while the second is based on feedback gathered from disabled people to inform DPA's advocacy on a proposed new legislation prohibiting discrimination at the workplace (Disabled People's Association, 2024). Both reports are informed by the lived experiences of disabled people, which are copiously referred to in the reports through direct quotes and narratives.

As a starting point, un(der)-employment is a serious problem facing disabled people in Singapore. According to government statistics, for the period between 2022 and 2023, the employment rate of disabled people between the working ages of 15 and 64 was 32.7%, while the labour force participation rate was 36.3%. This contrasts with a labour force participation rate of 70% among the general population during the same period. When asked why they were not working, disabled people outside the labour force largely cited 'too old/ poor health/ disabled' (76.2%) and 'education/training related' (12.7%) as the main reasons. How this data is interpreted would depend on whether disability is understood through the prism of the individual or the social model. In this regard, EM4 interprets this to mean that those disabled people outside the labour force are not "work-capable" without any acknowledgement of the role that social and other barriers play in determining whether a person can or wishes to participate in the labour force (2022, p. 84). In contrast, a 2018 UN report on disability inclusion in Asia and the Pacific noted that countries with a higher labour force participation rate tend to also boast higher employment rates, which suggests that disabled people are more willing and able to participate in the labour market if efforts are made to foster an inclusive and accessible working environment (United Nations Economic and Social Commission for Asia and the Pacific, 2018, p. 17).

The foregoing recalls Victor Zhuang's (2021) characterisation of Singapore's project of disability inclusion as constructing the figure of the "included" disabled, whose body is "productive and conforming" (p. 477). In contrast, he notes that "bodies that are not uniform, and which do not conform to this norm of work and the ideal of productivity are discarded and put aside … [t]he unproductive disabled body is then excluded within the nation" (Zhuang, 2021, p. 483). Indeed, EM4 purports to focus on promoting inclusive employment for those disabled people who, in its words, have the "potential to work"; this is to be achieved by, first, increasing the number of inclusive employers and employment models and, second, preparing disabled people for "jobs of the future" (2022, p. 88).

EM4 does not attribute the fact that employers are not willing to hire or retain disabled people to discriminatory attitudes or prejudice, but calls attention instead to their lack of "awareness, expertise or willingness to provide reasonable accommodations" (2022, p. 86). In fact, the word 'discrimination' does not appear at all in the section on inclusive employment, nor did EM4 propose any recommendation to empower disabled people in requesting accommodations within the workplace. In this regard, though EM4 was published a year after the government announced plans to enact a new workplace discrimination legislation (Lim, 2021), there was no reference to this legislation and how it can help to address the barriers that disabled people face in accessing employment. This is curious, when juxtaposed against the White Paper on Singapore Women's Development, which was published several months before EM4 and addressed how the new legislation would "reduce and remove barriers that hinder women's career progress" (Ministry of Social and Family Development, 2022, p. 30).

Informed by the lived experiences of disabled people themselves, both of DPA's reports focus on discrimination as the key barrier that disabled people face in the employment context. Whereas EM4 cast employers as simply ignorant or unaware about how they could include disabled people in their workplaces, DPA's 2018 report reveals a darker reality of blatant ableism, prejudice and exploitation. Some respondents reported being underpaid because employers and employment agencies knew that the disabled workers had no bargaining power (pp. 8–9), while others shared how they were shamed or mocked for their disabilities (pp. 9–10). Juxtaposed against these lived experiences, EM4's silence on the scourge of workplace discrimination that disabled people face is jarring.

For a long time, the Singapore government resisted the use of legislation to address workplace discrimination, preferring the 'business-case' approach, which highlights the benefits of workplace diversity (Chia & Lim, 2010). This finally changed in 2021, when the government announced that it would enact a new workplace discrimination legislation with the primary intention to protect local workers from so-called "nationality discrimination" (Yang, 2026). Drawing on the lived experiences of its members and other disabled people in this consultation process, DPA participated in consultations with the TCWF and emphasised the need for a comprehensive definition of discrimination that covered all forms of discrimination. Ultimately, however, its recommendations were rejected in TCWF's final report to the government, which proposed to only legislate against direct discrimination but not the other forms of discrimination. According to the TCWF, legislating against other forms of discrimination, particularly indirect discrimination and the denial of reasonable accommodations, "imposes very wide legal obligations on employers" and "risks creating a more litigious workplace" (Tripartite Committee on Workplace Fairness, 2023, pp. 16, 31).

In response, DPA consolidated its findings into the 2024 report, which detailed how disabled people regularly encountered indirect discrimination and the denial of reasonable accommodations within the workplace, which then affected their ability to secure a job and remain employed (Disabled People's Association, 2024). For example, the report detailed the experience of a blind respondent who was not afforded accommodations despite requesting for them and subsequently penalised for poor performance (p. 13). Another respondent who is Deaf recounted the challenges she faced both professionally and socially due to her colleagues' reluctance to communicate via written means (p. 14). The report also highlighted how, contrary to the TCWF's concern of a more litigious workplace, many disabled people are reluctant to request an accommodation out of fear that they would be discriminated against or, worse, dismissed if they disclosed their disability to their employers (p. 15). The law was eventually passed as the Workplace Fairness Act in 2025, based on the TCWF's recommendations, and it remains to be seen how far this new legislation can and will go, if at all, in addressing ableism and disability discrimination at the workplace.

As this section has shown, the combination of Singapore's technocratic approach to policymaking and the cultural dominance of the individual model of disability have augmented the marginalisation of and disregard for the lived experiences of disabled people in the policymaking process. As a result, the underlying barriers that disabled people face in the employment context are misapprehended, and the proposed solutions fail to address those barriers. It is therefore not enough that disabled people are able to participate in the policymaking process; instead, their inputs, particularly their lived experiences, must be meaningfully recognised and incorporated. The right to participate, therefore, cannot be viewed solely through the lens of *formal* involvement but also *substantive* engagement. In societies like Singapore, this must involve not only a rethinking of how disabled people are perceived but also how the policymaking process is designed as well as the relationship between the technocratic elite and citizens.

6.4 Conclusion

In analysing the jurisprudence on the CRPD's right to participate through the lens of Fraser's framework of participation parity, this chapter shines a spotlight on how the involvement of disabled people in decision-making processes may be undermined as a result of how disability and the policymaking process are conceived. Future scholarship should explore how other factors may result in the misrecognition of disabled people and the marginalisation of their lived experiences in the policymaking process. These insights can hopefully help representative organisations, disability rights practitioners and policymakers develop strategies to effectively incorporate the lived experiences of disabled people.

In addition, this chapter has demonstrated how an interdisciplinary approach may also offer fruitful avenues for further research into the ways by which disabled people exercise the right to participate. In this regard, the distinction between descriptive and substantive representation demands greater scrutiny of whether representative organisations and disabled individuals who are involved in decision-making processes necessarily act in the interests of those whom they purport to represent. If so, how? The scholarship on the hierarchy of disabilities (Deal, 2003) further complicates this question by calling attention to the diversity of lived experiences within the category of disability and the risk that the right to participate may be more accessible to some groups over others. In Singapore's case, all three NMPs have been wheelchair users whose experience of disability may differ from others with sensory or developmental disabilities. How then can a sole representative organisation or disabled individual offered a seat at the policymaking table fully and meaningfully represent the unique and diverse experiences of all disabled people and communities? These are difficult questions that may not have any (straightforward) answers, but which nonetheless we must grapple with.

From an international human rights perspective, greater clarity on how the right to participate is exercised on the ground can assist the CRPD Committee in providing clearer guidance to state parties on the relationship between the right to participate and the role of lived experiences in the implementation and monitoring of the CRPD. For example, Newton et al. (2024, p.89) propose the concept of 'lived expertise' as a form of "authority grounded in experience and sustained through awareness of additional forms of experiential and institutional knowledges", while Meltzer et al. (2021) developed a framework on how lived experience should be included as a form of evidence in policymaking processes. This reveals another transformative aspect of the CRPD, which demands not only a paradigm shift in how disability and disability policy are imagined but also of the policymaking process itself.

References

Barr, M. D. (2020). The Singapore school: Technocracy or less. In *China's 'Singapore Model' and Authoritarian Learning*. Routledge.

Calder, G. (2012). Disability and misrecognition. In S. Thompson & M. Yar (Eds.), *The Politics of Misrecognition*. Routledge.

Chaney, P. (2015). Institutional ableism, critical actors and the substantive representation of disabled people: Evidence from the UK Parliament 1940–2012. *The Journal of Legislative Studies*, *21*(2), 168–191.

Charlton, J. I. (2000). *Nothing About Us Without Us: Disability Oppression and Empowerment.* University of California Press.

Chia, A. & Lim, A. (2010). Singapore: Equality, harmony and fair employment. In A. Klarsfeld (Ed.), *International Handbook on Diversity Management at Work Country Perspectives on Diversity and Equal Treatment*. Edward Elgar Publishing.

Committee on the Rights of Persons with Disabilities. (2018). General Comment No. 7 (2018) on the participation of persons withdisabilities, including children with disabilities, through the irrepresentative organizations, in the implementation and monitoring of the Convention (CRPD/C/GC/7). UN Docs.

Danermark, B. & Gellerstedt, L. C. (2004). Social justice: Redistribution and recognition – a non-reductionist perspective on disability. *Disability & Society*, *19*(4), 339–353.

Deal, M. (2003). Disabled people's attitudes toward other impairment groups: A hierarchy of impairments. *Disability & Society*, *18*(7), 897–910.

Degener, T. (2016). Disability in a human rights context. *Laws*, *5*(3), Article 3.

Disabled People's Association. (2024). *Achieving Fairness in Employment for Persons with Disabilities in Singapore.* https://dpa.org.sg/wp-content/uploads/2024/04/Achieving-Fairness-in-Employment-for-Persons-with-Disabilities-in-Singapore.pdf

Disabled People's Association & Institute of Policy Studies. (2018). *Discrimination Faced by People With Disabilities in the Workplace*. https://www.dpa.org.sg/wp-content/uploads/2018/07/Discrimination-Faced-by-People-with-Disabilities-at-the-Workplace-Study-1.pdf

Enabling Masterplan Steering Committee. (2022). *Enabling Masterplan 2030*. https://www.msf.gov.sg/docs/default-source/enabling-masterplan/emp2030-report-(final2).pdf?sfvrsn=8032eb4d_3

Fraser, N. (1999). Social justice in the age of identity politics: Redistribution, recognition, and participation. In L. Ray & A. Sayer (Eds.), *Culture and Economy after the Cultural Turn* (pp. 25–52). SAGE Publications Ltd.

Fraser, N. (2013). *Fortunes of Feminism: From State-Managed Capitalism to Neoliberal Crisis*. Verso Books.

Kanter, A. S. (2007). The promise and challenge of the United Nations Convention on the rights of persons with disabilities. *Syracuse Journal of International Law and Commerce*, *34*(2), 287–322.

Khan, H. (1997). A brief assessment of Singapore's economic miracle. In *The ASEAN Region in Transition*. Routledge.

Knight, A. (2015). Democratizing disability: Achieving inclusion (without assimilation) through 'participatory parity'. *Hypatia*, *30*(1), 97–114.

Leong, H. K. (2000). Citizen participation and policy making in singapore: Conditions and predicaments. *Asian Survey*, *40*(3), 436–455.

Lim, M. Z. (2021, 29 August). NDR 2021: Fair employment guidelines to become law, new tribunal to deal with workplace discrimination. *The Straits Times*. https://www.straitstimes.com/singapore/politics/ndr-2021-fair-employment-guidelines-to-become-law-new-tribunal-to-deal-with

Löve, L. E. (2023). Exclusion to inclusion: Lived experience of intellectual disabilities in national reporting on the CRPD. *Social Inclusion*, *11*(2), 94–103.

Lowe, K., Barajas, J. & Coren, C. (2023). 'It's annoying, confusing, and it's irritating': Lived expertise for epistemic justice and understanding inequitable accessibility. *Journal of Transport Geography*, *106*, 103504.

Meltzer, A., Dickinson, H., Malbon, E. & Carey, G. (2021). Why is lived experience important for market stewardship? A proposed framework for why and how lived experience should be included in stewarding disability markets. *Evidence & Policy*, *17*(2), 335–347.

Ministry of Social and Family Development. (2016). *Initial Report Submitted by Singapore under Article 35 of the Convention* (CRPD/C/SGP/1). United Nations.

Ministry of Social and Family Development. (2022). *White Paper on Singapore Women's Development*. https://www.msf.gov.sg/docs/default-source/celebrating-sg-women-document/white-paper-on-singapore-womens-development.pdf?sfvrsn=708177eb_3

Mladenov, T. (2016). Disability and social justice. *Disability & Society*, *31*(9), 1226–1241.

Mladenov, T. (2017). Postsocialist disability matrix. *Scandinavian Journal of Disability Research*, *19*(2), 104–117.

Newton, G., Zappavigna, M., Drysdale, K. & Newman, C. E. (2024). From lived experience to lived expertise: How donor-conceived witnesses claim and sustain epistemic authority. *Journal of Pragmatics*, *221*, 89–104.

Ng, K. (2014, 13 August). New NMP to advocate for greater inclusion of people with disabilities. *TODAYOnline*. https://www.todayonline.com/singapore/new-nmp-advocate-greater-inclusion-people-disabilities

Orozova, R., Battalova, A. & Bagdasarova, N. (2023). A critical analysis of the disability movement in Kyrgyzstan: Trying to be heard. *Europe-Asia Studies*, *75*(2), 232–251.

Petri, G., Beadle-Brown, J. & Bradshaw, J. (2017). 'More honoured in the breach than in the observance' – self-advocacy and human rights. *Laws*, *6*(4), Article 4.

Radermacher, H., Sonn, C., Keys, C. & Duckett, P. (2010). Disability and participation: It's about us but still without us! *Journal of Community & Applied Social Psychology, 20*(5), 333–346.
Reher, S. (2022). Do disabled candidates represent disabled citizens? *British Journal of Political Science, 52*(2), 520–534.
Robinson, S., Valentine, K. & Idle, J. (2021). Disability and family violence prevention: A case study on participation in evidence making. *Evidence & Policy, 17*(2), 315–333.
Rodan, G. (2009). New modes of political participation and Singapore's Nominated Members of Parliament. *Government and Opposition, 44*(4), 438–462.
Rodan, G. (2018). *Participation Without Democracy: Containing Conflict in Southeast Asia*. Cornell University Press.
Rodan, G. & Jayasuriya, K. (2007). The technocratic politics of administrative participation: Case studies of Singapore and Vietnam. *Democratization, 14*(5), 795–815.
Safta-Zecheria, L., Tănăsan, G. & Petri, G. (2024). Between a shrinking and a shifting space: The symbolic inclusion of the disability movement in policy-making in Romania. *Revista de Asistenta Sociala, XXIII*(1), 153–165.
Sartor, C. (2023). Mental health and lived experience: The value of lived experience expertise in global mental health. *Cambridge Prisms: Global Mental Health, 10*, e38.
Tan, K. P. (2012). The ideology of pragmatism: Neo-liberal globalisation and political authoritarianism in Singapore. *Journal of Contemporary Asia, 42*(1), 67–92.
Tripartite Committee on Workplace Fairness. (2023). *Building Farier & More Harmonious Workplaces: Tripartite Committee on Workplace Fairness Final Report*. https://www.mom.gov.sg/-/media/mom/documents/press-releases/2023/tripartite-committee-on-workplace-fairness-final-report.pdf
United Nations Economic and Social Commission for Asia and the Pacific. (2018). *Building Disability-Inclusive Societies in Asia and the Pacific: Assessing Progress of the Incheon Strategy*. United Nations.
Yang, D. W., Zhuang, K., Goggin, G. & Wong, M. E. (2023). From enabling access to enabling rights: Singapore's practical approach to disability policy. In S. Robinson & K. Fisher (Eds.), *Research Handbook on Disability Policy*. Edward Elgar Publishing.
Zhuang, K. (2010). Enabling the Singapore story: Writing a history of disability. In Bruce Lockhart & T. S. Lim (Eds.), *Monograph 42: Studies in Malaysian & Singapore History: Mubin Sheppard Memorial Essays* (p. 36). MBRAS.
Zhuang, K. (2021). The included: Disability-led arts within inclusion in Singapore. *Journal of Literary & Cultural Disability Studies, 15*(4), 471–487.
Zhuang, K. (2021). The included: Disability-led arts within inclusion in Singapore. *Journal of Literary & Cultural Disability Studies, 15*(4), 471–487.

7 Indonesia's digital disability inclusion: From regulation to policymaking and practice

Muhammad Novsyaroni Umar, Galuh Fitri Amalia Susilo and Muhammad Karim Amrullah

7.1 Introduction

This chapter provides a Global South perspective on lived experience policymaking by relying on Indonesian narratives of disability. People with disabilities are amongst the most marginalised minorities (Adioetomo et al., 2014; Ditchman et al., 2013; Kusumastuti et al., 2014; Malik et al., 2021; Purwanta, 2012; Suharto et al., 2016; Trevisan, 2017). They experience prejudice (Tsaputra, 2016), and stigma, leading into vulnerability (Adioetomo et al., 2014; Kusumastuti et al., 2014; Satriana et al., 2021). Accessibility needs for people with disabilities are different from those for non-disabled people (Amrullah, 2017). Aside from continuing challenges related to physical accessibility, those with disabilities also face inequality related to aspects of non-physical accessibility and social inclusion. This results in, for example, biased media representation, where they are portrayed as pitiful and helpless within some media coverage (Tsaputra, 2016). In addition, information services required by people with disabilities (Ellis & Kent, 2016; Hersinta, 2020) are often inaccessible in many contexts. These accessibility and inclusion issues impact the fulfilment of their rights (Widinarsih, 2018) in the context of Indonesia's ratification of the United Nations Convention on the Rights of Persons with Disabilities (UNCRPD) (Edwards & McCarthy, 2007).

Like other people, studies have shown that people with disabilities are living in a digital society (Ellis & Kent, 2016; Goggin & Newell, 2005; Tollan, 2020). Therefore, understanding inclusion in relation to the emergence of the internet has been a crucial part of contemporary disability studies (Ellis et al., 2018a, 2018b; Goggin & Newell, 2005). The limited public narrative on the emergence of a digital divide for people with disabilities has shown that it is crucial to address disability inequality (Goggin, 2018), including inclusive digital policies (Lindsay, 2010). This includes Indonesians with disabilities who have been using digital technology for decades, but who are often limited in this usage because of accessibility concerns (Bexley, 2015; Hersinta, 2020; Pearson & Trevisan, 2015; Rofasita, 2017).

The government of Indonesia has crafted a robust policy framework to advance gender equality and the inclusion of persons with disabilities. The development of a national inclusive policy regarding people with disabilities started with the signing and ratifying of the UNCRPD, signed by Indonesia on 30 March 2007 and ratified into law in 2011. The convention explicitly mentioned that people with disability should be eliminated from any barriers that hinder their full and equal participation in society (Irwanto et al., 2010). This includes digital participation, which allows Indonesians with disabilities to access their digital presence in an accessible way.

Within disability research, Smith-Merry (2019) emphasises the need for disability inclusion, as most research has historically marginalised the voices of people with disabilities (Swartz, 2009). Disability scholars like Ellis et al. (2018a) and Goggin in Ellis et al. (2018b) have emphasised the urgency of merging critical disability studies with technological perspectives and emphasising disability lived experiences. From the perspective of research focusing on the Global South, Hersinta (2020) and Sri and Astuti (2021) called for more lived experience-led research in digital inclusion in Indonesia. Sri and Astuti (2021) specifically highlight the crucial participation of disabled people in the research phase of policymaking. This chapter provides this perspective and offers a lived experience-led perspective on disability inclusion in Indonesian policymaking.

In this chapter, the authors analyse the main Indonesian digital disability policy, which relates to Article 24 of Indonesian Law 8/2016 regarding disability rights in producing and obtaining information digitally. In doing so, this chapter intersects disability studies, law, public policy, and social media scholarship. To develop this chapter, the authors analysed Indonesian disability digital policy from the perspective of the lived experiences of people with disabilities and parents of disabled people who have founded disability-led and parent-led organisations. These people took part in digital disability activism and collaborated with policymakers in relation to the campaign to fulfil Indonesian disability rights on digital accessibility and inclusion. This chapter specifically highlights two Indonesian disability organisations led by different actors, both disabled and non-disabled, namely Difapedia and Jendela Ibu. To provide diverse lived experiences, the authors involved two people – Khanif and Riris – in the development of the chapter. Both were born with disabilities and have initiated a disability support group called Difapedia, which is based in Purbalingga and Yogyakarta. To add a parental perspective, the perspectives of Ifta and Sandy were included as they have established Jendela Ibu to empower the parents of disabled children in aiding their children to their health care rights, which have been ignored for a long time. Both organisations have criticised Indonesian society for discriminating against those with disability, and their activism has contributed to influencing Indonesia's disability policymaking.

7.2 Disability lived experiences in Indonesia

From an Indonesian sociocultural perspective, disability is a complex issue (Thohari et al., 2019) with Indonesians with disability living under sociocultural challenges related to negative cultural understandings of disability (Madyaningrum et al., 2022). Indonesians born with diverse disabilities are, for example, socially regarded as karma (Hersinta, 2020), and their families are blamed for their existence (Kusumastuti et al., 2014). In addressing such challenges, Indonesians with disabilities have formed support groups to empower each other (Madyaningrum et al., 2022). Parents who raise children with disabilities have also been involved in fostering parent support groups to support each other (Behl et al., 2016; Bray et al., 2017; Efendi, 2018).

Disability groups that disabled actors lead are often aimed at building a positive social representation of disability (Cahyadi & Setiawan, 2021; Nugroho, 2011) by self-representing themselves (Mineur et al., 2017). While Riris was born deaf, Khanif experienced a non-congenital disability in which he lost his hearing when he was ten years old, making his world silent. They built Difapedia as part of their self-representation. As well as self-representation, disability-led organisations are also believed to empower disabled members (Madyaningrum et al., 2022; Mineur et al., 2017; Seubert, 2022). Difapedia empowers disabled people and advocates for disability rights, especially in relation to digital accessibility and transferring digital skills.

Families who have disabled children are often challenged socioeconomically (Ammari et al., 2014). To provide support for tackling those challenges, parent support groups were established (Behl et al., 2016; Bray et al., 2017; Efendi, 2018). Ifta and Sandy raised two sons with special needs. Their experience drove them to initiate Jendela Ibu in response to the challenges experienced by parents who have children with special needs. The main aim of parent-led disability organisations is to ensure that every child has access to equal rights (Carey et al., 2019). Jendela Ibu assisted and educated parents to help their disabled children fulfil their rights.

This chapter addresses these Indonesian disability stakeholders' views on inclusive digital policy. The discussion relies on data from two focus group discussions, four formal interviews, and a virtual informal interview. Through these oral methodologies, this chapter presents dual perspectives on lived experiences in relation to Indonesian digital disability policymaking, its implementation, and its impact on disability stakeholders. In this chapter, we have specifically chosen to focus on the use of Instagram as both organisations have utilised Instagram as a campaigning tool, through @ difapedia and @jendelaibu respectively. Instagram enables a visual representation of diversity (Laestadius, 2018; Leaver et al., 2020). While international disability organisations have used Instagram as an advocacy tool for over a decade, and this has been discussed elsewhere (Bexley, 2015), this chapter provides a new lens by focusing on an Indonesian disability organisation's perspective on its use in these ways.

7.3 From UNCRPD to Indonesian law and policy

The enactment of disability rights in Indonesia must be considered in the context of the UNCRPD. The UNCRPD aims to protect disabled people from inequalities by emphasising the rights and needs of people with disabilities. As signatories to the convention, countries around the world, including Indonesia, use this convention to build inclusive policies to help people with disabilities live and gain equal rights to other citizens. Regarding digital accessibility, Article 9, section 1, parts A and B of the UNCRPD also includes non-physical accessibility, and therefore covers inclusive technology and digital spaces for people with disabilities.

Indonesia's ratification of UNCRPD can be viewed in relation to Indonesian laws to provide legal protection for the digital rights and needs of people with disabilities. Following Indonesia's ratification of the UNCRPD in 2011, the country gained significant momentum in addressing disability rights. This international agreement brought to the forefront Indonesia's obligations to ensure equal rights and opportunities for individuals with disabilities. The UNCRPD provided a clear framework for reforming the nation's disability laws to align with international human rights standards, emphasising a rights-based approach that promotes equality, inclusion, and the full participation of people with disabilities in all aspects of society, including digital rights.

Indonesia, as a legal and democratic state, clearly guarantees human rights for all people and citizens, as stated in the 1945 Constitution of the Republic of Indonesia. By ratifying the UNCRPD, Indonesia has built its inclusive legal system through Indonesian Law No. 8/2016 on Disability Law. Article 5 Paragraph (1) Letter M of the law emphasises disability rights to accessibility regardless of the form. Article 2 Letter H of the law underlines accessibility as a crucial part of implementing and fulfilling disability rights. In accordance with the UNCRPD, the law mentions technological inclusion to ensure non-physical accessibility for Indonesians with disabilities.

Central to its approach to inclusion, Indonesia has recently emphasised formulating and implementing the Gender Equality, Disability, and Social Inclusion (GEDSI) framework in its policymaking processes. The emphasis on GEDSI extends to subnational levels, including provincial governments, as mandated by Ministerial Regulation No. 15/2008 from the Ministry of Home Affairs. The GEDSI framework at the national level has evolved into a perspective that promotes a more inclusive approach aimed at including vulnerable groups, particularly Indonesians with disabilities. The regulation underscores the critical importance of incorporating the GEDSI framework to ensure inclusivity across all sectors, aligning with the understanding that full societal participation must be prioritised (Supanji, 2023). This framework has also been a solid basis for implementing inclusive information services for people with disabilities. This includes a regulation by Indonesia's Ministry of Communication and Information Technology regarding accessible information and communication services. This regulation is required to provide a diverse range of communication assistance for disabled people. In fulfilling inclusive informational rights, public institutions and services need to have the proper perspective and knowledge of all types of disabilities in accordance with the Disability Law and UNCRPD. In this case, the purpose of the GEDSI framework in policymaking is to emphasise to all elements of government and society that people with disabilities have equal rights as part of Indonesian society, just like other citizens. This understanding should guide efforts to fulfil these rights.

In policymaking, the formulation and evaluation processes are among the most crucial steps in a policy cycle (Gerston, 2014). Despite their recognised importance, the literature considering the creation and evaluation of disability policies in Indonesia remains insufficient. At the same time, the implementation phase represents a pivotal moment that can either effectively translate decisions into actions or lead to the failure or breakdown of the policy (Davis & Althaus, 2020). One potential constraint in policy implementation is the set of beliefs and preferences held by the implementing institution, referred to as the 'dominant coalition' as defined by Montjoy and O'Toole (1979). This shows that existing regulations and policies reflect the desires and knowledge of policymakers rather than people with disability. In Indonesia, general policymaking remains ineffective, and policy processes have demonstrated minimal engagement with people with disabilities (Maliki, 2022). This limitation is also shown in Indonesia's digital policies and their resulting lack of a focus on disability inclusion (Sri & Astuti, 2021). The next section of the chapter discusses digital activism for inclusion, which is related to policymaking processes on digital inclusion.

7.4 Indonesian digital activism: From disability to policy

The media industry is a critical factor in disability representation, and has the potential to educate and raise awareness regarding disability (Nurhaqiqi, 2019). However, in reality, Indonesians with disabilities are still portrayed as pitiful and helpless in some media coverage (Tsaputra, 2016), leading them to be seen through sympathetic eyes instead of inclusive ones (Nurhaqiqi, 2019). These negative portrayals also occur in digital platforms where Indonesians with disabilities are seen as powerless individuals within social media narratives (Umar, 2024). As a result, there is limited government engagement of people with disabilities digitally and their voices are absent from policymaking processes on digital inclusion (Sri & Astuti, 2021).

The rise of digital media has widened disability representation in comparison to traditional media (Ellis et al., 2015; Ellis & Kent, 2016; Goggin & Newell, 2005) as people with disabilities have used social media platforms to self-represent themselves and connect with fellow disabled users (Shpigelman & Gill, 2014). Over the past ten years, disabled Indonesians have been increasingly active users of digital technology (Bexley, 2015; Hersinta, 2020; Pearson & Trevisan, 2015; Rofasita, 2017). This includes increased numbers of disability activists (Hersinta, 2020) and organisations (Bexley, 2015) that have established a social media presence for broader disability awareness and inclusion.

Internationally, digital media has been used in similar ways. In Sweden, for example, Twitter has been used for collective protest through 10,000 tweets on disability policy using #funkpool. This public presence amplifies the voices of people with disability where they have been ignored previously, thereby decreasing an imbalance in power relations and including people with disabilities in social processes (IIneland et al., 2019). A similar protest movement was raised through Facebook in the United Kingdom to battle the lack of media representation in a Paralympic event (Pearson & Trevisan, 2015). In terms of groups, Facebook users have been building virtual communities for empowerment; for example, Facebook groups in America have successfully built inclusive online communities of disabled and non-disabled users (Shpigelman & Gill, 2014). Facebook has also mediated the social relations of American users with intellectual disabilities. While the number within this group of users is limited, the relations formed through Facebook have fostered a space for e-inclusion and social networks (White & Forrester-Jones, 2020).

Social media likewise has a crucial role in communicating disability in Indonesia (Bexley, 2015; Hersinta, 2020). For instance, Twitter provides a platform useful as a mediating space for neurodiversity movements by autistic users who challenge traditional views on autism by offering progressive perspectives about the diversity of human experiences (Hersinta, 2019). In addition, Facebook has facilitated the parents of children with cerebral palsy not only to get connected as parental peers but also to aid them in advocating for their children's rights (Rofasita, 2017). The emergence of social media has also provided space for disabled people in Indonesia for disability activism, amplifying their voices and impacting disability policymaking through the increasing involvement of people with disabilities in the process (Hasfi & Rahardjo, 2019). Digital activism bridges the shift from the charitable approach traditionally embedded in institutional perceptions of Indonesians with disabilities (Irwanto et al., 2010).

Instagram users can visualise diversity (Leaver et al., 2020), which includes users with disabilities, within their posts and this is an important way of increasing the social visibility of people with disability and their needs (Tollan, 2020). Both Difapedia and Jendela Ibu have taken part in increasing disability representation in the digital space using Instagram, as reflected in the disability and inclusion content they include on Instagram. Khanif mentioned that Difapedia has found that Instagram is the most suitable platform for their digital presence. Riris added that Difapedia uses Instagram to diversify disability content and spread positive information for users with disabilities. Jendela Ibu also uses their Instagram account to post content on disability inclusion.

With its visual features, Instagram allows users to post diverse content (Laestadius, 2018; Leaver et al., 2020). Both Difapedia and Jendela Ibu used Instagram as a portfolio to introduce their inclusive programmes. Ifta mentioned that Jendela Ibu actively posts content on Instagram related to their programmes and assistance for parents of children with special needs. For Difapedia, Riris added that they also posted posters and reports of their digital skills programmes. Instagram's visuality has been a driving force for its potential for human virtual connection and empowerment (Leaver et al., 2020). While Jendela Ibu can reach more parents of children with special needs, Difapedia reaches more disabled peers. With this connection, they can empower their audiences and amplify their experiences and needs in a public way, to counter their absence in other aspects of social life, including within policymaking.

7.5 Indonesian disability policymaking: Who is involved?

Indonesia has implemented the 'no one left behind' principle in its development programmes (Supanji, 2023). Pro-disability policies in the country originated from legislative measures such as Indonesian Law No. 4/1997 on Persons with Disabilities, which was then replaced by Indonesian Law No. 8/2016. Both regulations cover Indonesians with disabilities. Stemming from the ratification of the UNCRPD, the policy underwent a transformation, shifting the primary focus from health-related aspects of disability and a 'charity' approach to a framework anchored in performance against social welfare indicators (Ayuningtyas et al., 2021). In response, Mursalim and Haq (2022) argue that Indonesia's Ministry of Communication and Information Technology has gone through policymaking processes to provide accessible and inclusive digital practices. This effort is shaped by an affirmative programme rooted in the principles of the GEDSI framework (Irwanto et al., 2010).

One example of Indonesia's commitment to disability rights is the National Action Plan for Persons with Disabilities (RAN-PD), which aims to significantly enhance the participation of individuals with disabilities across various sectors, including the digital space. Through affirmative government measures, these policies seek to create opportunities for meaningful engagement in a safer and more accessible environment. Furthermore, Indonesia's commitment to the UNCRPD's provisions on accessibility and equal access to information and communication technologies has intensified political pressure on the government to address digital exclusion, ensuring that the digital landscape becomes inclusive for all.

As discussed above, a critical factor in such successful implementation of disability laws through such policy and the longevity of this change lies in the initial policy formulation process. The Multiple Streams Framework highlights the interplay of three key processes: the problem stream, the policy stream, and the politics stream (Kingdon, 2013, p. 87). The problem stream involves recognising issues through indicators, focusing events, or feedback mechanisms which together spotlight societal challenges (Kingdon, 2013, pp. 90–92). The policy stream focuses on the generation and refinement of proposals within policy communities, where feasible and acceptable solutions compete for attention (Kingdon, 2013, pp. 116–118). The politics stream encompasses the broader political environment, including shifts in public opinion, election results, and changes in government leadership (Kingdon, 2013, pp. 145–147). When these streams converge, often facilitated by policy entrepreneurs, policy windows open, enabling significant legislative change (Kingdon, 2013, p. 166).

The policy stream highlights domestic advocacy's pivotal role in policymaking (Kingdon, 2013). Indonesia's approach to disability policymaking can be considered in relation to this framework. The country's ratification of the UNCRPD marked a critical moment in the problem stream by recognising the need for comprehensive disability policies. In the policy stream, diverse disability stakeholders, such as disability organisations, civil society groups, and disability rights advocates, have been instrumental in proposing policy solutions. As covered in this chapter, disability-led organisations like Difapedia and Jendela Ibu advanced proposals by advocating for digital literacy training and digital inclusion policies. However, challenges in the politics stream, including bureaucratic inertia and limited political will, have hindered effective policy implementation. Aligning these streams through proactive government engagement and meaningful stakeholder participation remains essential for fostering sustainable disability policy reforms. They have persistently pushed for a shift from the outdated charity model to a human-rights-based approach, which recognises individuals with disabilities as equal citizens with the right to access public services, employment, and education. This shift is essential in realising the UNCRPD's goals and fostering a more inclusive society.

Despite policy efforts aimed at promoting inclusivity, stigmatisation and structural barriers within Indonesia's digital sector continue to hinder the meaningful participation of marginalised groups, especially individuals with disabilities. These persistent obstacles reinforce power imbalances and limit opportunities for these communities to engage effectively in the digital economy. For example, symbolic inclusion remains a common issue where institutions superficially address diversity without making substantial structural changes (Montjoy & O'Toole, 1979). This impedes the ability of people with disability to contribute meaningfully to the national development of policy initiatives related to digital inclusion and digital economy. Without structural reforms, such as inclusive policies, accessible technologies, and equitable digital education, these groups will continue to face significant barriers, perpetuating inequalities in Indonesia's digital landscape. Addressing these gaps is essential to achieving true inclusivity and sustainable growth in the nation's digital transformation journey.

With its complexity, the policy implementation process, especially in relation to digital inclusion, has brought about little to no change for people with disabilities (Mursalim & Haq, 2022). Difapedia's programmes provide support, which both counteracts and highlights the lack of understanding and implementation of digital accessibility (Figure 7.1). Riris comments that disability digital policy is lacking in implementation as it does not suit the needs of Indonesians with disabilities. In the United States, people with intellectual disabilities can maintain their mutual virtual relations through Facebook (White & Forrester-Jones, 2020), which is the opposite of Jendela Ibu's members with special needs, including their parents. As Ifta and Sandy pointed out, this may be due to the lack of digital skills in people with disability, which is reflected in the lack of disability digital policy implementation to improve digital literacy.

Source: @difapedia Official Instagram Account https://instagram.com/difapedia.

Figure 7.1 Difapedia's digital skills training for disabled participants

7.6 Disability activists vs. policymakers in Indonesia

Despite inclusive regulations, the comments above show that Indonesians with disabilities face inequality in digital accessibility (Tsaputra, 2016). Effective mechanisms for the formulation and monitoring cycle of inclusive policies are still lacking (Maliki, 2022). Many government agencies fail to engage disability groups, whose involvement is crucial for addressing the incomplete implementation and poor coordination of policy (Blomkamp et al., 2018).

While there has been some progress towards greater inclusivity, the involvement of marginalised groups in the media and digital spaces remains minimal. The disability inclusion framework established by Indonesian Law No. 8/2016 mandates the involvement of Indonesians with disabilities in policymaking processes related to their inclusion, including digital inclusion. Unfortunately, this regulation is relatively recent and unfamiliar to many individuals with disabilities. A survey conducted by Ayuningtyas et al. (2021) revealed that 59.1% of people with disabilities are not adequately informed about their constitutional rights, as their accessibility needs were not being fulfilled. Article 28 F of the 1945 Constitution of the Republic of Indonesia also states that everyone has the right to communicate and obtain information to develop their personality and social environment. The Article constitutionally mandates rights to communication and freedom for all people, including people with disabilities as both individuals and as integral members of society.

The challenge of achieving digital inclusion in Indonesia is further complicated by the structure of its bureaucracy and organisational framework. Maliki (2022) highlights that formulation and monitoring mechanisms for inclusive policymaking remain ineffective, with many agencies failing to fulfil their mandated duties to involve disability groups. This issue aligns with research from the Knowledge Sector Initiative, a joint effort between Australia's Department of Foreign Affairs and Trade and Indonesia's Ministry of National Development Planning, which underscores a recurring trend of incomplete implementation and coordination challenges. Even in broader terms, governmental bodies often struggle to align their efforts with other regulations and objectives (Blomkamp et al., 2018), contributing to the slow pace of digital transformation and inclusion. Consequently, local governments in less developed regions struggle to raise awareness, advocate effectively for this demographic, and create meaningful action plans at the regional level.

Policy is also made against the background of a deeply ingrained charitable approach in institutional perceptions of people with disabilities (Irwanto et al., 2010). As a result, individuals with disabilities continue to face segregation, raising ongoing concerns about their ability to participate meaningfully in policymaking processes. Compounding this issue is the persistent negative stigma surrounding people with disabilities in Indonesia. Poerwanti (2017) notes that a common misconception exists, linking physical disabilities with diminished intellectual capabilities. Such attitudes perpetuate the association of disability with illness or dependency, leading to discriminatory practices and the neglect of their needs.

With the emergence of technology, people with disability face digital inequalities (Wahab, 2019), but the accessibility of digital technology also serves as a valuable medium for the social participation of disabled people (Goggin & Newell, 2005; Lindsay, 2010). Difapedia focuses on the digital sector in tackling digital inequalities, as it has a crucial role in the disability movement. Difapedia works with Indonesia's Ministry of Communication and Information Technology to overcome the issue of digital inaccessibility. One of their essential programmes is conducting workshops on transferable digital skills for people with disabilities. Khanif mentions that the workshops focus on digital marketing and social media content creation. The workshops have also assisted local micro, small and medium enterprises in digitalisation. For those who cannot participate in person, Difapedia has also held webinars on disability and the digital world.

Disability stakeholders can foster social inclusion by engagement with technology (Lindsay, 2010), as Difapedia and Jendela Ibu have utilised social media not only to promote disability inclusion through digital content but also to challenge policymakers. Ifta states that their presence on Instagram has effectively mediated their voice to the policymakers. However, both organisations face challenges in producing impactful disability inclusion content. Their impact on policymakers was minimal and not easily heard by government. This could be because they do not engage in collective protests towards the government that might create a mass voice that the government must respond to. Ineland et al. (2019) explains that the Twitter protest in Sweden has successfully impacted policymakers to include people with disabilities in their policymaking processes. Khanif mentions that Instagram has been useful in disseminating digital inclusion and transferable digital skills and reaching more significant audiences, and so could be used for such purposes in Indonesia.

Digital accessibility requires two elements. First, access given by policymakers through the provision of equitable digital resources is rooted in the involvement of disability stakeholders in policymaking processes. Second, the ability or digital skills of people with disabilities also has an important role in tackling the digital divide. Hence, in order to achieve digital equality and disability inclusion, joint commitment is needed to both increasing the accessibility of digital resources and increasing digital skills (Wahab, 2019). Khanif and Sandy comment that Indonesian disability activism is challenging as there are limited human resources from disability stakeholders to help with content production, reflecting a lack of digital skills.

Ifta hopes that the government focuses on improving digital inclusion for Indonesians with disabilities. She criticises the government's habit of providing food subsidies and basic necessities as its dominant response to people with disabilities, linking disability to poverty. She thinks that this approach should be ended and suggests that because of its limited scope the government should instead make a greater effort to assist those with disabilities to enhance their digital skills and increase digital accessibility. She added that people with disabilities require more skills development assistance to be independent, and to be better integrated with so-called 'normal society'. For Riris, this challenge is becoming more complex because of a lack of disabled people's understanding towards inclusive policy due to their low literacy skills. Therefore the government should also work on improving the literacy of people with disability.

A disability-related digital divide fosters social movements for digital disability inclusion (Ellis & Kent, 2016) within policy, as promoted by disability organisations (Madyaningrum et al., 2022). Wahab (2019) emphasises that the formation of an inclusive digital policy should involve people with disabilities. With a focus on digital inclusion, Difapedia, which Khanif founded, has been involved in local policymaking. This involvement considered Khanif's lived experience as a person with disability and his contribution to assisting local disabled people. Within the local government of Purbalingga region in Central Java, Indonesia, he was appointed as a committee member to consult on local disability regulation and policymaking. For instance, he was involved in bringing disability perspectives to the formulation of Purbalingga's Regional Regulations. In addition, he also contributed to formulating the National Action Plan for Human Rights and Regional Government Work Plan in relation to disability.

Riris mentioned that Difapedia has assisted more than 20 participants as part of their digital skills training. This is in addition to participants who joined digital literacy seminars they have run in collaboration with Indonesia's Ministry of Communication and Information Technology. The number of participants continues to increase, which shows the important role of Difapedia in the community, but also the limited digital literacy which leads to this increasing demand, and which in itself reflects the poor implementation of disability digital policy. Alongside Difapedia, Jendela Ibu has also witnessed the digital divide between disabled people and their parents, and the broader community. Although they are not directly involved in policymaking, their Instagram activism has effectively influenced policymakers. An example of this is when local governments have publicly recognised their advocacy, and its impact on their decision-making processes towards being more inclusive and disability friendly. This impact of social media on policy is also reflected in previous literature, which has indicated that Instagram is an effective social media platform for advocating for disability inclusion (Cahyadi & Setiawan, 2021). An impactful online presence on Instagram is also experienced by Difapedia, as mentioned by Khanif and Riris, respectively. Beyond the policy context, Ifta added that social media has aided the organisation in recruiting and empowering more members and in raising awareness of disability inclusion more broadly.

7.7 Towards digital inclusion: Recommendations

Before concluding this chapter, the authors would like to provide recommendations to Indonesian policymakers in relation to digital disability inclusion. These are also recommendations of areas that need, at the same time, to be the topic of further academic research on lived experience in policy. It is essential that we move forward to enhance government knowledge and capacity to actively participate in GEDSI initiatives at both national and regional levels. According to Fuller (2010), three primary challenges regarding opportunities for individuals with disabilities to participate in society include society's bias towards people with disabilities, negative perceptions of their capacity, and financial constraints faced by companies in facilitating access to employment for people with disabilities. These constraints need to be addressed by the government to improve the ability of people with disability to participate in policymaking and society more generally.

The implementation of the GEDSI framework in relation to digital inclusion should aim to enhance technological accessibility. This approach should encourage the development and distribution of affordable assistive technologies and ensure that mainstream digital platforms comply with accessibility standards (Sri & Astuti, 2021). The GEDSI framework can also be utilised as a means to promote government affirmative action by implementing interventions to empower individuals and institutions to promptly and effectively apply inclusive mindsets and behaviours within their teams (Katz & Miller, 2016).

In addition, the government should include people with disabilities in the implementation of its digitisation-related policy. This is important because it will allow policy to better reflect the needs and interests of people with disabilities at the point of policy creation rather than addressing implementation failures down the road. This will also make the policy implementation more cost-effective as it will reduce unwanted consequences for costly corrections as a result of failing implementation. Importantly, this involvement will also build mutual trust, which is crucial to fostering an inclusive society.

One of Australia's best practice examples of digital inclusion is the National Disability Insurance Scheme (NDIS) Digital Inclusion Strategy, which focuses on providing accessible digital services for people with disabilities (NDIS, 2023). The NDIS is Australia's national support programme for people with disabilities, offering funding for services and support (NDIS, 2021). The NDIS Digital Inclusion Strategy aims to ensure that all services and platforms associated with the scheme are digitally accessible to everyone, particularly individuals with disabilities. The strategy promotes inclusion by removing barriers and enhancing access to online services for participants, providers, and stakeholders (NDIS, 2023).

A vital aspect of this initiative is the application of Web Content Accessibility Guidelines standards for web accessibility, ensuring that platforms are usable by people with various disabilities – visual, auditory, or physical (W3C, 2024). This approach can be applied to government websites, public service apps, and e-learning platforms to make them more inclusive. Such initiatives can strengthen policy implementation by ensuring that existing laws and policies on disability inclusion are effectively enforced and monitored and provide the necessary funding and resources for ongoing support. This holistic approach also supports community and advocacy efforts by providing funding and resources to disability advocacy organisations and fostering collaboration between the government, the private sector, and civil society. By doing so, it bridges gaps in the current system and enhances the overall effectiveness of digital inclusion policies.

Within an Indonesian context, Difapedia and Jendela Ibu have become exemplary organisations as advocacy groups working towards digital inclusion for Indonesians with disabilities. They have bridged the divide between government and people with disabilities in the digital inclusion policies. Their efforts have shown the lack of involvement of people with disability by the government in the policymaking process, leading to the minimal impact of policy on the digital inclusion of people with disabilities. As a result, Indonesia's effort in forming digital inclusion policies and ensuring their implementation has not been effective. While other countries have specific documents, such as Australia's NDIS Digital Inclusion Strategy, specific documents remain absent in Indonesia. Creating such documents is a reflection of inclusive policymaking. Learning from Australia, Indonesia could adapt an holistic approach which results in inclusion, not only by engaging with disability organisations but also by evaluating the actual condition on the ground to really know the needs of people with disabilities. Through collaboration, targeted policy, and proper implementation, digital inclusion can be realised.

7.8 Conclusion

Just like a marathon, Indonesia keeps running towards its goal of bringing an inclusive society to people with disabilities, by increasing the accessibility of the digital world. While there are still many problems, all the individuals working within advocacy organsiations who contributed their experiences to this chapter agree that Indonesia's digital disability policy has been progressing over the past decade. Both organisations included in this chapter have been influential as disability communities that have influenced policymakers. While Difapedia has been involved in policymaking towards the digital inclusion of people with disability, Jendela Ibu has not been directly involved but has affected local government decision-making by encouraging it to at least consider disability inclusion in its policymaking.

This chapter emphasises that disability involvement is required in every policy formulation and evaluation aspect so that existing policies can accommodate the needs of people with disability. Fulfilling disability rights will not be possible without listening to and understanding the needs of those with disabilities because they experience first-hand the barriers and challenges of the digital divide. With that, they have the knowledge of how best to accommodate their digital inclusion, which might otherwise be overlooked by people who do not have this lived experience. By involving them in the policymaking process, implementing digital inclusion will accelerate the fulfilment of their digital rights and finally foster equitable digitalisation.

The lack of meaningful changes and adaptability in inclusive policy to dismantle the stigma around people with disabilities in their digital presence highlights the complex challenges of programme implementation at the institutional level. This may result from a failure to engage policy end users during the policy design phase. Although civil society organisations like Difapedia and Jendela Ibu have initiated efforts, substantial systemic changes remain absent.

The policymaking process to boost digital inclusion for people with disabilities in Indonesia is dynamic and ongoing. It requires a comprehensive approach that includes setting clear objectives, engaging diverse stakeholders, securing legislative approval, implementing initiatives, and continuously monitoring and refining policies. Disability-friendly policies must involve diverse parties and, most importantly, people with disabilities. By fostering collaboration between the government, the private sector, civil society, and international organisations, Indonesia can make significant strides towards creating a more inclusive digital society for people with disabilities.

In conclusion, this chapter provided insight into how disability organisations in Indonesia – Difapedia and Jendela Ibu – were involved in disability digital policymaking processes. We also demonstrated how disability organisations have supported local governments in improving digital literacy and skills among Indonesians with disabilities. While this chapter has discussed an organisational perspective, consideration of people with disabilities as digital users was limited. Therefore, future research needs to delve into the opinions of people with disabilities in relation to digital policy, questioning whether they feel represented in existing policy and the efficacy of policy implementation.

References

Adioetomo, S. M., Mont, D., & Irwanto. (2014). Persons with Disabilities in Indonesia: Empirical Facts and Implications for Social Protection Policies. Jakarta: TNP2K.

Ammari, T., Morris, M. R., & Schoenebeck, S. Y. (2014). Accessing Social Support and Overcoming Judgment on Social Media among Parents of Children with Special Needs. www.aaai.org

Amrullah, M. K. (2017). Urgensi Keterlibatan Difabel dalam Perumusan Kebijakan Desa. *Jurnal Difabel Sigab*, *4*(4).

Ayuningtyas, D., Rachmawati, R., Larasanti, A., Margaretha, C., Hasibuan, S. U., & Ayuni, Q. (2021). The law on persons with disabilities: How far have we gone? (Case study in Indonesia). *Journal of Legal, Ethical and Regulatory Issues*, *25*(1), 1–19.

Behl, D., Desgeorges, J., & White, K. R. (2016). The role of family-led disability organizations in supporting families with hearing-related concerns. *Journal of Early Hearing Detection and Intervention*, *1*(1). http://www.familyvoices.org

Bexley, A. (2015). Social Media Ignites Disability Movement in Indonesia. Asia Foundation. https://www.pressreleasepoint.com/social-media-ignites-disability-movement-indonesia

Blomkamp, E., Sholikin, M. N., Nursyamsi, F., Lewis, J. M., & Toumbourou, T. (2018). *Understanding Policymaking in Indonesia: In Search of a Policy Cycle*. Melbourne: The University of Melbourne.

Bray, L., Carter, B., Sanders, C., Blake, L., & Keegan, K. (2017). Parent-to-parent peer support for parents of children with a disability: A mixed method study. *Patient Education and Counseling*, *100*(8), 1537–1543. https://doi.org/10.1016/j.pec.2017.03.004

Cahyadi, A. & Setiawan, A. (2021). Disability and social media: Exploring utilization of instagram as a tool for disability advocacy. *Al-Balagh: Jurnal Dakwah Dan Komunikasi*, *5*(2), 223–250. https://doi.org/10.22515/al-balagh.v5i2.2746

Carey, A. C., Block, P., & Scotch, R. K. (2019). Sometimes allies: Parent-led disability organizations and social movements. *Disability Studies Quarterly*. *39*(1) https://dsq-sds.org/article/id/1463/

Davis, G. & Althaus, C. (2020). *The Australian Policy Handbook*. Routledge. https://doi.org/10.4324/9781003117940

Ditchman, N., Werner, S., Kosyluk, K., Jones, N., Elg, B., & Corrigan, P. W. (2013). Stigma and intellectual disability: Potential application of mental illness research. *Rehabilitation Psychology*, *58*(2), 206–216. https://doi.org/10.1037/a0032466

Edwards, B. & McCarthy, J. D. (2007). Resources and social movement mobilization. In *The Blackwell Companion to Social Movements* (pp. 116–152). Blackwell Publishing Ltd. https://doi.org/10.1002/9780470999103.ch6

Efendi, M. (2018). The implementation of inclusive education in Indonesia for children with special needs: Expectation and reality. *Journal of ICSAR ISSN*, *2*(2), 142–147.

Ellis, K., Garland-Thomson, R., Kent, M., & Robertson, R. (2018a). *Interdisciplinary Approaches to Disability* London: Routledge. https://doi.org/10.4324/9781351053228

Ellis, K., Garland-Thomson, R., Kent, M., & Robertson, R. (2018b). Manifestos for the future of critical disability studies. In *Manifestos for the Future of Critical Disability Studies* (Vol. 1). Taylor and Francis. https://doi.org/10.4324/9781351053341

Ellis, K., Goggin, G., & Kent, M. (2015). Disability's digital frictions: Activism, technology, and politics. *The Fibreculture Journal*, *26*, 7–31. https://doi.org/10.15307/fcj.26.188.2015

Ellis, K. & Kent, M. (2016). *Disability and Social Media*. London: Routledge. https://doi.org/10.4324/9781315577357

Fuller, S. K. (2010). Employment for the Developmentally Disabled via One-Stop Centers. Capella University.

Gerston, L. N. (2014). *Public Policy Making*. London: Routledge. https://doi.org/10.4324/9781315701387

Goggin, G. (2018). Disability and digital inequalities: Rethinking digital divides with disability theory. In M. Ragnedda & G. W. Muschert (Eds.), *Theorizing Digital Divides* (pp. 63–74). Routledge.

Goggin, G. & Newell, C. (2005). Introduction: The intimate relations between technology and disability. *Disability Studies Quarterly*, 25(2), 1–4.

Hasfi, N., & Rahardjo, T. (2019). The disabled people virtual communities in social media from the perspective of public sphere theory. *Jurnal Komunikasi Ikatan Sarjana Komunikasi Indonesia*, 4(2), 65–76. https://doi.org/10.25008/jkiski.v4i2.327

Hersinta. (2019). Tweeting Autism – A Framing Analysis of Twitter Conversations on Autism in Indonesia. Proceedings of the 4th International Conference on Contemporary Social And Political Affairs (ICoCSPA 2018), August 2018, 142–152. https://doi.org/10.5220/0008818101420152

Hersinta. (2020). Communicating Autism on the Internet. The Emerging of Neurodiversity Movement in Indonesia. Thesis. Curtin University. https://espace.curtin.edu.au/handle/20.500.11937/82188

Ineland, J., Gelfgren, S., & Cocq, C. (2019). Negotiating authority: Disability, interactions and power relations on Twitter. *Scandinavian Journal of Disability Research*, *21*(1), 238–249. https://doi.org/10.16993/sjdr.591

Irwanto, Kasim, E. R., Fransiska, A., Lusli, M., & Okta, S. (2010). The Situation of People with Disability in Indonesia: A Desk Review. Centre for Disability Studies: Universitas Indonesia.

Katz, J. H. & Miller, F. A. (2016). Defining Diversity and Adapting Inclusion Strategies on a Global Scale Lessons from the Field, for the Field. www.kjcg.com

Kingdon, J. W. (2013). *Agendas, Alternatives, and Public Policies* (Updated). Pearson Education.

Kusumastuti, P., Pradanasari, R., & Ratnawati, A. (2014). The problems of people with disability in indonesia and what is being learned from the world report on disability. *American Journal of Physical* Medicine & Rehabilitation, *93*(1), S63–S67. https://doi.org/10.1097/PHM.0000000000000025

Laestadius, L. (2018). Instagram. In L. Sloan & A. Quan-Haase (Eds.), *The SAGE Handbook of Social Media Research Methods*. SAGE Publications Ltd.

Leaver, T., Highfield, T., & Abidin, C. (2020). *Instagram: Visual Social Media Cultures*. Polity.

Lindsay, S. (2010). Disability and the digital divide: Gaps and future directions. In C. Evans (Ed.), *Internet Issues: Blogging, Digital Divide and Digital Libraries*. Nova Science Publishers.

Madyaningrum, M. E., Sonn, C. C., & Fisher, A. T. (2022). Disability organizations as empowering settings: Challenging stigmatization, promoting emancipation. *American Journal of Community Psychology*, 69(3–4), 474–483. https://doi.org/10.1002/ajcp.12560

Malik, F., Abduladjid, S., Mangku, D. G. S., Yuliartini, N. P. R., Wirawan, I. G. M. A. S., & Mahendra, P. R. A. (2021). Legal protection for people with disabilities in the perspective of human rights in Indonesia. *International Journal of Criminology and Sociology*, *10*, 538–547. https://doi.org/10.6000/1929-4409.2021.10.62

Maliki. (2022). Perencanaan dan Penganggaran Inklusif Disabilitas melalui Rencana Aksi Daerah Penyandang Disabilitas (Peraturan Menteri PPN/Kepala Bappenas Nomor 3 Tahun 2021).

Mineur, T., Tideman, M., & Mallander, O. (2017). Self-advocacy in Sweden – An analysis of impact on daily life and identity of self-advocates with intellectual disability. *Cogent Social Sciences*, 3(1), 1–16. https://doi.org/10.1080/23311886.2017.1304513

Montjoy, R. S., & O'Toole, L. J. (1979). Toward a theory of policy implementation: An organisational perspective. *Public Administration Review*, 39(5), 465–476. https://doi.org/10.2307/3109921

Mursalim, S. W. & Haq, F. N. (2022). Decent work inclusive policy for persons with disabilities in Indonesia. *Jurnal Ilmiah Ilmu Administrasi Publik*, *12*(2), 450. https://doi.org/10.26858/jiap.v12i2.38581

NDIS. (2021). Australia's Disability Strategy 2021–2031 [National Disability Insurance Agency]. https://www.ndis.gov.au/understanding/australias-disability-strategy-2021-2031

NDIS. (2023). Implementation Report Summary Australia's Disability Strategy 2021–2031 [National Disability Insurance Agency]. https://www.disabilitygateway.gov.au/document/10151

Nugroho, Y. (2011). Citizens in @ction Collaboration, Participatory Democracy and Freedom of Information – Mapping Contemporary Civic Activism and the Use of New Social Media in Indonesia. University of Manchester and HIVOS Regional Office Southeast Asia.

Nurhaqiqi, H. (2019, 7 October). Difable Literacy: Analysis of Difable Representation in Indonesian Media. https://doi.org/10.4108/eai.30-7-2019.2287625

Pearson, C. & Trevisan, F. (2015). Disability activism in the new media ecology: Campaigning strategies in the digital era. *Disability & Society*, *30*(6), 924–940. https://doi.org/10.1080/09687599.2015.1051516

Poerwanti, S. D. (2017). Pengelolaan Tenaga Kerja Difabel untuk Mewujudkan Workplace Inclusion. *INKLUSI*, *4*(1), Article 1. https://doi.org/10.14421/ijds.040101

Purwanta, S. A. (2012). Penyandang Disabilitas. In E. Riyadi and S. Nurhidayat (Eds.), *Vulnerable Group: Kajian dan Mekanisme Perlindungannya* (pp. 257–213). Pusat Studi Hak Asasi Manusia Universitas Islam Indonesia (PUSHAM UII).

Rofasita, S. (2017). Sharing experience dan resiliensi: Studi atas Facebook group orang tua anak cerebral palsy. *Jurnal INKLUSI*, *4*(1), 119. https://www.researchgate.net/publication/321485603_Sharing_Experience_dan_Resiliensi_Studi_atas_Facebook_Group_Orang_Tua_Anak_Cerebral_Palsy

Satriana, S., Huda, K., Saadah, N., Hidayati, D., & Zulkarnaen, A. (2021). Covid-19 Impacts on People with Disabilities in Indonesia: An In-Depth Look. Kementarian PPN/Bappenas and Australian Government. https://www.dfat.gov.au/sites/default/files/covid19-impact-pwd-indonesia.pdf

Seubert, F. J. (2022). 'Sanitise your hands with rainbows!' Encouraging self-representation in times of crisis: Inclusive reflections on Covid-19, together with women with learning disabilities from East London. *Research in Drama Education*, *27*(4), 443–457. https://doi.org/10.1080/13569783.2022.2049223

Shpigelman, C. N. & Gill, C. J. (2014). Facebook use by persons with disabilities. *Journal of Computer-Mediated Communication*, *19*(3), 610–624. https://doi.org/10.1111/jcc4.12059

Smith-Merry, J. (2019). Inclusive disability research. In P. Liamputtong (Ed.), *Handbook of Research Methods in Health Social Sciences* (pp. 1935–1952). Springer Singapore. https://doi.org/10.1007/978-981-10-5251-4_129

Sri, E. & Astuti, S. A. (2021). The Indonesian digital policy: Lessons from PRCs. In *United Nations Conference on Trade and Development*, 1–26. https://unctad.org/system/files/official-document/BRI-Project_RP10_en.pdf

Suharto, S., Kuipers, P., & Dorsett, P. (2016). Disability terminology and the emergence of 'diffability' in Indonesia. *Disability and Society*, *31*(5), 693–712. https://doi.org/10.1080/09687599.2016.1200014

Supanji, T. H. (2023). Pemerintah Penuhi Hak Penyandang Disabilitas di Indonesia. Kementerian Koordinator Bidang Pembangunan Manusia Dan Kebudayaan Republik Indonesia. https://www.kemenkopmk.go.id/pemerintah-penuhi-hak-penyandang-disabilitas-di-indonesia

Swartz, L. (2009). Building disability research capacity in low-income contexts: Possibilities and challenges. In *Disability and International Development: Towards Inclusive Global Health* (pp. 91–103). Springer.

Thohari, S., Movement, S., & Model, S. (2019). Promoting 'difabel', promoting social model of disability in Indonesia. *Study of Disability Movement in Yogyakarta*, 3(1). https://bjss.ub.ac.id/index.php/bjss/article/view/58/35

Tollan, K. (2020). *Exploring the Development of Identity and Community Amongst Disabled Youth on Instagram*. Brock University.

Trevisan, F. (2017). Crowd-sourced advocacy: Promoting disability rights through online storytelling. *Public Relations Inquiry*, *6*(2), 191–208. https://doi.org/10.1177/2046147X17697785

Tsaputra, A. (2016). Portrayals of people with disabilities in Indonesian newsprint media (A case study on three Indonesian major newspapers). *Indonesian Journal of Disability Studies*, 3(1), 1–11. http://IJDS.ub.ac.id

Umar. (2024). We belong to you, but you don't represent us. A Javanese (Indonesian) experience of disabilities. In *Indigenous Disability Studies* (pp. 242–255). Routledge. https://doi.org/10.4324/9781032656519-30

W3C. (2024). *WCAG 2 Overview*. Web Accessibility Initiative (WAI). https://www.w3.org/WAI/standards-guidelines/wcag/

Wahab, R. A. (2019). Narrowing the digital divide of people with disabilities to ensure the technology and social inclusion. Masyarakat telematika dan informasi. *Jurnal Penelitian Teknologi Informasi Dan Komunikasi*, *10*(2), 50. https://www.researchgate.net/publication/337851229_Narrowing_The_Digital_Divide_of_People_With_Disabilities_To_Ensure_The_Technology_and_Social_Inclusion

White, P. & Forrester-Jones, R. (2020). Valuing e-inclusion: Social media and the social networks of adolescents with intellectual disability. *Journal of Intellectual Disabilities*, *24*(3), 381–397. https://doi.org/10.1177/1744629518821240

Widinarsih, D. (2018). Disability Inclusion and Disability Awareness in Muslim Society: An Experience of Indonesians Muslim with Disability in Performing Worship. https://doi.org/https://doi.org/10.2991/icddims-17.2018.20

8

From experience to policy: The influence of lived experience on disability transport policy in Sydney, Australia

Miguel Loyola and Jennifer Kent

8.1 Introduction

This chapter aims to explore the role of lived experience in shaping disability transport policy using Australia's largest city, Sydney, as a case study. By integrating the first-hand accounts of individuals with lived experience of disability, this chapter seeks to highlight the practical insights and unique challenges that can inform and enhance policymaking processes. The significance of incorporating lived experiences lies in the co-development of more inclusive, empathetic, and effective transport policies that truly address the needs of the disability community.

8.1.1 Context and background

As Australia's largest and most populous city, Sydney is a major urban hub known for its diverse demographics and vibrant economy. It is also a city facing significant challenges in providing accessible services to all its residents. Sydney's current disability transport system is constrained by fragmented funding, inadequate availability of accessible vehicles, and limited operating hours (Vogel et al., 2020). Accessible transport is crucial for the independence and social and economic inclusion of people with disabilities, enabling them to access essential services, employment opportunities, and social activities. These issues significantly impact the mobility and independence of individuals with disabilities, restricting their ability to engage in everyday activities and participate in the community.

Despite some improvements in public transportation infrastructure, critical gaps remain in the creation of a truly inclusive system. This chapter makes an important contribution of knowledge to this volume by focusing on the importance of lived experience in disability policy for transport. It emphasizes the need for inclusive approaches that reflect the real-world experiences of individuals with disabilities. By examining the specific context of the city of Sydney, Australia, this chapter provides research and policy insights that can contribute to the development of more effective, responsive, and inclusive transport policies both locally and internationally.

Following this introduction, the chapter is organized into several key sections. We begin with the Conceptual Framework, which explores the traditional and contemporary approaches to transport research, emphasizing gaps in the use of inclusive and user-centred methodologies and outlining our approach, which is defined by a series of in-depth interviews with service providers. In the next section – Challenges in Disability Transport – we examine the specific issues facing Sydney's disability transport system as a case study. This is followed by a discussion on the Impact of Lived Experience on Perceptions and Practices, which highlights how first-hand accounts reveal critical service limitations and the necessity for more responsive policies. We then turn to the Role of Lived Experience in Community Transport Organizations, discussing how these insights can inform the design of more inclusive and effective services. The chapter concludes with a section on Policy and Research Implications and Recommendations, which addresses the broader impact of our findings for transport policy and offers suggestions for future improvements.

8.2 Conceptual framework

8.2.1 Historical dominance of utilitarian approaches in transport research and practice

Traditional transport research has predominantly focused on utilitarian approaches, emphasizing efficiency and cost-effectiveness as primary objectives (Lyons & Davidson, 2016; Marsden & Reardon, 2017). These methodologies often prioritize quantitative metrics such as travel time savings, cost-benefit analysis, and network optimization. While these approaches have contributed to the development of efficient transport systems, they frequently overlook the nuanced needs of diverse populations, particularly individuals with disabilities.

The utilitarian paradigm in transport research tends to marginalize non-standard travel behaviours and experiences (Sheller, 2018), failing to account for the varied and often complex mobility needs of different demographic groups. For example, the emphasis on peak-hour efficiency and cost minimization can result in the underprovision of services during off-peak hours, a critical time for many individuals with disabilities who require flexible and accessible transport options. This approach's limitations are evident in the persistent accessibility issues and gaps in service provision that disproportionately affect those with mobility challenges.

Contemporary research highlights the importance of inclusive and user-centred approaches in transport planning (Lucas, 2012; Schwanen et al., 2012; Lyons et al., 2016). Moreover, research by Loyola et al. (2023) underscores the importance of narratives in understanding and implementing transport policies. They argue that narratives are crucial methodological tools for capturing the values and experiences of individuals, providing deeper insights into the lived realities of diverse travellers. By incorporating these personal stories, especially those from individuals with direct or indirect disabilities, which are understood as lived experiences into transport research and policymaking, we can begin to address the shortcomings of utilitarian approaches and move towards more inclusive transport solutions.

8.2.2 The necessity of comprehending diversity and listening to travellers' voices

Recognizing and accommodating diverse mobility needs is essential for developing transport policies that are truly inclusive and effective. Incorporating the voices of those who actually travel, especially individuals with disabilities, can lead to more equitable and responsive transport systems. Kent et al. (2021) highlight the significance of understanding 'messy trips' – those journeys which do not fit into neat, predictable patterns. Their research emphasizes the value of qualitative methods in capturing the complexities of real-life travel experiences, which are often missed by traditional quantitative approaches.

Listening to travellers' voices can reveal critical insights into the barriers and challenges faced by different population groups (Currie et al., 2010). For instance, individuals with disabilities may require specific accommodations such as accessible vehicles, flexible scheduling, and trained staff. By engaging with these travellers and incorporating their feedback into policy development, transport systems can become more adaptive and user-centred.

Moreover, qualitative research methods, such as in-depth interviews and participatory workshops, can uncover the unique needs and preferences of travellers that are not captured by standard surveys and statistical analyses (Ritchie & Spencer, 2002; Smith et al., 2021). These insights are invaluable for designing transport services that genuinely meet the needs of all users, fostering greater social inclusion and mobility equity. By moving beyond utilitarian approaches and incorporating the rich narratives of individuals, we can develop transport systems that are not only efficient but also inclusive and just.

In the coming sections, we focus on the major perspectives concerning the integration of lived experiences of disability in the context of transport organizations. To gather these perspectives, desktop research and semi-structured interviews were conducted with stakeholders from organizations working on disability transport. Specifically, interviews included three stakeholders from a community transport organization, which is an NGO; one stakeholder from Community Transport Organisation, the peak body for community transport in New South Wales, Australia; and one stakeholder from a government organization dealing specifically with disabled transport. Due to confidentiality agreements, more detailed information about these organizations cannot be disclosed.

These interviews revealed core beliefs highlighted in public and academic discourse. For example, advocacy groups for people with disabilities often emphasize the necessity of incorporating lived experiences to co-develop policies that genuinely reflect the needs and challenges faced by individuals with both visible and invisible disabilities. Conversely, policymakers and transport providers may stress the operational benefits and practical insights gained from engaging with these first-hand accounts. By identifying and analysing these primary perspectives, we can better understand the dynamics that shape disability transport policy. This foundational understanding sets the stage for the coming sections, where the direct or indirect lived experiences of individuals with disabilities provide invaluable insights into how these policies impact their daily lives.

8.3 Challenges in disability transport

8.3.1 Fragmented and uncoordinated funding sources

Fragmented and uncoordinated funding poses a major challenge in the provision of disability transport services. The complexity arises from the presence of multiple funding bodies, such as the National Disability Insurance Scheme (NDIS), the Taxi Transport Subsidy Scheme (TTSS), and various state government programmes. These funding sources often operate in isolation, lacking a unified framework that promotes seamless integration and comprehensive service delivery. Consequently, individuals with disabilities encounter inconsistent and inadequate transport options.

The absence of coordination among these funding streams results in a fragmented approach that emphasizes eligibility criteria and subsidy allocation over addressing the actual transportation needs of users. For instance, Respondent 1 pointed out: "There's the NDIS, the TTSS for taxis, and a state government pot of money. None of it works together. It's not person-centred." This disjointed system fails to consider the holistic needs of individuals with disabilities, leading to significant gaps in transport service provision and accessibility.

Furthermore, the reliance on multiple funding sources imposes administrative burdens on both service providers and users. Providers must navigate complex bureaucratic procedures to secure funding, while users may find it difficult to understand and access the various schemes available. Respondent 2 emphasized this issue, stating: "We throw money at it to hide it ... We talk to it. We don't talk with it." This highlights the need for a more integrated and user-friendly funding approach. A unified approach could streamline administrative processes, reduce redundancy, and improve the overall effectiveness of transport services. By fostering collaboration among funding entities, policymakers can develop a more person-centred and efficient transport system that better serves people with disabilities (Krahn & Drum, 2007; Bezyak et al., 2017; Martens, 2018).

8.3.2 Availability and accessibility issues

Issues related to the availability and accessibility of transport services, particularly wheelchair-accessible vehicles and 24/7 services, significantly impede the mobility and autonomy of individuals with disabilities. Despite improvements in public transportation infrastructure, the availability of wheelchair-accessible options remains inconsistent and often insufficient. This shortfall limits the daily activities, employment opportunities, and social engagement of people with disabilities, highlighting a critical deficiency in the current transport system.

In numerous areas, the lack of wheelchair-accessible transport is a widespread problem. Respondent 1 noted: "In some places, there is zero wheelchair accessible transport ... It's very limiting for people living with a disability." This scarcity forces individuals to rely on less reliable and often more costly alternatives, such as private hire services, which may not always meet their specific needs. Additionally, the limited operating hours of accessible transport services exacerbate the situation, leaving individuals with disabilities without viable options during off-peak times or late hours. The impact of these accessibility issues on daily life is profound. For example, individuals with disabilities may face substantial barriers in accessing essential services, employment opportunities, and social activities. Respondent 2 illustrated this disparity, stating: "It shocked me how poor it is. We think public transport is accessible, but it's accessible for those who are able to walk." This reality reflects a broader systemic failure to cater to the diverse needs of all users within the public transport system.

Previous research corroborates these findings, indicating that accessible transport is vital for social inclusion and quality of life for people with disabilities (Kastenholz et al., 2015; Bjerkan & Øvstedal, 2020). The lack of accessible transport options can lead to increased isolation and dependency, further marginalizing individuals with disabilities. Addressing these challenges necessitates a comprehensive approach involving policy reforms, greater investment in accessible infrastructure, and ongoing engagement with the disability community. By prioritizing the development of inclusive transport services, policymakers can ensure that all individuals, regardless of their mobility needs, have equitable access to opportunities and experiences that contribute to a fulfilling life.

8.4 Impact of lived experience on perceptions and practices

8.4.1 Highlighting service limitations

Lived experiences provide critical insights into the limitations of current transport services for individuals with disabilities. These first-hand accounts highlight specific issues that might otherwise be overlooked in policy development and service design. One significant limitation frequently identified is the inadequate hours of operation for accessible transport services. This constraint can severely limit the mobility and independence of individuals who rely on these services for their daily activities. For instance, Respondent 1 emphasized: "Listening to people with lived experience has made me reflect on the hours of operation that we work ... we need to do better." This statement underscores the disconnect between service provision and the actual needs of users, suggesting that extending operating hours could significantly enhance accessibility and convenience for people with disabilities. Similarly, Respondent 2 remarked: "I want better for those that need this ... Their needs are quite different, and we haven't taken that into account." This reflects a broader systemic issue where transport services are not sufficiently tailored to meet the diverse needs of all users. A lack of flexible and responsive transport services can exacerbate social exclusion and limit opportunities for participation in community life. The literature supports these observations, indicating these issues (Church et al., 2000; Kenyon et al., 2002).

8.4.2 Transportation insecurity and social participation

Transportation insecurity significantly impacts social inclusion and participation for individuals with disabilities. When reliable and accessible transport options are unavailable, it hinders their ability to engage in community activities, access essential services, and maintain social connections. The resulting isolation can exacerbate feelings of marginalization and limit opportunities for personal and professional growth.

Respondent 3 highlighted the varied needs of individuals with different disabilities, stating: "Different disabilities mean different transport needs. Some clients have anxiety and need reassurance about schedules and staff." This emphasizes the necessity for transport services that are not only physically accessible but also sensitive to the emotional and psychological needs of users. Ensuring that staff are well-trained and that schedules are reliable can provide the reassurance needed to alleviate anxiety and promote greater confidence in using public transport. Respondent 4 further elaborated on the importance of understanding and addressing individual needs: "Safety and understanding the client's needs are critical. We rely on feedback from families and drivers to improve services." This underscores the importance of a feedback loop involving all stakeholders, including families and service providers, to continuously refine and improve transport services. While the contributions of these allies are invaluable, it is crucial to recognize that individuals with disabilities themselves are the most important voices in informing transport policies and practices about their unique needs. By incorporating their direct feedback, services can become more responsive and better tailored to the specific needs of individuals, thereby enhancing their overall experience and participation in society.

8.5 Role of lived experience in community transport organizations

8.5.1 Designing person-centred services

Incorporating lived experience into the design of community transport services is crucial for developing systems that genuinely meet the needs of individuals with disabilities. By involving people with first-hand experience in the planning and implementation stages, transport services can become more empathetic and effective, addressing real-world challenges in a more nuanced manner.

Respondent 1 emphasized the value of this approach, stating: "Having people with lived experience involved ensures the services meet real needs." This insight highlights the importance of a user-centred design process where the voices of those directly affected by transport policies are heard and integrated. Such involvement can lead to more practical solutions that improve accessibility and convenience, ultimately enhancing the user experience. Furthermore, Respondent 3 noted: "It's very important for them to have a voice and for us to support them in the best way possible." This underscores the necessity of empowerment and active participation of individuals with disabilities in service design. By providing a platform for their input, community transport organizations can foster a sense of ownership and accountability among users, leading to more sustainable and user-friendly services.

The benefits of a person-centred approach are well-documented in academic literature, which demonstrates that services designed with direct input from users are more likely to be effective and inclusive (Chowdhury et al., 2018; Beresford, 2020). Such approaches not only improve the quality of services but also promote social inclusion by recognizing and valuing the contributions of individuals with disabilities, such as their unique insights into accessibility needs, the identification of service gaps, and the development of innovative solutions that might otherwise be overlooked (Priestley et al., 2010; Larkin et al., 2015).

In practice, this means engaging with people with disabilities through regular consultations, feedback sessions, and participatory design workshops. By understanding their unique perspectives and challenges, transport services can be tailored to address specific needs, whether that involves modifying physical infrastructure, adjusting service hours, or improving staff training. For instance, service providers might implement flexible scheduling to accommodate varying needs or invest in technology that enhances communication between drivers and passengers.

Additionally, a person-centred approach can help to identify and mitigate potential barriers before they become significant issues. This proactive stance ensures that transport services remain adaptable and responsive to changing needs, fostering an environment of continuous improvement. Involving people with lived experience of disability in the evaluation of services also provides valuable insights into the effectiveness of existing policies and practices, enabling organizations to make informed decisions about future developments. By embracing the perspectives of those with lived experience, community transport organizations can build more resilient and responsive systems. This collaborative approach ensures that transport services are not only functional but also empowering, providing individuals with disabilities with the support and accessibility they require to lead independent lives.

8.5.2 Invisible disabilities and transportation needs

Invisible disabilities, though not immediately apparent, profoundly impact individuals' experiences with transportation (Velho, 2021). Addressing these disabilities requires heightened awareness and tailored support to ensure inclusive and effective transport services. Recognizing and accommodating these needs is crucial for fostering a truly inclusive transport environment.

8.5.3 Awareness and support

Individuals with invisible disabilities face unique challenges, such as difficulty in accessing appropriate accommodations, heightened anxiety in crowded or unfamiliar environments, and the need for more flexible and personalized support, when using transportation services (Bezyak et al., 2020; Niwa et al., 2022). These disabilities, which may include anxiety disorders, autism, and sensory impairments, are not immediately visible, making it difficult for others to recognize and understand the needs of these individuals. This lack of awareness often results in inadequate support and accommodations, exacerbating the difficulties faced by those with invisible disabilities.

Respondent 1 highlighted this issue, stating: "There are a lot of people with stress-related anxiety around transport ... It's more common than we think." This statement underscores the prevalence of invisible disabilities and the significant impact they can have on an individual's ability to use public transport. Without proper understanding and support, individuals with these conditions may experience heightened anxiety and distress, leading to avoidance of public transport altogether. Respondent 2 echoed this sentiment, noting: "We don't see all disabilities, and they're not all visual ... We don't understand the needs because we don't live it ourselves." This observation points to a critical gap in knowledge and empathy among transport service providers and the general public. Increasing awareness about invisible disabilities is essential for fostering a more inclusive and supportive transport environment.

While general training programmes for transport staff can play a crucial role in bridging the gap, academic literature supports the importance of awareness and tailored support for individuals with invisible disabilities. By educating staff about the nature of invisible disabilities and effective strategies for support, transport services can become more accessible and accommodating. This is consistent with the findings of Conover et al. (2021), Olkin et al. (2019), and Kattari et al. (2018) who emphasize the need for targeted awareness, public campaigns, and support initiatives like implementing comprehensive training modules to help staff better understand the experiences of those with invisible disabilities, offering discreet communication tools such as badges, lanyards, or apps that allow individuals to signal their need for assistance without having to disclose their condition publicly, and establishing clear, universally applied protocols for accommodating requests related to invisible disabilities. Such approaches thereby promote consistency and sensitivity in transport service delivery for people with invisible disabilities.

8.5.4 Person-centred approaches

Implementing person-centred approaches in transport services is essential for addressing the needs of individuals with invisible disabilities. These strategies focus on tailoring support to the unique requirements of each individual, ensuring a more inclusive and responsive service. Staff education plays a critical role in this approach. One respondent emphasized: "Educating staff about non-visible disabilities is crucial. Routine and clear communication can help reduce anxiety for clients." Comprehensive training programmes that equip transport staff with the necessary skills to recognize signs of distress, provide discreet and respectful assistance, and adapt their communication methods based on individual needs can significantly alleviate anxiety and enhance comfort for individuals with invisible disabilities.

Understanding specific triggers and needs is another key component. One respondent noted: "Knowing the triggers and needs of individuals with autism or other invisible disabilities is key to providing effective support." Personalized care in transport services facilitates greater social inclusion and participation for individuals with invisible disabilities. Creating environments that minimize stress through measures such as quiet spaces and flexible scheduling can greatly improve the travel experience for these passengers. In practice, person-centred strategies might also include personalized travel plans and ongoing collaboration with disability advocacy groups, ensuring services remain responsive to evolving needs. By focusing on these tailored strategies, transport services can provide a more supportive and accommodating environment for all passengers.

8.6 Transport policy and research implications and recommendations

8.6.1 Integrating lived experience in transport policy development

First-hand accounts provide invaluable insights into the transport challenges faced by individuals with disabilities thereby significantly enhancing the policymaking process. By listening to those directly affected, policymakers can better understand transport policy issues and develop more nuanced and responsive measures that address the diverse needs of the disability community.

Lived experiences of disability can inform policymakers about the practical implications of transport services and highlight areas requiring improvement. For instance, understanding the limitations of current transport services, such as inadequate operating hours and inaccessible infrastructure, can guide the development of policies that better cater to these needs. As one respondent noted: "Listening to people with lived experience has made me reflect on the hours of operation that we work ... we need to do better." This feedback can help shape policies that ensure transport services are available and accessible when needed.

For an international audience, the Australian city of Sydney case study exemplifies how integrating lived experiences of disability into policy development can lead to significant improvements. Australia, like many other countries, grapples with the challenge of creating inclusive transport systems that accommodate diverse needs. By establishing mechanisms for ongoing consultation and engagement with the disability community, such as regular feedback sessions, advisory committees, and public forums, policymakers can ensure that policies are grounded in the realities of those they aim to serve.

Additionally, adopting a person-centred approach in the design and implementation of transport services is essential. This involves tailoring services to meet the unique needs of individuals rather than applying a one-size-fits-all solution. Personalized travel plans, flexible scheduling, and improved staff training are examples of how policies can be designed to better accommodate the diverse needs of the disability community. If done correctly, Sydney could serve as a model for other regions aiming to integrate lived experiences into their policy frameworks. Sharing best practices and successful models internationally can facilitate the development of more inclusive and effective transport policies globally.

8.6.2 Impact of the American with Disabilities Act (ADA) and related research opportunities

The ADA has significantly influenced transport services in the US by mandating equitable access and accommodations for individuals with disabilities. This legislation ensures that transport contracts must meet specific accessibility standards, thereby promoting inclusive service delivery. As Respondent 1 highlighted: "The American with Disabilities Act underpins how American or US contracts federal contracts for transport service delivery ... It means that when a contract is given to deliver a bus service, those buses must be delivered in an equitable way."

In the state of New South Wales (NSW), Australia, the Disability Inclusion Act and the Transport for NSW Disability Inclusion Action Plan serve similar purposes. These frameworks aim to enhance accessibility and inclusion in transport services by incorporating the perspectives and needs of individuals with disabilities into policy development. However, greater government investment in co-designed research is needed to evaluate the effectiveness of these initiatives and identify areas for improvement.

Ongoing studies should focus on how well these frameworks integrate lived experiences and whether they effectively address the diverse needs of the disability community. Additionally, exploring the impact of these policies on the daily lives of individuals with disabilities can provide valuable insights for future policy development. By conducting co-designed research and continually refining these frameworks, researchers and policymakers can respectively advance transport services in NSW and beyond that are inclusive and responsive to the needs of all users.

8.7 Conclusion

Throughout this chapter, we have examined the critical challenges and potential solutions in disability transport, emphasizing the importance of integrating lived experiences of disability into policy development. The fragmentation and uncoordinated funding of disability transport services in Sydney, highlighted by respondents, reveal significant gaps that need addressing to ensure comprehensive and person-centred service delivery. Inadequate availability and accessibility of transport options further exacerbate the difficulties faced by individuals with disabilities, limiting their social and economic participation and independence.

Lived experiences of disability provide invaluable insights into the above-mentioned systemic transport issues, offering practical perspectives on service limitations and the necessity for extended operating hours. These first-hand accounts also emphasize the diverse needs of individuals with invisible disabilities, underscoring the importance of awareness and tailored support. Person-centred approaches in service design, as discussed, are crucial for creating inclusive, accessible and responsive transport systems. In addition, the demonstrated impact of legislative frameworks, such as the US ADA and the Disability Inclusion Act in NSW, underscores the importance of legal mandates in promoting accessibility and equity. These frameworks highlight the need for continuous research and policy refinement to better integrate lived experiences and address the evolving transport needs of the disability community.

Future research should focus on evaluating the effectiveness of current legislative frameworks and transport policies in addressing the diverse needs of individuals with disabilities, particularly in different regional and international contexts. Studies should investigate how well these policies integrate lived experiences of disability and identify areas for improvement to ensure more inclusive and responsive transport services. Additionally, exploring the broader implications of transportation insecurity on social inclusion and economic participation can provide valuable insights for policymakers in both urban and rural settings across various countries and regions. International collaboration and sharing of best practices, as exemplified by the ADA, can facilitate the development of more effective and inclusive transport policies globally. By adopting successful models and tailoring them to local contexts, capital cities like Sydney can enhance their transport systems to better serve individuals with disabilities.

The ongoing importance of lived experience of disability in shaping and co-producing inclusive transport policies cannot be overstated. Policymakers must continue to engage with the disability community through regular consultations and feedback mechanisms, ensuring that transport policies remain grounded in the realities of those they aim to serve. By prioritizing person-centred approaches and fostering an environment of continuous improvement, transport authorities, policymakers, and community stakeholders can create transport systems that truly meet the needs of all users, promoting social and economic inclusion, and enhancing the quality of life for individuals with disabilities.

References

Beresford, P. (2020). PPI or user involvement: Taking stock from a service user perspective in the twenty first century. *Research Involvement and Engagement*, 6, 1–5.

Bezyak, J. L., Sabella, S. A., & Gattis, R. H. (2017). Public transportation: An investigation of barriers for people with disabilities. *Journal of Disability Policy Studies*, *28*(1), 52–60.

Bezyak, J. L., Sabella, S., Hammel, J., McDonald, K., Jones, R. A., & Barton, D. (2020). Community participation and public transportation barriers experienced by people with disabilities. *Disability and Rehabilitation*, *42*(23), 3275–3283.

Bjerkan, K. Y. & Øvstedal, L. R. (2020). Functional requirements for inclusive transport. *Transportation*, *47*(3), 1177–1198. https://doi.org/10.1007/s11116-018-9939-7

Chowdhury, S., Hadas, Y., Gonzalez, V. A., & Schot, B. (2018). Public transport users' and policy makers' perceptions of integrated public transport systems. *Transport Policy*, *61*, 75–83. https://doi.org/10.1016/j.tranpol.2017.10.001

Church, A., Frost, M., & Sullivan, K. (2000). Transport and social exclusion in London. *Transport Policy*, *7*(3), 195–205.

Conover, K. J., Acosta, V. M., & Bokoch, R. (2021). Perceptions of ableist microaggressions among target and nontarget groups. *Rehabilitation Psychology*, *66*(4), 565.

Currie, G., Richardson, T., Smyth, P., Vella-Brodrick, D., Hine, J., Lucas, K., Stanley, J., Morris, J., Kinnear, R., & Stanley, J. (2010). Investigating links between transport disadvantage, social exclusion and well-being in Melbourne – Updated results. *Research in Transportation Economics*, *29*(1), 287–295.

Kastenholz, E., Eusébio, C., & Figueiredo, E. (2015). Contributions of tourism to social inclusion of persons with disability. *Disability & Society*, *30*(8), 1259–1281.

Kattari, S. K., Olzman, M., & Hanna, M. D. (2018). 'You look fine!' Ableist experiences by people with invisible disabilities. *Affilia*, *33*(4), 477–492.

Kent, J. L., Mulley, C., Goh, L., & Stevens, N. (2021). Public transport and travel with dogs. In *The Routledge Handbook of Public Transport* (pp. 381–392). Routledge.

Kenyon, S., Lyons, G., & Rafferty, J. (2002). Transport and social exclusion: Investigating the possibility of promoting inclusion through virtual mobility. *Journal of Transport Geography*, *10*(3), 207–219.

Krahn, G. L., & Drum, C. E. (2007). Translating policy principles into practice to improve health care access for adults with intellectual disabilities: A research review of the past decade. *Mental Retardation and Developmental Disabilities Research Reviews*, *13*(2), 160–168.

Larkin, M., Boden, Z. V., & Newton, E. (2015). On the brink of genuinely collaborative care: experience-based co-design in mental health. *Qualitative Health Research*, *25*(11), 1463–1476.

Loyola, M., Nelson, J. D., Clifton, G., & Levinson, D. (2023). Narratives in transport research: A thematic and functional analysis. *Transportation Research Interdisciplinary Perspectives*, *17*, 100754. https://doi.org/https://doi.org/10.1016/j.trip.2023.100754

Lucas, K. (2012). Transport and social exclusion: Where are we now? *Transport Policy*, *20*, 105–113. https://doi.org/10.1016/j.tranpol.2012.01.013

Lyons, G. & Davidson, C. (2016). Guidance for transport planning and policymaking in the face of an uncertain future. *Transportation Research Part A: Policy and Practice*, *88*, 104–116.

Lyons, G., Jain, J., & Weir, I. (2016). Changing times – a decade of empirical insight into the experience of rail passengers in Great Britain. *Journal of Transport Geography*, *57*, 94–104.

Marsden, G. & Reardon, L. (2017). Questions of governance: Rethinking the study of transportation policy. *Transportation Research Part A: Policy and Practice*, *101*, 238–251. https://doi.org/10.1016/j.tra.2017.05.008

Martens, K. (2018). Ageing, impairments and travel: Priority setting for an inclusive transport system. *Transport Policy*, *63*, 122–130.

Niwa, N., Niwa, T., Akiyama, T., & Takeshiima, K. (2022). A basic study on the issues of facility planning and human support for smooth transportation of persons with invisible disabilities, including people with dementia and people with autism spectrum disorder. *Journal of Architecture and Planning (Transactions of AIJ)*, *87*(802), 23962407.

Olkin, R., Hayward, H. S., Abbene, M. S., & VanHeel, G. (2019). The experiences of microaggressions against women with visible and invisible disabilities. *Journal of Social Issues*, *75*(3), 757–785.

Priestley, M., Waddington, L., & Bessozi, C. (2010). Towards an agenda for disability research in Europe: Learning from disabled people's organisations. *Disability & Society*, *25*(6), 731–746.

Ritchie, J. & Spencer, L. (2002). Qualitative data analysis for applied policy research. In *Analyzing Qualitative Data* (pp. 173–194). Routledge.

Schwanen, T., Banister, D., & Anable, J. (2012). Rethinking habits and their role in behaviour change: The case of low-carbon mobility. *Journal of Transport Geography*, *24*, 522–532.

Sheller, M. (2018). *Mobility Justice: The Politics of Movement in an Age of Extremes*. Verso Books.

Smith, J. A., Larkin, M., & Flowers, P. (2021). *Interpretative Phenomenological Analysis: Theory, Method and Research*. Sage.

Velho, R. (2021). 'They're changing the network just by being there': Reconsidering infrastructures through the frame of disability studies. *Disability Studies Quarterly*, *41*(2).

Vogel, R. K., Ryan, R., Lawrie, A., Grant, B., Meng, X., Walsh, P., Morris, A., & Riedy, C. (2020). Global city Sydney. *Progress in Planning*, *136*, 100426.

9 What is the problem with private supported boarding houses? Resident perspectives on the Queensland Parliamentary Inquiry

Elroy Dearn, Neil Turton-Lane and Matilda Alexander

9.1 Introduction

Western democracies have embraced the principle of deinstitutionalization since the late 20th century, shifting the focus from supporting people in institutional settings to smaller, community-based housing and support (Perry, 2016). Article 19 of the United Nations Convention on the Rights of Persons with Disabilities outlines the right of people with disabilities to housing choice and to not be required to live in segregated environments. It is well-established that institutional care models restrict the freedom, choice, and control that people with disabilities have over their lives. As a signatory to the CRPD, the Australian government has made a policy commitment to promoting individuals' choices about where they live and with whom (Department of Social Services, 2021; National Disability Insurance Agency, 2015). In this context, private supported boarding houses are an anathema; an institutional setting out of step with Article 19 of the CRPD (Dearn et al., 2022).

Until now, the policy problem of private supported boarding houses has largely been framed by government and policy makers as a safeguarding issue. Policy solutions that follow have been to enhance regulation and increase subsidisation to these settings to improve standards and enhance legislative protections. The voices of residents have largely been absent from the discussion. The Queensland Parliamentary Inquiry (QPI) sets a new benchmark for the inclusion of resident voices in policy making on this issue. This article showcases resident submissions to the QPI into supported accommodation. Adopting a key question from Carole Bacchi's policy problematisation framework, we pose the question: What is the policy problem from the perspective of residents who live in these settings? In prioritising residents' perspectives, we argue that the problem is revealed to be not only a safeguarding issue, but a problem with the model itself. The solutions suggested by resident perspectives contrast with the common policy solutions to address the problem of private supported boarding houses. The narratives shared by residents underscore the value of framing the policy problem from the perspective of residents who live in these settings.

In the first section of this chapter, we provide background to this issue, outlining the characteristics of private supported boarding houses and elucidating the policy challenge. We explore the findings of numerous related reviews and inquiries, highlighting the notable absence of resident input and introducing the QPI. In the next section, we outline our approach to the analysis of the QPI submissions, introducing Bacchi's, 'What is the problem represented to be?' approach for analysing policy problems and the methodology. In the main body of the chapter, we provide findings from our analysis of 45 public resident submissions to the QPI. In the discussion, we discuss the insights gleaned from resident submissions, concluding by arguing that the representation of what the problem is from the resident perspective provides a different solution to what has commonly been produced.

9.2 Background

9.2.1 Characteristics of private supported boarding houses

Private supported boarding houses are a type of for-profit supported accommodation for people with disabilities, which (similar to Canada, the UK, and New Zealand) emerged in Australia during deinstitutionalisation to accommodate people who, due to government failings, had no alternative housing and support (Dearn et al., 2022; Drake, 2014). In Victoria they are known as supported residential services (SRS), in NSW they are called Licenced Boarding Houses, and in Queensland they are referred to as Residential Services Level 3. Specific legislative frameworks govern private supported boarding houses across state jurisdictions, but state facilities share similarities (Council to Homeless Persons, 2024; Dearn et al., 2022; Drake, 2014). Private supported boarding houses were designed with low staffing ratios to accommodate large numbers of residents who are provided with support with activities including meals, laundry, assistance with the taking of medication, and personal care in a congregate or institutional framework.

These settings have been described as a 21st-century poorhouse (Dearn & Brophy, 2020) with residents, most of whom experience psychosocial disability, effectively living in poverty on as little as AU$7 per day (Dearn et al., 2022). Research from different jurisdictions shows that people living in private supported boarding houses have higher rates of hospital readmission than people discharged into their own home (Browne et al., 2004); have higher rates of mortality than the general population (Segal & Kotler, 1993); live in chronic poverty (Christophers, 1999; Drake, 2010; Green, 2001), and have negligible opportunities for participation and recovery (Andrews, 2014; Chopra & Herrman, 2011; Christophers, 1999; Drake, 2010; Kerman, 2012). Life in private supported boarding accommodations in Australia today closely mirrors the depiction provided by a Canadian survivor of psychiatric care who lived in a boarding house during the 1990s and who described the:

> lack of personal control … the overly narrow lens used to define who they are and what they're capable of, the refusal to recognise and address the impact of poverty, isolation and the social determinants of health ensure a broken population who will remain that way. (Capponi, 2013)

9.2.2 Inquiries and reviews into private supported boarding houses

Government inquiries over four decades have documented the failings of private supported boarding houses and the inadequacy of this model to meet the needs of people with psychosocial disability (Barbour, 2011; Burdekin, 1993; Commonwealth of Australia, 2023, 2022; Green, 2001; Richmond, 1983; State of Victoria, 2021). As early as 1983, the NSW Richmond Report into health services for people with psychiatric illness (Richmond, 1983) and the 1993 national Burdekin inquiry into the human rights of people with mental illness (Burdekin, 1993) both noted issues regarding standards of care, physical care and neglect, lack of disposable income, and lack of rehabilitation support in private supported boarding houses. In 2011, a NSW Ombudsman report found that 'the current legislation governing licenced boarding houses and the standards expected in such facilities are inadequate to protect already vulnerable residents from harm and violations of their fundamental human rights' (Barbour, 2011, p. i). In 2021, the summary finding from the Victorian Mental Health Royal Commission reported that a lack of adequate housing and support options for people with mental illness had led 'to an increased reliance on privately operated supported residential services to accommodate this cohort at the point of discharge, despite these services neither being adequately resourced nor intended to provide this form of support' (State of Victoria, 2021, p. 409).

Calls have been made to gradually eliminate the privately supported boarding house model and for alternative options to be explored. For example, in Victoria more than two decades ago, David Green, former Victorian Public Advocate, suggested replacing the supported residential services model with publicly owned housing for financially disadvantaged individuals with ongoing care needs (Green, 2001). Similarly, the findings of the Burdekin Inquiry argued against the use of boarding houses as an accommodation option for people with mental illness (Burdekin, 1993). In NSW, Gabrielle Drake's study into licensed boarding houses recommended the 'staged deinstitutionalisation of licenced boarding houses and the resourcing of accommodation and support models' (Drake, 2010, p. 225). Again, in 2021, the Victorian Royal Commission into Victoria's Mental Health System in 2021 reiterated that the existing private supported boarding house model is unsuitable for addressing the needs of people with mental illness (State of Victoria, 2021).

However, instead of working towards the elimination of these settings, incremental safeguarding approaches continue to be the primary solution across states, including Queensland, NSW, South Australia, and Victoria (Dearn, 2024). In New South Wales, a comprehensive assessment of boarding houses resulted in the introduction of the new *Boarding Houses Act 2012* with more protections for residents. Similarly, an inquiry into the regulation of supported residential services in Victoria led to the tightening of regulations under the *Supported Residential Services (Private Proprietors') Act 2010*.

In Queensland, the current review of supported accommodation (which has a focus on level 3 services) is focused on evaluating whether regulations under the *Residential Services (Accreditation) Act 2002* effectively address service provision and regulatory adequacy.

Despite some reductions in the number of these facilities over time, likely due to stricter regulations and the deregistration of substandard settings, ongoing reports continue to highlight the failures of such segregated housing and their incompatibility with Australia's obligations under Article 19 of the CRPD to provide people with disabilities with non-segregated living options (Council to Homeless Persons, 2024).

9.2.3 Representation of people with disabilities in policy relating to private supported boarding houses

Critical to the exploration of any policy issue is the voice of people who will be most affected. Despite enduring scrutiny and incremental policy changes, resident voices have not been central in the framing of the problem of private supported boarding houses. The construction of the problem from the perspective of policy makers and safeguarding bodies has in most states led to legislative solutions framed within a safeguarding or regulatory framework. Whilst in Queensland and Victoria a secondary response included funding to provide support to residents,[1] the intention of these programmes has been to support residents in situ rather than to support pathways into alternative accommodation. In their analysis of competing policy priorities that government is presented with in achieving rights for people living in private supported boarding houses, Fisher et al. noted that 'policies to fulfill rights through support were not successful where the breach of an immediate realisation right such as housing remained unaddressed' (Fisher et al., 2013, p. 520).

The CRPD principles call for participation of people with disabilities in all levels of decision-making, stating that 'persons with disabilities should have the opportunity to be actively involved in decision-making processes about policies and programmes, including those directly concerning them' (Convention on the Rights of Persons with Disabilities, 2007). This principle underscores the need for full and active participation and representation of people with disabilities in policy making (Fisher & Robinson, 2010; Löve et al., 2017). This understanding is linked to the idea that policy problems are socially constructed, with people's knowledge of the world influenced by their different social locations. This underscores the importance of drawing on the lived experiences of those affected (Löve et al., 2017).

Disability advocates have consistently called for better representation in policy that affects them and inclusion in both setting the agenda and defining issues that impact

[1] Victoria introduced the Supporting Accommodation for Vulnerable Victorians Initiative in 2012 and Queensland introduced a pilot scheme, the Resident Support Program, in 2003–2004, both intended to supplement the support able to be provided to residents in private supported boarding houses.

their lives. However, people with disabilities have often been overlooked in policies that impact them and have not had equal access to policy processes (Robinson et al., 2014). While government policy processes usually give priority to certain groups over others, representation significantly influences the shaping of policy issues and outcomes (Bacchi, 2009).

Resident voices have not been central in the framing of the problem of private supported boarding houses. Exceptions have been Drake's review of the implementation of the NSW *Boarding House Act 2012* and Fisher and Robinson's review of policies and practices for referral into Queensland private residential facilities, both of which prioritised residents' perspectives (Drake, 2018; Fisher & Robinson, 2010). The Royal Commission into Violence, Abuse, Neglect and Exploitation of People with Disability prioritised lived experience perspectives in its investigation into homelessness, including experience in boarding houses, hostels, and other arrangements (Commonwealth of Australia, 2023). However, few residents participated. In Victoria and other states, the voice of residents has largely been absent in considering the future of private supported boarding houses. With the future of these settings now a national issue (Council to Homeless Persons, 2024), resident perspectives are more important than ever.

9.2.4 The Queensland parliamentary inquiry into supported accommodation

The QPI marks a pivotal shift in representative policy making by prioritising resident input into the future of private supported boarding houses. In October 2023 the Queensland Legislative Assembly supported a motion for the Community Support and Services Committee to inquire into and report on the provision and regulation of supported accommodation in Queensland. The inquiry was initiated on the recommendation of the Public Advocate's report, *Safe, Secure and Affordable? The Need for an Inquiry into Supported Accommodation in Queensland* (Queensland Public Advocate, 2023). The Inquiry terms of reference specifically called for the views of residents and former residents to be included, allocating a role for two non-government advocacy organisations to support residents to contribute their views (Queensland Community Support and Services Committee, 2024). Queensland Advocacy for Inclusion (QAI) and Queenslanders with Disability Network (QDN) were engaged by the Department of Housing to support level 3 residents to tell their story and link them with services and supports. Members of the parliamentary committee visited 14 residential services to speak directly to residents and residential service providers, including in regional areas. QAI and QDN produced plain English guides and fact sheets to assist residents to engage in the inquiry. More than 700 residents were engaged throughout the parliamentary process.

By the time the submissions closed, the committee had received 147 submissions from current and former residents (including 68 written submissions and 79 audio submissions made with the assistance of advocates). Many submissions were confidential and were not made public. The QPI website contains 49 publicly available resident submissions. Our analysis of 45 of these submissions is the focus of this chapter.

9.3 Approach

9.3.1 What is the problem represented to be?

Carole Bacchi's, 'What is the problem represented to be?' approach challenges the conventional wisdom that policy problems are fixed and known (Bacchi, 2009). In Bacchi's understanding, policy problems are constructed, and governments, in reacting to what are assumed to be known problems, leave the problem itself unexamined. At the heart of Bacchi's framework lies the idea that policy agents construct policy problems in ways that normalise intractable issues, and that these formulations lead to a specific shape for solutions. She argues that to achieve real societal transformation, the way that the problem is represented needs critical examination. Her policy problematisation framework demands a reconceptualising of what are understood to be known problems. In this chapter, based on the publicly available resident submissions from the QPI website we answer the key question posed by Bacchi's policy problematisation framework: What is the policy problem represented to be?

9.3.2 Method and data analysis

Publicly available resident submissions were downloaded from the QPI inquiry website (N=49). Residents were supported in their submission writing process by advocates from QDN (N=34), QAI (N=10), and unknown support (N=1). Most submissions were a transcription of an interview between the advocate and the resident. Two submissions were excluded due to insufficient data and two submissions were excluded because they did not relate to the experience of residential services but to living in a group home. Of the 45 submissions analysed, 43 were determined to be from current residents and two were from former residents.

Data were extracted from the 45 submissions by two authors into an Excel spreadsheet based on the key themes occurring in transcripts of open-ended conversations between residents and advocates. The key identified themes related to home, food, safety, sharing with others, conflict, supports, standards, money, and fees. Submissions were categorised as broadly positive or broadly negative, or neither positive nor negative, based on responses to the themes raised. Data from the 45 submissions were thematically analysed using Clark and Braun's method of thematic analysis to identify patterns across data in relation to the lived experience, views, and perspectives of residents (Clarke & Braun, 2017).

9.4 Findings

The classification of the submissions revealed that 23 were broadly negative, 17 were broadly positive, and five were neither positive nor negative. While the broad classification tells one story, the thematic analysis provides additional insight into the complexity of residents' experiences, thereby facilitating a deeper understanding of the policy problem. This section discusses four key themes that emerged from the thematic analysis: standards, living in an institutional model, housing choices, and the experience of support.

9.4.1 Theme 1: Standards

Over half of the resident submissions raised issues and concerns about standards, amenities, and fees, ranging from facilities being run-down, inadequate cooling, insufficient meals, and the lack of affordability of level 3 facilities.

Many submissions noted that facilities were run-down, in particular bathrooms and toilets. One person noted that they would like to see improvements in facilities:

> I would like those improvements to be some more bathrooms and a general improvements of the state of the building in which we live. (s170)

Another noted that the residence didn't meet expected standards:

> My room has mould everywhere, and the paint is peeling from the ceiling. I know there is a lot of asbestos in there as well and this worries me. (s14)

Several submissions noted that their rooms were too hot and needed air conditioning:

> There's no air conditioning or places where we can go to cool off during summer. (s31)
>
> Needs quite a few upgrades like some air conditioning in the bedrooms. (s182)

Whilst some people liked the food and noted that they enjoyed the meals, more than half of the resident submissions were not satisfied with the food. Issues included an inadequate amount of food, poor nutritional quality, high sugar content, or food not meeting their dietary requirements of tastes:

> Residents almost never receive hot meals. When they do, it is only ever chicken. No variety in proteins provided. The vast majority of meals provided are very simple. i.e. vegemite sandwiches or lettuce and cheese sandwiches. Occasionally I have to go and buy my own food just to get a break from the same food provided. (s14)
>
> The tea and coffee was never enough for everyone even in terms of the sugar and the milk was powdered. I had to buy my own fridge and stock it with my own food out of my own pocket. (s151)
>
> Meals are unfit. Some food is not cooked properly and is not quality food ... The food is high in sugar content and so many people have put on weight since living there. I think this all needs to be looked into. (s31)

However, there was little choice about what was provided, as noted in this submission:

> I don't eat porridge. I hate it. Absolutely hate porridge. It would be great if we had something else ... But it'd be great if we had, like, Weetbix, cereal, you know? You know even, for

> breakfast, you know, something like eggs on toast, you know, or bacon, you know, would be great, you know. (s188)

Many submissions raised the high cost of fees of living in residential services. These were viewed as excessive and not leaving people with enough money to meet their other costs:

> And outright robbery of NDIS [National Disability Insurance Scheme] level for accommodation take everyone's pensions. And not leaving anyone with any money to live off for general basic needs like a toothbrush and some toilet paper. (s21)

> The cost of living. I'm paying $930 per fortnight, which is roughly about 85% of my income, and does not leave me very much at the end of the day to pay for bills or anything else I have outstanding. (s111)

Some submissions noted that they were paying for services that they were not receiving:

> They make you pay for supports you don't get like laundry and room cleaning, laundry services. (s24)

9.4.2 Theme 2: Living in an institutional model

The second theme raised throughout the submissions related to the institutional nature of the environment. Nearly half of all submissions spoke to their limited everyday choices living in an institutional environment, including living with large numbers of other people, sharing living spaces such as bedrooms and bathrooms, the lack of choice over who they lived with, unwelcome conflict, and the experience of exclusion from life outside the residential service.

Many residents spoke of having to live with large numbers of people with complex needs and their capacity to cope:

> There's 61 of us and we've all got a mental and or physical disability and I feel like some days we can cope and others you can't. (s101)

> When I first moved here, I was petrified because I'm not used to living amongst such a large group of people. (s183)

The difficulty sharing spaces including bedrooms, bathrooms, and dining facilities was raised in some submissions:

> I shared a room with a bloke who would regularly come home at 3 a.m. high on drugs. This made me relapse eventually [I ended up] in a mental health facility from drug induced psychosis, so this really affected me. (s151)

> Sitting in the mess hall with other residents during a mealtime makes me anxious. There is generally about eight of us sitting around a table during communal meals and I feel like I have to be careful about what I say in that sort of interaction. (s183)

Conflict between residents was raised in many submissions, which involved people both witnessing violence or being intimidated and/or assaulted by other residents:

> Living is ok right now [today] but before I was really upset because people keep barging in and telling me off. Sometimes, other residents who live here go crazy and it's really scary to be around. When that happens, I just walk away and turn off and go back to bed. It's the only way to deal with it. (s63)

> Sexual assaults I've reported a couple of these ... that have happened inside and other facilities I've lived in. People living together in environments that have mental health patients, disabled patients, elderly, young, drug addicts, sex offenders and little old ladies living under the same roof. (s21)

Highlighting the sense of segregation of residential services, several people spoke to the experience of exclusion:

> The reason my supported accommodation needs to be supported and improved is because we live in these places, and we want the government to listen and basically, I want them to hear us out. I don't want to hear their ideas, but I want to them to hear us out. Like in every other place in Brisbane, residents feel that their self is excluded. (s162)

> My main thing is that I don't get to go out and be part of the world. I know I'm part of the world. I know I'm part of the world ... I'm not asking for the world. All I'm asking is to be heard. (s159)

Other residents noted the feeling of lack of autonomy due to locked doors and being unable to self-medicate:

> There's an 8 p.m. curfew. They lock the doors. (178)

> They seem to really strip me of my autonomy here. I can't self-medicate, although I've been doing that for 20 years. All of a sudden they've got to be doled out to me every day. (s178)

9.4.3 Theme 3: Housing choices

The third theme raised in submissions relates to housing choices, revealing a level of complexity which spoke to people's housing history, lack of housing choices, and how living in residential services compared to other places that they had lived.

Around a quarter of people reported an overall positive experience, actively stating that they liked living there: 'I like living here' (s47), 'I'm happy here. I hope to stay another couple of years' (s179). Others spoke of living in supported accommodation as a negative experience, feeling 'stripped of autonomy' (s178), with one person noting that 'they would be better off in jail as far as living conditions go' (s187).

For some people, there was a contradiction between their objective experience and their subjective experience. One submission stated, 'Yeah, it's good, I love it' (s190), but they reported that the food is 'yucky' (s190) and that conflict with another resident was leading them to 'go in my room and start crying and being lonely and everything' (s190). Another submission noted that, while they hoped to stay living in their current residence and were 'quite happy here', it 'has its problems, could be improved, people come in off [the] street' (s54).

Many submissions provided valuable insights into places they had previously lived, helping to explain why people might report a level of satisfaction in residential services:

> I've lived in one other supported accommodation … and that was terrible. This is much, much nicer and safer. (s54)
>
> Owners and support staff here are kind, caring and helpful … other places seem interested in money. (s73)
>
> It's a lot better than a boarding house, which I was at. (s167)

There was a strong sense that the lack of suitable housing choices was what had ultimately led some people moving into residential services, rather than being able to live independently in the community as they desired:

> I ended up living here because there weren't a lot of options, and I didn't want to live in a share house arrangement – I wanted my own space … I play the lotto with the hope that I win some day and can buy a nice house. (s183)
>
> I had no say in the matter … So so here I am … but I've been looking around to find another place … normal two bedroom. You know with garage and bathroom. Totally just simple. (s187)

The tenuousness of people's housing security and lack of alternative options were noted in some submissions, with people conscious of their precarious housing situation and the limited housing options available to them:

> We want the government to listen and basically I want them to hear us out. I don't want to hear their ideas, but I want to them to hear us out. Like in every other place in Brisbane, residents feel that their self is excluded. They're not allowed to say stuff. They live in fear of eviction every day. (s162)
>
> They said I could go back out on the streets if I didn't like it … I'd rather be homeless than ever go back there … some of the people living there are trapped there because there is nowhere else to go. They are horrible places, but they have no other options. (s151)

Under the National Disability Insurance Scheme (NDIS), which is Australia's individualised funding scheme for people with disabilities caused by a permanent impairment, some people are now eligible for funding to live independently. One of these funding streams is Supported Independent Living (SIL) funding. Several submissions highlighted the participants' strong interest in moving into more independent living arrangements.

> I'm hoping or trying to get another SIL house at least or some other form of accommodation that's a little friendlier to my needs. (s182)
>
> I wanna be right near the beach. Yeah, you know. Have my own place, something that even if there's a unit or a caravan, you know. (s188)
>
> but … what I want to do in the future is I plan to get off public trust and then when I've got my finances independently again, maybe get a job for a couple days a week and try to integrate back into normal society. (s167)

Other submissions noted that the lack of appropriate housing options made this transition difficult to achieve:

> The biggest problem with transitioning to my own place is finding housing because it's so hard. I don't have a great rental history so it's really hard to find a place that will take you and it takes years to get social housing. (s151)
>
> I've been looking around to find another place … but it's very hard to find a place right now. (s187)

9.4.4 Theme 4: The experience of support

Resident submissions provided perspectives on the support received in residential services, with over half of the submissions addressing interactions with staff. Whereas half reported feeling supported and well cared for, the other half expressed feeling unsupported, citing concerns such as inadequate staff training, limited support for people with mental illness, and insufficient responsiveness to conflicts and feedback. Disparities in support received through alternative funding sources was raised as an issue.

One submission touched on the power imbalance between staff and residents and how this made them feel like they had little control over their lives:

> Power imbalance between the people that work here and the residents. There's definitely an us and them not everyone together … It's called assisted living but it's quite authoritarian, actually it's really a 'we'll tell you what's going on and you'll do it'. (s171)

A key issue raised in many submissions was the lack of staff responsiveness to conflict between residents. Several submissions noted that when conflict between residents arises that police are never called, and people are left to fend for themselves:

> The police are never called. I believe they should be called. (s31)
>
> It gets put upon other residents to deal with issues and call the police and to get ourselves looked after. There is no responsibility. I believe that has been lacking since day one and I believe they should shut it down or fix it. (s173)

Whilst some residents noted they felt supported by staff, many people noted that they were not listened to and there was no feedback system:

> The owner of the house has not been listening to any of the residents' complaints when he's been around, and we would like him to start listening more to what we have to say because we live here, and we'd like him to respect us as residents. (s111)

> So, it's the instead of working with management and sharing ideas about how things should work better for everyone, for the staff, for the residents, we're just told no, this is the way it is. (s178)

One resident noted that there was not enough support for people with mental illness and that staff had insufficient training:

> I find often when we send someone to hospital in the ambulance whose having a mental breakdown ... invariably they are sent home in a cab by themselves at 3.00 a.m. in the morning ... even the person working here at night doesn't know someone that's come back, it makes it difficult. (s101)

Some submissions noted the difference it made to be in receipt of external funded support, such as the NDIS, rather than reliant on the minimal support able to be provided by facilities:

> Before I joined the NDIS, I found it very hard to do anything, but since I've been on it, my life has changed a lot. I go out all the time, I have travel assistance from the inreach staff and through NDIS, so if it wasn't for them ... I probably would be like a mushroom in a corner. (s164)

However, others noted the ways in which a lack of funding created barriers to community participation:

> A lot of these people do have NDIS, and they have their own worker, all the stuff. Yeah. You know, for me it's the opposite. You know, I don't have any NDIS yet. And I wish I had a support worker to help me get out you know, have a coffee. You know, do something, you know, go to library or something like that. (s188)

> I look at people who live here, that go along with NDIS, they go along with Auscare. They go out places. They do things. They do them on a regular basis as well and I feel left out and I'm sure that most other people here that are not on the NDIS or not with Auscare, I'm sure that they feel left out as well. (s159)

> Maybe a few extra trips for people that aren't on the NDIS because it seems a little unfair that if you're not on the NDIS is you can't really be included. (s54)

9.5 Discussion

Resident submissions to the QPI provide valuable insights into the problems residents face living in Queensland level 4 residential services. Responding to Carole Bacchi's policy problematisation framework, the key question addressed is: What is the policy problem purported to be?

Resident submissions document significant concerns relating to safeguarding, including issues with standards, amenities and fees, run-down environments, inadequate cooling, and insufficient meals. This is consistent with findings from decades of inquiries relating to private supported boarding houses, which highlight inadequate oversight, inadequate protections, poor standards of care, lack of disposable income for residents, and substandard environments (Burdekin, 1993; Commonwealth of Australia, 2023 ; Richmond, 1983; State of Victoria, 2021).

A more persistent problem reported by residents is the institutional nature of the model and the disconnect between support available and their needs. This aligns with research identifying private supported boarding houses as being untherapeutic and segregated, with institutional models out of step with contemporary expectations and human rights (Dearn et al., 2022; Drake, 2014; Fisher et al., 2013; McVilly et al., 2022). The Queensland Public Advocate report to the QPI described how limited housing options both compelled residents to accept these settings and hinders their ability to leave (Queensland Public Advocate, 2023). As shown in submissions, many residents stated they would prefer to live in independent non-segregated environments in which they have control over where they live and with whom. This preference is supported by research indicating that housing choice is crucial for recovery (Nelson et al., 2007), and that given the opportunity, many people with psychosocial disability would choose to live independently (Fisher et al., 2013; Forchuk et al., 2006; Harvey et al., 2012; Nelson et al., 2007). However, there is often a discrepancy between residents' housing preferences and their living situation (Fisher et al., 2021; Harvey et al., 2012).

Bacchi's framework asks for a critical examination of the underlying assumptions and power dynamics embedded within policy representations, considering who benefits and who is marginalised or excluded by the current framing of the problem (Bacchi, 2009). The problem representation of private supported boarding houses by government and policy makers as a safeguarding problem assumes a safeguarding solution. The perspective of residents gives an alternative problem representation, providing different perspectives and voices often overlooked in the dominant narrative. Reframing the problem from the perspective of residents provides deeper insight into the challenges and complexities they face living in these settings, in securing appropriate and accessible housing, obtaining necessary funding and support, and navigating the transition out of institutional care.

The Queensland Supported Accommodation Inquiry sets a new benchmark for the proactive engagement of residents in inquiries into private supported boarding houses. Despite decades of reviews in states across Australia, rarely has the voice of residents been so central. Residents are often assumed to be a 'hard to reach' and 'vulnerable' group, unable to participate in such reviews. The QPI revealed that when given the opportunity, residents can and will participate in such inquiries, providing important perspectives on how they view the experience of living in such facilities.

Bacchi's framework suggests that when tackling seemingly intractable policy problems, it is critical to reframe the policy problem from different perspectives, rather than reacting to the problem as fixed – which often leads to the same types of solutions. A reframing of the problem of private supported boarding houses from the perspective of residents calls for a reassessment of the way in which the problem is represented. In the context of private supported boarding houses, these findings call for deinstitutionalisation policies.

Private supported boarding houses have largely remained unaffected by broader policy shifts and there is an absence of a comprehensive national policy addressing this issue (Drake & Herbert, 2015). Based on the plethora of evidence of the failings of these settings, and consistent with Australia's obligations under Article 19 of the CRPD, we argue that it is now time to reconsider private supported boarding houses as a human rights problem. Considered from this perspective, these settings fail to deliver what is entailed under Article 19 – the right to live independently and to be included in the community.

9.6 Conclusion

Private supported boarding houses have long been regarded as a safeguarding problem by government policy makers. Consequently, policy responses have focused on regulation and subsidies to both enhance legislative protections and improve standards. Residents' voices have largely been absent from these discussions. By prioritising residents' perspectives, we contend that the issue extends beyond safeguarding to a fundamental problem with the model itself. The narratives shared by residents emphasise the importance of framing the policy problem from the viewpoint of people who live in such settings.

Private supported boarding houses are simply unable to deliver on the realisation of the CRPD positive right to live independently and be included in the community. This chapter advocates for a re-evaluation of the problem of private supported boarding houses based on the perspectives of those most impacted by such policies – residents themselves. It recommends a research agenda focused on lived experience, prioritising collaborative and consumer-driven studies to address the housing needs and preferences of people living in these settings.

9.6.1 Limitations

This study analysed 45 out of 49 publicly available submissions from former and current residents on the QPI website. However, there were 88 other confidential resident submissions that were not made public. Based on QAI's experience with residents' reluctance to speak up due to fear of reprisal, the public submissions likely represent a more positive depiction of residents' actual experiences. Previous research has found that people with disabilities need assistance to feel safe when speaking up about their experiences of poor support (McVilly et al., 2022; Meltzer et al., 2017). Illustrating this, QAI found that residents had mixed reactions to the offer of sharing their stories with the parliamentary inquiry. Some residents who felt comfortable speaking publicly appreciated having their basic needs met and were more likely to voice concerns. However, other residents were too fearful to speak up, or were unwilling or unable to participate. Some residents expressed that they feared repercussions from the service provider and were reluctant to make submissions, even with assurances of confidentiality. Similarly, while several service providers welcomed QAI's team and encouraged resident engagement with the inquiry, others were more uncomfortable, and some actively discouraged their proposed visits, downplaying the ability of their residents to engage and/or presuming they would not be interested in doing so. One provider refused QAI's request to arrange a follow-up visit to residents. Many of the people QAI engaged with, some of whom did not submit their view publicly, spoke of their desire to live elsewhere, yet had been 'stuck' in the facility for years, with seemingly little to no access to support to move elsewhere. One confidential submission from a resident shared: 'I feel like it's very important that I share my story because I really feel like living in such a bad environment like this is an injustice. I would love to get out of here.'

References

Andrews, K. (2014). Pension-level supported residential services and their influence in the occupational participation and recovery of residents with mental illness [Master's thesis]. Monash University. https://doi.org/10.26180/4625896

Bacchi, C. (2009). Analysing policy: What's the problem represented to be? Pearson Australia.

Barbour, B. (2011). More than board and lodging: The need for boarding house reform: A special report to Parliament under Section 31 of the Ombudsman Act 1974. NSW Ombudsman.

Browne, G., Courtney, M., & Meehan, T. (2004). Type of housing predicts rate of readmission to hospital but not length of stay in people with schizophrenia on the Gold Coast in Queensland. *Australian Health Review*, 27, 65–72. https://doi.org/10.1071/AH042710065

Burdekin, B. (1993). Human rights and mental illness: Report of the national inquiry into the human rights of people with mental illness (Vol. 1). Australian Human Rights and Equal Opportunity Commission.

Capponi, P. (2013). Kitty Lundy memorial lecture. https://www.youtube.com/watch?v=FzjngOEhAlU

Chopra, P. & Herrman, H. (2011). The long-term outcomes and unmet needs of a cohort of former long-stay patients in Melbourne, Australia. *Community Mental Health Journal*, 47(5), 531–541. https://doi.org/10.1007/s10597-010-9351-z

Christophers, M. (1999). Qualitative study of people with mental illness in supported residential services [Master's thesis]. Monash University.

Clarke, V. & Braun, V. (2017). Thematic analysis. *The Journal of Positive Psychology*, 12(3), 297–298. https://doi.org/10.1080/17439760.2016.1262613

Convention on the Rights of Persons with Disabilities, Pub. L. No. A/RES/61/106 (2007).

Council to Homeless Persons. (2024). No other option? Supported residential services and private supported boarding houses and homelessness. *Parity*, *2*(37). https://search.informit.org/toc/par/37/2

Dearn, E. (2024). No other option?: Supported residential services, private supported boarding houses and homelessness. *Parity*, *37*(2), 7–9. Council to Homeless Persons. https://search.informit.org/doi/10.3316/informit.T2024081600006701922368803

Dearn, L. & Brophy, L. (2020, September). Stop the pandemic neglect of people living in supported residential services. Croakey. https://www.croakey.org/stop-the-pandemic-neglect-of-people-living-in-supported-residential-services/

Dearn, Ramcharan P., Weller, P., Brophy, L., & Johnson, K. (2022). Supported residential services as a type of 'total institution': Implications for the National Disability Insurance Scheme. *Australian Journal of Social Issues*, ajs4.233. https://doi.org/10.1002/ajs4.233

Department of Social Services. (2021). Australia's Disability Strategy 2021–2031. Commonwealth of Australia, 72.

Commonwealth of Australia (2023) Royal Commission into Violence, Abuse, Neglect and Exploitation of People with Disability. Final report: Vol. 7. Inclusive education, employment and housing. https://disability.royalcommission.gov.au/publications/final-report-volume-7-inclusive-education-employment-and-housing.

Drake, G. (2010). The privatisation of the back-wards: The accommodation of people with intellectual disability and people with mental illness in licensed boarding houses in Sydney [PhD thesis]. Curtin University. https://espace.curtin.edu.au/handle/20.500.11937/1087

Drake, G. (2014). The transinstitutionalisation of people living in licensed boarding houses in Sydney. *Australian Social Work*, 67(2), 240–255. https://doi.org/10.1080/0312407X.2013.843714

Drake, G. (2018). Evaluation of the Boarding Houses Act 2012: Final report. Australian Catholic University and Newtown Neighbourhood House.

Drake, G. & Herbert, J. L. (2015). Leaving a licensed boarding house: Transcending trans-institutionalisation with person-centred transitions. *Disability & Society*, 30(4), 583–596. https://doi.org/10.1080/09687599.2015.1037952

Fisher, K. R., Robinson, S., & Harris, S. P. (2013). Can policy to address some disability rights mitigate weak approaches to others? *International Journal of Public Administration*, 36(7), 512–521. https://doi.org/10.1080/01900692.2013.772633

Fisher, K. R., Purcal, C., Jones, A., Lutz, D., Robinson, S., & Kayess, R. (2021). What place is there for shared housing with individualized disability support? Disability and Rehabilitation, 43(1), 60–68. https://doi.org/10.1080/09638288.2019.1615562

Fisher, K. & Robinson, S. (2010). Will policy makers hear my disability experience? How participatory research contributes to managing interest conflict in policy implementation. *Social Policy and Society*, 9(02), 207-220. https://doi.org/10.1017/S1474746409990339

Forchuk, C., Nelson, G., & Hall, B. (2006). 'It's important to be proud of the place you live': Housing problems and preferences of psychiatric survivors. *Perspectives in Psychiatric Care*, 42(1), 42–52.

Green, D. (2001). Advice to the Department of Human Services on supported residential services. Department of Human Services, Melbourne.

Harvey, C., Killackey, E., Groves, A., & Herrman, H. (2012). A place to live: Housing needs for people with psychotic disorders identified in the second Australian National Survey of Psychosis. *Australian & New Zealand Journal of Psychiatry*, 46(9), 840–850. https://doi.org/10.1177/0004867412449301

Kerman, N. (2012). From this point forward: Ending custodial housing for people with mental illness in Canada. Community Support Research Unit, Centre for Addiction and Mental Health.

Löve, L., Traustadóttir, R., Quinn, G., & Rice, J. (2017). The Inclusion of the lived experience of disability in policymaking. *Laws*, 6(4). https://doi.org/10.3390/laws6040033

McVilly, K., Ainsworth, E., Graham, L., Harrison, M., Sojo, V., Spivakovsky, C., Gale, L., Genat, A., & Zirnsak, T. (2022). Outcomes associated with 'inclusive', 'segregated' and 'integrated' settings: Accommodation and community living, employment and education. A research report commissioned by the Royal Commission into Violence, Abuse, Neglect and Exploitation of People with Disability. University of Melbourne.

Meltzer, A., Robinson, S., Proud, Y., & Fisher, K. (2017). Literature and practice review: Support to make decisions that promote personal safety and prevent harm. Social Policy Research Centre, UNSW.

National Disability Insurance Agency. (2015). Optimising the 'user cost of capital' for housing as part of delivering the NDIS sustainably and efficiently. Canberra. Australia. https://www.aph.gov.au/~/media/Committees/Senate/committee/ndis_ctte/Correspondence/EC15-000321%20-%20Bonyhady.pdf?la=en

Nelson, G., Sylvestre, J., Aubry, T., George, L., & Trainor, J. (2007). Housing choice and control, housing quality, and control over professional support as contributors to the subjective quality of life and community adaptation of people with severe mental illness. *Administration and Policy in Mental Health and Mental Health Services Research*, *34*(2), 89–100. https://doi.org/10.1007/s10488-006-0083-x

Parliament of Victoria. (2009). Inquiry into supported accommodation for Victorians with a disability and/or mental illness. Victorian State Government.

Pearce, C. (2009, 25 September). Failing our vulnerable: The bleak lives of those in our private sector care homes. *The Age Newspaper.*

Perry, B. L. (2016). *50 Years after Deinstitutionalization: Mental Illness in Contemporary Communities* (1st edn, Vols 1–17). Bingley: Emerald Publishing Limited.

Queensland Community Support and Services Committee. (2024). Inquiry into the Provision and Regulation of Supported Accommodation in Queensland. Report no.44, 57th Parliament. Queensland Parliament. https://share.google/hXaGucdbupYvGGKUQ

Queensland Public Advocate. (2023). 'Safe, secure and affordable'? The need for an inquiry into supported accommodation in Queensland.

Richmond, D. T. (1983). Inquiry into Health Services for the Psychiatrically Ill and Developmentally Disabled, March 1983. Division of Planning and Research, Department of Health N.S.W.

Robinson, S., Fisher, K. R., & Strike, R. (2014). Participatory and inclusive approaches to disability program evaluation. *Australian Social Work*, *67*(4), 495–508. https://doi.org/10.1080/0312407X.2014.902979

Segal, A. & Kotler, P. (1993). Sheltered care residence: Ten-year personal outcomes. *American Journal of Orthopsychiatry*, *63*(1), 80–91. https://doi.org/10.1037/h0079409

State of Victoria. (2021). Royal Commission into Victoria's mental health system, final report, volume 1: A new approach to mental health and wellbeing in Victoria (No. Parl Paper No. 202, Session 2018–21 (document 2 of 6)). www.rcvmhs.vic.gov.au

10 The research agenda for assisted dying policy for psychiatric disability

Sam Sam and Jennifer Smith-Merry

10.1 Introduction

This chapter argues for a new person-centred research agenda for assisted dying for people with severe mental distress that contextualises academic research within evolving policy and legal contexts and lived experience. It is informed by one of the author's lived experiences of severe, protracted, and treatment-resistant mental illness. Lived experience has rarely entered debates in policy making around suicide and medical assisted dying (Pronk et al., 2022) but the scant research which does exist has shown that people with lived experience of considering assisted dying can provide important reflections to reform the systems surrounding assisted dying (Jeanneret et al., 2024). There remains an absence of inclusion of lived experiences of people with severe mental distress in policy making relating to assisted dying. This chapter counters this absence by intertwining our discussion of policy and research with Sam's personal reflections on the topic. Sam's lived experiences are italicised and interspersed in the discussion in order to keep that perspective at the forefront of thinking through how we research and make policy in this area.

> *I am not in 'temporary' crisis. My suffering is long-standing and intolerable.* Sam

Westermair et al. (2022) observe that even with evidence-based treatment, some people with severe and persistent mental distress never get better; the probability of improvement declines with each successive treatment, and the probability of side effects increases. The frequent alternative, suicide, can be painful, lonely, and violent (Dembo et al., 2018). As anthologised in Rooney et al. (2018) there are an estimated six other people who are psychologically harmed (by risk of depression, substance abuse, and even suicide) for every successful suicide attempt.

> *If or when I choose to end my life, my options are limited. I do not want to traumatise others with my dead body, nor burden others with criminal or civil penalties for unlawfully assisting with my death. I do not want to test and risk closing for others the loopholes in the law around palliative sedation after voluntarily stopping eating and drinking. I do not want to injure and disable myself in a botched suicide attempt either, because that could reduce my chance of*

> *a more successful attempt. If assisted dying is easier to access than suicide, there will be less harm to myself or others.* Sam

Another alternative, assisted dying, is a more regulated, less stigmatised alternative to suicide (Hawke et al., 2024), both for the individual and their friends and family (Verhofstadt et al., 2021). Assisted dying, while called various terms in different contexts, occurs "when a person seeks assistance from a health practitioner to receive medication that will end their life" (Jeanneret et al., 2024). It has been argued that the loved ones of assisted dying patients have a less difficult experience than when someone dies by suicide (Rooney et al., 2018). For the individual, it is viewed as offering greater control over the time, manner, and pain of death (van Wijngaarden et al., 2016).

Assisted dying is widely advocated for as a public good in many contexts and this has led to widespread legal change to decriminalise assisted dying in various settings, in particular where people have life-limiting illnesses of short duration (e.g. terminal cancer or motor neurone disease). In many contexts the legislation has also extended to situations where people do not have a life-limiting illness of short duration, such as changes to assisted dying legislation in Canada (Health Canada, 2022). These legal changes have been brought about by social movements that have asserted that individuals have a right to choose the manner of their death in order to limit pain and suffering.

However, in most contexts, a line is often drawn around advocacy for assisted dying in the context of people with severe mental distress. This group is often specifically excluded from arguments for legislative reform, which limits assisted dying where mental illness is the sole diagnosis, or even a contextual issue (Jeanneret et al., 2024). Mental illness as a sole diagnosis was, for example, 'temporarily' excluded from the Canadian legislation, and its inclusion has been postponed on multiple occasions because of an inability to resolve critical issues related to its inclusion (currently postponed until 2027).

At the heart of concerns about the inclusion of mental illness as a sole diagnosis is the fear that people with a mental illness are not competent to consent to assisted dying, and that incurability and irreversibility is difficult to determine, with these being key concepts in legal determinations of the validity of assisted dying (Health Canada, 2022). There is also a concern that individual choices for assisted dying in the context of mental illness are a reflection of the entrenched social marginalisation and disadvantage of people with mental illness that should be addressed by government. There is thus a concern that seeking assisted dying "may mask profound unmet needs" that should be met (Health Canada, 2022, p. 11).

> *I have a long history accessing treatments and social support which have not resolved my suffering. I hope that the next trial succeeds, for spontaneous recovery, and for breakthrough treatments.* Sam

In some settings it is easier to receive support for assisted dying than social and health supports for mental illness.

In their systematic review, Favron-Godbout and Racine (2023) identify five broad areas of concern related to the inclusion of people with mental illness as a sole underlying condition to access assisted dying: concerns related to the societal context (e.g. stigma, discrimination, and social determinants of health), concerns related to the health-care system (e.g. lack of access to services), concerns related to the continuum of care (e.g. quality of care), concerns relating to discussing assisted dying (e.g. transference and countertransference, or how clinicians react to requests for assisted dying), and concerns related to assisted dying practices themselves (e.g. assessments of requests for assisted dying). Despite these concerns limiting access in many settings, access to assisted dying for people who have a sole diagnosis of mental illness is legal in some settings, such as in the Netherlands and Belgium (Kim et al., 2016).

10.2 Bringing assisted dying into conversation with lived experience

Recentring a lived experience perspective does not mean removing all other perspectives but brings to the fore lived experiences as central within any area of policy development and resulting legal reforms. In the rest of this chapter we propose the following person-centred research agenda (titled 'SAM') for assisted dying in the context of severe mental distress. SAM has three elements that should be considered in research in order to improve the evidence.

1. **S**afeguarding decision-making
2. **A**ssessment of irremediability
3. **M**ethodological innovation

Each should be considered within an overarching understanding of the centrality of lived experience. A failure to consider lived experience will mean that policy making continues to be developed without a focus on the voices of those impacted most by the decisions made to allow or restrict assisted dying. Each SAM theme represents a key dimension of policy making. Together this framework prioritises lived experience in the context of (1) the key issues framing debates (safeguarding decision-making and assessment of irremediability), and (2) the processes of evidence gathering and utilisation important for policy decision-making (via methodological innovation and evidence-based practice). For each of those research themes we have recommended research questions that further develop key questions and prioritise lived experience. These research questions are not exhaustive but provide an example of how researchers may approach research in order to fill some of the gaps in evidence around this important policy issue.

10.2.1 Safeguarding decision-making

As outlined in a systematic review undertaken by Nicolini et al. (2020), there are eight categories of reasons for and against assisted dying: (1) mental and physical illness and suffering, (2) decisional capacity, (3) irremediability, (4) goals of medicine and psychiatry, (5) consequences for mental health care, (6) psychiatric euthanasia and assisted suicide, (7) self-determination and authenticity, and (8) psychiatric euthanasia and assisted suicide and refusal of life-sustaining treatment. Foremost amongst these (reasons 1 and 2) are safeguards for ensuring capacity but also trusting the decision-making of people with mental illness and enabling decision-making in the context of assisted dying. These concerns relate to the inherent characteristics of depression. As Holmes (2021) writes:

> Persistent low mood, characteristic of major depression, drives a negative appraisal of the world, including what it will be like in the future. If depression is affecting the weighing up of options regarding the future, then the patient may be considered not to have a full, 'pre-depression' level of judgement and therefore to have impaired capacity. (Holmes et al., 2021)

Research and policy that does not foreground the lived experiences of all intended beneficiaries risks unintended or malicious consequences because it dehumanises the decision-making.

> *The question is not, can we reason, but can we suffer? The question is not whether we should be able to make decisions, but how?* Sam

There are risks in taking decision-making away from the individual, but also heightened vulnerabilities which need to be safeguarded. People with disabilities have been targeted by eugenics, including being prevented from having children in Australia (Dunn, 2018). In Alberta, Canada the *Sexual Sterilisation Act* passed in 1928 permitted the sterilisation of individuals identified as mentally diseased or mentally defective. The Act was amended in 1937, removing the requirement for the individual's consent, and again in 1942 to permit the sterilisation of persons who had not been institutionalised (Grekul et al., 2004). This history alerts us to serious concerns about decision-making that does not include the views of the people with disability themselves. This makes it essential that we bring lived experience further into our consideration of any policy that impacts on the life course of people with disability, including people with mental illness.

Favron-Godbout and Racine (2023) have argued that the concerns of some people opposed to assisted dying can be the subject of safeguards to make the practice more acceptable. Evidence of the effectiveness of such safeguarding is essential. Evidence-based practice is important in all areas of medicine, but we lack evidence for practice in relation to key areas of the practice of assisted dying in relation to mental illness. An example of an area that currently lacks evidence but is essential to putting policy and legislation into practice is psychiatry's relationship to the autonomy of patients regarding death.

Decision-making about the capacity of individuals experiencing severe mental distress is a core facet of legislative approaches to mental health that consider compulsory treatment. Although attitudes to assisted dying for terminal illness have liberalised over recent decades, psychiatrists are increasingly expected to prevent suicide in their patients (Burgess & Hawton, 1998). Even where assisted dying for people with severe mental distress is presently legal, they may not get the best care with appropriate guidelines and oversight over professional practice.

Bringing lived experience to the fore in relation to these issues necessitates a consideration of the following research questions:

1. In what situations do people report their decision-making was impaired due to their mental illness and, conversely, in what situations are they able to make sound decisions?
2. What assessment tools can evaluate decision-making capacity in individuals with mental illness considering assisted dying?
3. Where can mental health services be better allocated to prevent people with severe mental distress feeling that they need to turn to assisted dying?
4. What safeguards are necessary to prevent exclusion from assisted dying?
5. Should refusal of appropriate treatment preclude eligibility for euthanasia and assisted suicide?
6. How can we balance the importance of treatment with respecting a person's right to refuse treatment?
7. What are the reasons for treatment refusal, considering potential side effects, and individual experiences?
8. How should systems balance suicide prevention with a potential right to choose medical assistance in dying?

10.3 Assessment of irremediability

> *Assisted dying may reduce the duration of someone's life, but may also reduce the duration of their suffering.* Sam

This research theme focuses on one of the key dilemmas in decision-making around assisted dying in relation to mental distress – the concept of irremediability. As summarised in van Veen et al.'s (2020) review, and within Health Canada's (2022) expert panel on *MAiD and Mental Illness* (MAiD = medical assistance in dying) which met to discuss concerns about how mental illness is considered in relation to Canadian assisted dying legislation, there is ongoing debate over when a person's condition should be considered irremediable. This debate needs to be further informed by the lived experience of people who currently, or have previously, considered their conditions to be irremediable.

Will further treatment attempts expedite my end-of-life choice or resolve it? When I am already suffering, who can tell me the uncertain benefit or harm of further treatment will be tolerable? Sam

Nicolini et al. (2023) found that neither statistics nor clinicians can reliably predict who will recover from treatment resistant depression: "lack of treatment-response does not necessarily entail lack of long-term recovery." Even chronically depressed patients improve with or without treatment in the longer term. The majority of chronic severely depressed persons who have tried many evidence-based treatments actually do enter remission (Salzer et al., 2018). It is important to hear from people with lived experience who have experienced remission including those who have considered suicide or would have used assisted dying had it been available, alongside those who have never experienced remission.

Assisted dying guidelines are generally oriented around physical illnesses, overlooking the complexity of establishing incurability in psychiatry and the uncertain prognosis of mental health treatment (Schoevers et al., 1998). Psychiatrists are also reluctant to acknowledge treatment failure (Pienaar, 2016) and, for example, in the Netherlands many psychiatrists are not familiar with assisted dying and therefore are reluctant to participate (de Boer & Oei, 2011).

Given these concerns there is a need for improved psychiatric and assisted dying guidelines to facilitate the development of evidence-based palliative psychiatry. Guidelines can play a role in supporting psychiatrists to deliver evidence-based palliative care in light of these challenges. As contemplated by Pienaar (2016) this includes the development of, or variation in, a psychiatrist's scientific skills and coping with how outcomes are understood in relation to end-of-life dilemmas. In other words, how do they balance suicide prevention with assisted dying in practice settings? Better evidence is needed to be able to practise effectively where such dilemmas exist. In understanding the key aspects of these dilemmas evidence should reflect both sides of the practice dyad and consider both psychiatric practice and lived experience of receiving psychiatric support, or not receiving support where individuals need it.

We need to provide evidence that helps us to consider entrenched ways of thinking about the role of experts, including psychiatrists, in providing support in the context of mental illness and assisted dying and balance this with the lived realities of individuals. This will help us to develop a more relevant and nuanced approach to assisted dying. In order to further explore this topic we offer the following examples of research questions:

1. What are the views of those who have experienced remission after a long period of mental illness, and have considered suicide and assisted dying?
2. How should a person's reasons for refusal and the potential for side effects be taken into account in access to end-of-life options?
3. What specific waiting periods if any are appropriate, and should psychiatric consultation be required?

4. How to (and whether it is possible to) differentiate between people who have a chance of recovery and those who do not?
5. What level of 'false positive' of irremediableness and preventable death, if any, is acceptable?
6. How can guidelines better meet the needs of people with severe mental distress and psychiatrists in decision-making about assisted dying?
7. What professional oversight arrangements can best protect the interests of all parties in relation to assisted dying?

10.4 Methodological innovation

The purpose of this research theme is to ensure that we have the right evidence available in order to respond to the questions that we have proposed above. Fundamentally we need to develop approaches that recentre the individuals experiencing severe mental distress, their families, and communities alongside the legal and medical decision-making that currently dominates our evidence base. This means that we need to develop innovative methodologies to include lived experiences in research. Because of the nature of the topic, and entrenched stigmatised views about the capacity of people with mental illness to speak for themselves, it is important to think through how we enable research for policy making that actively challenges potential barriers to really *hearing* lived experiences.

> *Advocacy often highlights stories of recovery, those who manage their conditions, those new to care or with barriers to care. Those whose illnesses are unresponsive to treatment are overlooked.* Sam

Those who have recovered or experience milder and more transient mental illness are more able to share their stories and advocate from that perspective. This means that research will be more biased towards suicide prevention and recovery-focused approaches, rather than end-of-life options. There is therefore a need for the development of innovative research methodologies that compensate for this selection bias. This could include targeted recruitment strategies, such as oversampling individuals with severe mental illnesses for their lived experience, and advocacy to platform rarer voices, including those who have survived suicide attempts and those who plan to use assisted dying where (or when) available. This would help ensure less biased, more equitable, inclusive, and representative policies.

To further this research focus, we recommend the following research questions:

1. How can the lived experience of current and protracted suicidality be further incorporated into assisted dying research and policy making?
2. Can we understand which people who complete suicide would otherwise have opted for assisted dying?
3. How does suicide prevention and recovery-oriented practice intersect with the goals of palliative psychiatry?

4. What are the personal histories of those who choose to use assisted dying, to retrospectively understand opportunities for support that have been missed?

10.5 Concluding thoughts

By incorporating lived experience, research can be more responsive and respectful of individual experiences and where and how decision-making can be shared with people with severe mental distress when it comes to medical assistance in dying. The SAM framework we have articulated here provides a perspective on assisted dying in relation to mental illness that considers key dilemmas in decision-making and the need for effective evidence for making decisions. We hope that the list of research questions that we provide may inspire researchers to build their own programmes of research to centre lived experience in the development of crucial evidence for policy making.

References

Burgess, S. & Hawton, K. (1998). Suicide, euthanasia, and the psychiatrist. *Philosophy, Psychiatry, & Psychology*, *5*(2), 113–126.

de Boer, A. P. & Oei, T. I. (2011). Assisted suicide in psychiatry; current situation and notes on a recent case. *Tijdschr Psychiatr*, *53*(8), 543–550. (Hulp bij zelfdoding in de psychiatrie; stand van zaken en bespreking van een recente casus.)

Dembo, J., Schuklenk, U., & Reggler, J. (2018). 'For their own good': A response to popular arguments against permitting medical assistance in dying (MAID) where mental illness is the sole underlying condition. *Canadian Journal of Psychiatry*, *63*(7), 451–456. https://doi.org/10.1177/0706743718766055

Dunn, C. (2018). *Sterilisation of Girls with Disability: The State Responsibility to Protect Human Rights*. The University of Melbourne. https://wwda.org.au/wp-content/uploads/2018/09/Sterilisation-of-Girls-with-Disability-Cashelle-Dunn-2018-1.pdf

Favron-Godbout, C. & Racine, E. (2023). Medical assistance in dying for people living with mental disorders: A qualitative thematic review. *BMC Medical Ethics*, *24*(1), 86. https://doi.org/10.1186/s12910-023-00971-4

Grekul, J., Krahn, A., & Odynak, D. (2004). Sterilizing the 'feeble-minded': Eugenics in Alberta, Canada, 1929–1972. *Journal of Historical Sociology*, *17*(4), 358–384.

Hawke, L. D., Bastidas-Bilbao, H., Cappe, V., van Kesteren, M. R., Stewart, D. E., Gupta, M., Simpson, A. I. F., Campbell, B. H., Castle, D., Stergiopoulos, V., & Null, N. (2024). Medical assistance in dying for mental illness as a sole underlying medical condition and its relationship to suicide: A qualitative lived experience-engaged study: Aide Médicale à Mourir Pour Maladie Mentale Comme Seule Condition Médicale Sous-Jacente et Son Lien Avec le Suicide: Une Etude Qualitative Engagée Dans l'Expérience Vécue. *The Canadian Journal of Psychiatry*, *69*(5), 314–325. https://doi.org/10.1177/07067437231209658

Health Canada. (2022). *Final Report of the Expert Panel on MAiD and Mental Illness*. https://www.canada.ca/content/dam/hc-sc/documents/corporate/about-health-canada/public-engagement/external-advisory-bodies/expert-panel-maid-mental-illness/final-report-expert-panel-maid-mental-illness/final-report-expert-panel-maid-mental-illness.pdf

Holmes, A., Lange, P., Stewart, C., White, B., Willmott, L., Dooley, M., Philip, J., La Brooy, C., & Komesaroff, P. (2021). Can depressed patients make a decision to request voluntary assisted dying? *Internal Medicine Journal*, *51*(10), 1713–1716.

Jeanneret, R., Close, E., Willmott, L., Downie, J., & White, B. P. (2024). Patients' and caregivers' suggestions for improving assisted dying regulation: A qualitative study in Australia and Canada. *Health Expectations*, *27*(3), e14107.

Kim, S. Y., De Vries, R. G., & Peteet, J. R. (2016). Euthanasia and assisted suicide of patients with psychiatric disorders in the Netherlands 2011 to 2014. *JAMA Psychiatry*, *73*(4), 362–368.

Nicolini, M., Kim, S., Churchill, M., & Gastmans, C. (2020). Should euthanasia and assisted suicide for psychiatric disorders be permitted? A systematic review of reasons. *Psychological Medicine*, *50*, 1–16. https://doi.org/10.1017/S0033291720001543

Nicolini, M. E., Jardas, E. J., Zarate, C. A., Jr., Gastmans, C., & Kim, S. Y. H. (2023). Irremediability in psychiatric euthanasia: Examining the objective standard. *Psychological Medicine*, *53*(12), 5729–5747. https://doi.org/10.1017/s0033291722002951

Pienaar, W. (2016). Developing the language of futility in psychiatry with care. *South African Journal of Psychiatry*, *22*(1), 978. https://doi.org/10.4102/sajpsychiatry.v22i1.978

Pronk, R., Willems, D. L., & van de Vathorst, S. (2022). Feeling seen, being heard: Perspectives of patients suffering from mental illness on the possibility of physician-assisted death in the Netherlands. *Culture, Medicine, and Psychiatry*, *46*(2), 475–489. https://doi.org/10.1007/s11013-021-09726-5

Rooney, W., Schuklenk, U., & van de Vathorst, S. (2018). Are concerns about irremediableness, vulnerability, or competence sufficient to justify excluding all psychiatric patients from medical aid in dying? *Health Care Analysis*, *26*(4), 326–343. https://doi.org/10.1007/s10728-017-0344-8

Salzer, M. S., Brusilovskiy, E., & Townley, G. (2018). National estimates of recovery-remission from serious mental illness. *Psychiatric Services*, *69*, 523–528.

Schoevers, R. A., Asmus, F. P., & Van Tilburg, W. (1998). Physician-assisted suicide in psychiatry: Developments in The Netherlands. *Psychiatric Services*, *49*(11), 1475–1480. https://doi.org/10.1176/ps.49.11.1475

van Veen, S. M. P., Ruissen, A. M., & Widdershoven, G. A. M. (2020). Irremediable psychiatric suffering in the context of physician-assisted death: A scoping review of arguments. La souffrance psychiatrique irrémédiable dans le contexte du suicide assisté: Une revue étendue des arguments. *The Canadian Journal of Psychiatry*, *65*(9), 593–603. https://doi.org/10.1177/0706743720923072

van Wijngaarden, E. J., Leget, C. J. W., & Goossensen, A. (2016). Till death do us part: The lived experience of an elderly couple who chose to end their lives by spousal self-euthanasia. *The Gerontologist*, *56*(6), 1062–1071. https://doi.org/10.1093/geront/gnv060

Verhofstadt, M., Pardon, K., Audenaert, K., Deliens, L., Mortier, F., Liégeois, A., & Chambaere, K. (2021). Why adults with psychiatric conditions request euthanasia: A qualitative interview study of life experiences, motives and preventive factors. *Journal of Psychiatric Research*, *144*, 158–167. https://doi.org/10.1016/j.jpsychires.2021.09.032

Westermair, A. L., Buchman, D. Z., Levitt, S., Perrar, K. M., & Trachsel, M. (2022). Palliative psychiatry in a narrow and in a broad sense: A concept clarification. *Australian & New Zealand Journal of Psychiatry*, *56*(12), 1535–1541. https://doi.org/10.1177/00048674221114784

11 Decolonising the Indigenous disability sciences in Australia and New Zealand

Jemma Chao, Alix Beckett, Sarah Veli-Gold and John Gilroy

11.1 Introduction

Government policy and decision makers pride themselves as developing and implementing disability policy informed by the lived experience and expertise of Aboriginal and Torres Strait Islander peoples. However, there is limited research literature from the past century informed by the perspectives and lived experiences of Indigenous people living with a disability. The inclusion of wisdom and knowledge informed by lived experiences is just as important as the so-called objectivism of professionals. Just like mixing ingredients in a Kangaroo stew, there is a need for a mix and a balance of professionalism and the lived experience of people with disability in the disability human rights advocacy movement. This chapter is a contribution to this human rights movement from a decolonisation lens. Indigenous people with disability have been treated as the objects of disability science since before the invasion of their lands by Europeans. Australia and New Zealand are no exception.

The Indigenous peoples of New Zealand (Māori) and Australia (Aboriginal and Torres Strait Islander peoples) have progressed the decolonisation of Western sciences (Nakata, 2007; Tuhiwai Smith, 2012). John Gilroy, for example, as a world-leading Indigenous disability scholar, has led the decolonisation of disability studies through his lived experience as an Aboriginal person with a disability (e.g. Gilroy & Donelly, 2016; Gilroy et al., 2018; Gilroy, Ragen, et al., 2018; Gilroy, Uttjek, et al., 2018). Indigenous 'nations' and 'tribes' across the world have vast diverse cultures, languages, histories, and belief systems that makes defining the term 'Indigenous' insurmountable. The United Nations (UN) Declaration of the Rights of Indigenous Peoples (DRIP) continues to have a working definition of Indigenous persons, in large part because some governments either refuse to acknowledge indigeneity or they cannot establish a definition with Indigenous peoples. Having an agreed working definition, the World Health Organization (WHO) (United Nations, 2009) reported in 2010 that 370 million Indigenous people lived in 70 countries around the world.

The WHO has reported that Indigenous people experience worse rates of chronic disease and disability than non-Indigenous peoples. Schofield and Gilroy's (2015) research has showed that the rates of chronic disease and disability are largely linked to European invasion in countries such as Canada, the USA, Australia, and New Zealand. Colonisation is widely understood as a process whereby one ethnic or cultural group invades and occupies the lands of another. Underpinning the process of colonisation are ideals of the *superior human being*, a Social Darwinian ideal that subjugates Indigenous peoples through what Schofield and Gilroy (Schofield & Gilroy, 2015, p. 109) defined as "process of coercive alienation". The result is a dynamic of *relations of inequality*: Indigenous peoples live in poverty and the invader, non-Indigenous people, relish in affluence.

Indigenous scholars (Battiste, 2013; Gilroy, 2012; Kaomea, 2001; Moreton-Robinson, 2000; Nakata, 2007; Tuhiwai Smith, 2012) around the world have demonstrated how Western sciences continues to operate as a tool to falsely justify the invasion of Indigenous lands through a process of 'academic neo-imperialism' (Alatas, 2003; Gilroy & Donelly, 2016). Western scientific knowledge systems produced by the Invaders (Global north/metropole/West/Europe) and imposed on Indigenous peoples (global south/periphery/native) have constructed, evolved, and represented a version of Indigenous communities' reality without the permission or input of Indigenous peoples. Research on Indigenous peoples therefore serves the interests of the colonial elite (metropole/Global north/West) even though their interests do not benefit Indigenous peoples (Gilroy & Donelly, 2016).

Research by Gilroy et al. (Gilroy, 2009; Gilroy, 2010; Gilroy et al., 2021; Gilroy et al., 2013; Gilroy & Donelly, 2016; Gilroy, Lincoln, et al., 2018; Gilroy et al., 2023; Gilroy, Ragen, et al., 2018; Gilroy, Uttjek, et al., 2018), Grech and Soldatic (2016), and Ravindran et al. (2017) found that disability studies is no exception; Indigenous people with disability have been treated as the objects of disability science since before the invasion of their lands by Europeans. Research by Gilroy, Uttjek et al. (2018) found that disability scholars imposed their own definitions of normalcy (able-bodied, disability, handicap) and cultural values (Christianity, democracy), resulting in the desecration of Indigenous communities' graves and forced incarceration in institutions designed for people with mental illness and/or disability. Gilroy and Donelly's (2016, p. 548) review of Aboriginal and Torres Strait Islander disability research ethics found that "researchers have quantified, documented and reported on intellectual disability (identified variously in early research using terms such as 'intellectual handicap', 'mental retardation' or 'mental delay') and mental health conditions (also identified as insanity or mental illness) of so-called 'traditional' and 'non-traditional' people in Australian Indigenous communities". Regarding disability scholarship, Gilroy's (2012) historical analysis concluded:

> There are volumes of knowledge, a whole epistemological library in fact, on Indigenous people with a disability. This knowledge is not owned by Indigenous people, rather this library operates as a resource for non-Indigenous researchers and government decision makers to legitimate themselves as the controllers and bearers of the 'truth' on disability.

11.1.1 Research and policy

The colonial tool, research, is linked to government policy development and review processes. Gilroy's (2010) historical discourse analysis of Australian disability policy formulation/evolution since the Disability Services Act 1986 has shown that the voices of Aboriginal and Torres Strait Islander peoples were included and excluded over a 30-year period. In the government-led inquiry that informed the DSA, there were fewer than 100 words on Aboriginal and Torres Strait Islander peoples with disability. It was not until the late 2000s that the voices of Aboriginal and Torres Strait Islander peoples with disability were heard by researchers in government-led research. Similarly, research from Ravindran et al. (2017) found that there are slight differences in how Aboriginal and Torres Strait Islander peoples define disability and disability service provider policies.

This calls for a specific investigation into how research is undertaken so that it may be effectively translated into policy. Indigenous scholars have engaged in a global effort to decolonise the Western sciences through a process of decolonisation. Decolonisation is a process of deconstructing Western sciences' modus operandi that reinforces the oppression and subjugation of Indigenous peoples as lower-class peoples (Gilroy & Donelly, 2016). Essentially, the aim is to empower Indigenous peoples in the research process by having Indigenous values, ethics, and cultural values at the centre of scientific knowledge production.

This chapter forms part of that effort by addressing the research question of: To what degree are the voices of Indigenous people captured in disability research in Australia and New Zealand over the last century? Moreover, by providing Indigenous informed areas requiring disability research and policy attention, our chapter also offers a valuable contribution to this book's overarching goal of informing a research agenda for lived experience and disability policy.

In the sections to follow, we will start by describing the methods (i.e. how we collected and analysed data in a systematic review of the literature). We will then provide the results relating to our above-mentioned research question, which includes the following six themes from our thematic analysis: (1) financial impact; (2) caregivers/family; (3) culture and land; (4) informed perspectives; (5) stigma, stereotypes, and prejudice; and (6) access to services. Next, we offer a critical discussion of results before raising the limitations of our study. Importantly, we conclude by providing readers with Indigenous informed future disability research and policy directions.

11.2 Methods

Contributing to the global effort to decolonise the disability sciences, a systematic literature review of peer-reviewed published scientific literature was conducted by three Australian Indigenous peoples with lived experience to answer the question as raised above. The aim of a systematic review is to ascertain the quality of research and identify the findings of research within a particular discourse or discipline within disability studies. Within the context of a decolonising paradigm, the research team adopted Gilroy's (Gilroy et al., 2013; Gilroy & Donelly, 2016; Gilroy, 2009) Indigenous Standpoint Theory (IST). Gilroy's IST for disability research consists of nine domains:

1. Indigenous community inclusion: The research team consisted of only Aboriginal people with lived experience.
2. Colonisation is acknowledged as a social determinant of health.
3. Is based in a social justice model.
4. Acknowledges that Indigenous peoples live and operate within the Cultural Interface.
5. Foley's three tiers of Indigenous research are adopted. These tiers are the Physical World, Human World, and the Sacred World of Indigenous communities.
6. Acknowledges that all Indigenous communities are diverse.
7. Critiques disability and impairment research epistemology.
8. Focuses on cultural and community participation.
9. Research methodologies are agreed between all researchers.

We followed the PRISMA (Preferred Reporting Items for Systematic Reviews and Meta-Analyses) guidelines in this study. This approach included setting eligibility criteria, identifying and selecting scholarly publications, appraising and extraction of data, and conducting thematic analysis on included publications.

11.2.1 Eligibility criteria

Peer-reviewed published literature was identified by systematically searching seven databases in August 2022. We included studies published between August 1922 to August 2022. This was to capture the voices of Indigenous people over the last 100 years and whether there were any changes over time. Articles needed to contain original data specific to Indigenous people with a disability from Australia and New Zealand.

Studies were included if they fit the following criteria:

- Research about the voices/perspectives of Aboriginal and Torres Strait Islander peoples and/or Māori people with disability.
- Peer-reviewed publications.
- Lived experience of disability.
- Included Indigenous people from Australia and New Zealand as the research topic and/or participants.
- Carers of Aboriginal and Torres Strait Islander peoples and/or Māori people with disability.

Exclusion criteria consisted of:

- Research from workers perspectives.

- Research on Aboriginal and Torres Strait Islander and/or Māori people without inclusion of their voices/perspectives.
- Grey literature.
- Clinical reviews.

11.2.2 Search identification and selection

Defining disability research was challenging. The research team took a phase approach. Firstly, we had to consider where mental health fits within the definition of disability. Furthermore, social and emotional well-being and mental health are considered as disabilities in Indigenous health and disability research and policy. Reflecting on the literature and the recent Audit (Centre for Disability Research and Policy, 2014), we frame the experience of disability as a blend of the social/environmental factors together with human biology and how that interacts with the individual's life. This systematic review considered all studies that involved Aboriginal and/or Torres Strait Islander and/or Māori people with a disability, where disability had a life-long impact on activities of daily living.

Secondly, we worked with a librarian and renowned disability scholars to create the search string, which consisted of words for disability types, life-long mental illness, and Indigenous synonyms to those terms in use over many decades. The search string used phrases and words similar to the Australian audit of disability research (Centre for Disability Research and Policy, 2014) and Gilroy et al.'s (2018) recent discourse analysis of Aboriginal and Torres Strait Islander peoples with disability in the news media.

Using our new string search, we were able to combine our searches over seven databases (see below) to search literature. The found literature was then imported into EndNote X8. A total of 9,788 titles and abstracts were screened, by the authors (Author 1, Author 2), using the systematic review software Covidence. Papers that raised uncertainty of inclusion into this study were discussed further among Author 1, Author 2, and Author 3 until 100% agreement was achieved on inclusion or exclusion.

Databases/search strategies utilised:

- CINAHL, MEDLINE, PROQUEST, Scopus, Web of Science, Embase, and Informit
- A hand search was undertaken – this involved contacting key people in the research field and public databases (such as Centre for Disability Research and Policy library, Google and Google Scholar) for further peer-reviewed literature.

Thirdly, we conducted the search twice as the initial search found no papers from Māori perspectives. One reason for the lack of initial findings is that Māori terminology for disability differs to Aboriginal and Torres Strait Islander peoples' terminologies. Māori academics and researchers will use traditional language and phrases when talking about health or health concerns, therefore our original search wasn't applicable. As such, we engaged Māori colleagues who have knowledge and skills in health and disability services and research to obtain traditional words and terms for family, disability, colonisation, health, and the traditional words for common disabilities such as deaf, blind, wheelchair. These people are included in our acknowledgements. Reflecting our individual study time, this approach ensured that the voices of Māori community were included in this study. However, we were not able to apply Aboriginal and Torres Strait Islander families' words for disability due to the many hundreds of languages spoken across Australia.

11.2.3 Publication appraisal

Under the guidance of Author 4 we blended an Integrated Indigenous Australian analysis method utilising the CREATE evaluation tool, which is a tool that evaluates the level of influence and voice in the research process, with the Mixed Methods Assessment Tool (MMAT), which evaluates the quality of the research. The CREATE tool was developed by Aboriginal and Torres Strait Islander peoples and scholars as a decolonising screening template to ascertain the quality of Indigenous lore, cultural protocols, and ethics in research. The MMAT is a scholarly tool that is used to screen qualitative, quantitative, and mixed-method research publications (Hong et al., 2018; Pace et al., 2012; Pluye et al., 2009).

Given the size of the study, the research team blended the two tools together to focus on the question: How has the historic archive of disability science captured and represented the voices of Māori, Aboriginal, and Torres Strait Islander people with disability? This analytic tool was developed as we were focused on the level and type of inclusion of Indigenous peoples in the research archive.

Authors 1–3 had all included papers printed out and screened using the tool. All three authors discussed each paper and came to an agreement on each section of the tool for each paper. Specific colours were used on the hard copies whilst using the screening tool. Afterwards the findings were placed into an Excel spreadsheet.

11.2.4 Thematic analysis

The team adopted Braun and Clarke's six-phases for thematic analysis: (1) familiarisation of data; (2) initial codes; (3) searching for themes; (4) reviewing themes; (5) defining and naming themes; and (6) writing the paper. This approach was used in previous reviews that involved Authors 3 and 4 (Gilroy et al., 2023; Veli-Gold et al., 2023).

11.3 Results

11.3.1 Data extraction

Our search strategy found 26,380 articles. Of these, 15,899 were removed as duplicates, leaving 10,481 papers which fit within our criteria. On review of the literature, based on our inclusion/exclusion criteria we excluded 9,788 articles.

On further review and discussion between Authors 1, 2, and 3, when insignificant details on Indigenous voices were not included in the abstract this excluded additional

601 articles. After this analysis, all the authors agreed that the final review included 47 studies. Of these, 10 were Māori, while 37 were Aboriginal and/or Torres Strait Islander related. These results are presented in Figure 11.1 below, according to the PRISMA framework.

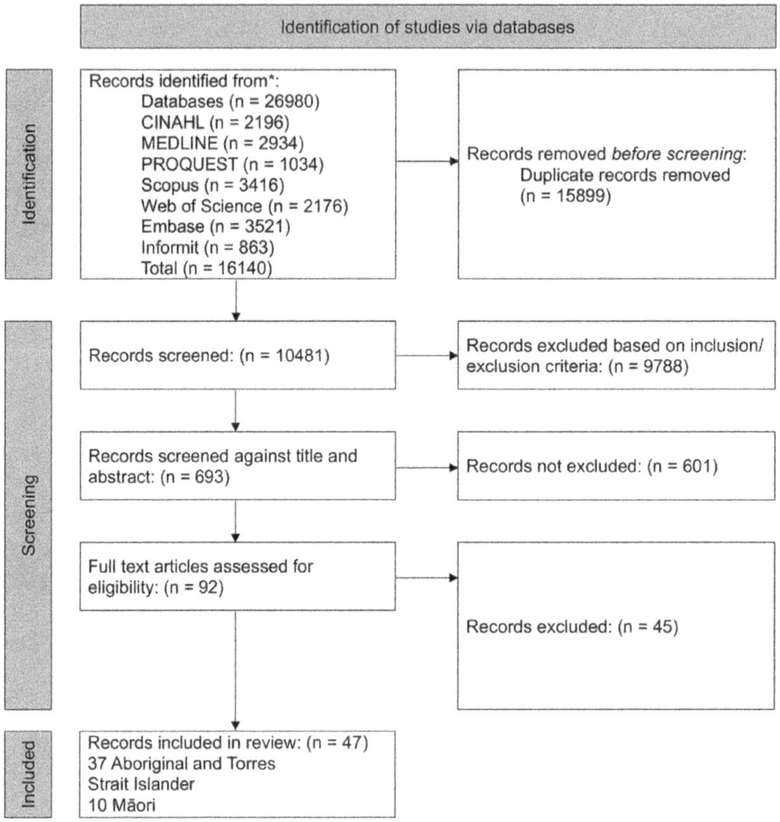

Source: Authors.

Figure 11.1 PRISMA flow diagram for the systematic review

11.3.2 Characteristics of the studies

Of the included studies, 37 were qualitative, three were quantitative, and seven studies were mixed-method reviews. The qualitative research studies utilised a variety of methods, including focus groups, yarning, case studies, and individual interviews. The studies cover a range of geographic regions, from remote to metropolitan. However, not all the studies used an approved classification tool to define what they meant by remote/rural, such as the Modified Monash Model.

Of the 47 studies, ten included data from workers and professionals, in addition to people with disability, and parents/carers of people with disability. The other papers collected data from people with a disability and/or parents/carers. One research paper did not report on the number of people who participated in the study. Although all the research projects methodologies were sound, seven of the studies did not report on the level of Indigenous governance of the research process. All the studies identified the important benefits the research provided for Indigenous peoples.

11.3.3 Thematic findings

Of the identified studies we found that a lot of the papers covered topics such as Finance, National Disability Insurance Scheme (NDIS), Access to Services, Housing and Homeless, Workforce, Education, Caregivers/Family, Youth/Children, Environmental Barrier, Barriers/Stereotypes, Trauma Informed, Lived Experience, Impacts on Daily Living, Awareness and Culture and Land. The review identified six (n=6) overarching themes from the 47 studies included in this research:

1. Financial impact
2. Caregivers/family
3. Culture and land
4. Informed perspectives
5. Stigma, stereotypes, and prejudice
6. Access to services

11.3.4 Financial impact

The included papers stated that the financial experiences of Indigenous people with disability are linked historically to colonisation, urbanisation, and systemic discrimination. People living with disabilities often face significant financial challenges that can impact their quality of life, independence, and overall well-being (McGruer et al., 2019).

The Indigenous populations experienced financial stress related to living with a disability. Thirteen of the papers that involved Aboriginal and Torres Strait Islander peoples (Armstrong et al., 2019; Cockram et al., 2007; DiGiacomo et al., 2017; Fitts & Soldatic, 2020, 2022; Grant et al., 2017; Hamilton et al., 2020; McInerney-Leo et al., 2022; Soldatic, 2018a, 2018b; Soldatic et al., 2017; Spurway & Soldatic, 2016; Townsend et al., 2019) and two that involved Māori peoples (Lambert et al., 2021; McGruer et al., 2019) reported that the financial challenges are linked to limited access to financial institutes such as banks, and credit unions. This is largely related to the larger number of Aboriginal and Torres Strait Islander peoples living in rural and remote areas.

In the two papers that focused on Māori people, the research reported that financial implications directly related to the lack of culturally appropriate disability services and support can lead to feelings of disconnection from their Māori culture and identity and disconnection from Whānau (family or community who live together in the same area). The Aboriginal and Torres Strait Islander focused papers reported that the Disability Support Pension programme is not sustainable for the cost-of-living pressures experienced by Aboriginal and Torres Strait Islander peoples living with a disability.

Overall, these 13 papers suggested that financial services and government income support programmes need to be more culturally responsive to the unique experiences and needs of Māori, Aboriginal, and Torres Strait Islander peoples living with disabilities. Governments and financial institutions must work together to increase access to financial services and adequate income support for those people living in remote and rural areas. The finance sector needs a better-trained workforce for the local Indigenous populations.

We also noted that injury and disability had a significant impact on the participants' ability to perform their job duties, and some were able to recover quickly while others were unable to return to work due to the severity of their injury (Lambert et al., 2021).

11.3.5 Caregivers/family

Twenty-two of the papers discussed the perspectives of family and/or caregivers who were looking after an Indigenous person living with a disability. Caregivers and family members played a vital role in supporting people with disabilities, providing the necessary care, advocacy, and assistance to live independently.

These papers reported on the unique challenges and stresses family members and carers faced when supporting Indigenous people with disabilities. Six papers (Ariotti, 1999; Armstrong, Coffin, et al., 2021; DiGiacomo et al., 2017; Fitts et al., 2019; Fitts & Soldatic, 2022; Greenstein et al., 2016a) reported that family and/or caregivers experienced serious emotional challenges related to caring for a person with a disability. The paper reported that caring duties can be emotionally demanding, especially when supporting people with complex needs and/or co-morbidities (such as challenging behaviours, balancing medical appointments, and managing daily routines) (Armstrong et al., 2019; Armstrong et al., 2015; Cockram et al., 2007). This also has a physical demand on the family and/or caregivers requiring manual labour, lifting, and transferring individuals depending on the severity of the disability (Jeffries-Stokes et al., 2004).

Nineteen of the papers spoke about the lack of financial support for families and caregivers and the strain that produces not only on the person they care about but also personally. The broader costs are significant, with expenses including medical equipment and home modifications (Ariotti, 1999; Armstrong, Coffin, et al., 2021; Armstrong et al., 2019; Armstrong et al., 2015; Blackburn, 2016; Cockram et al., 2007; Dew et al., 2020; DiGiacomo et al., 2017; Fitts et al., 2019; Fitts & Soldatic, 2022; Green et al., 2016; Greenstein et al., 2016a; 2016b; Jeffries-Stokes et al., 2004; Lambert et al., 2021; McGruer et al., 2019; McInerney-Leo et al., 2022; Sanders et al., 2011; Shen et al., 2018; Soldatic, 2018a; Spurling et al., 2021).

11.3.6 Culture and land

Over half of the papers reported on the significance of culture and land/country for Indigenous populations, and how deeply rooted in this their history, identity, and way of life is. Culture and land are fundamental aspects of Māori, Aboriginal, and Torres Strait Islander people's identity, well-being, and spirituality. Understanding the significance of these elements is crucial for Indigenous people living with a disability (Ariotti, 1999; Armstrong et al., 2012; Blackburn, 2016; Dew et al., 2020; Dew et al., 2019; Elder, 2013; Gibson et al., 2021; Gilroy et al., 2021; Graham et al., 2022; Green et al., 2016; S. Hamilton et al., 2020; Higgins et al., 2013; Lambert et al., 2021; McGruer et al., 2019; McInerney-Leo et al., 2022; McRae et al., 2019; Shen et al., 2018; Smiler & McKee, 2007; Soldatic, 2018b; Soldatic et al., 2017; Spurling et al., 2021; Spurway & Soldatic, 2016).

The research papers reported that culture and land/country are integral to the social and emotional well-being of Indigenous peoples. The invasion of Indigenous lands has contributed to the prevalence and experience of disability for Indigenous peoples in New Zealand and Australia. Māori people with disabilities are not being treated fairly under the Treaty of Waitangi. Since the Treaty was signed, it has been subject to interpretation and has led to ongoing conflicts over land ownership and use. Aboriginal and Torres Strait Islander cultures are connected metaphysically and physically to their traditional lands (Country), which have been passed down intergenerationally. The Australian government's policies, including the removal of children from their families (the 'Stolen Generations') has further prioritised Aboriginal and Torres Strait Islander peoples with disability's connection and engagement to culture and country.

11.3.7 Informed perspectives

The theme 'informed perspectives' was most important in relation to hearing the 'voices' (informed perspectives) of the experiences and challenges faced by Māori and Aboriginal and Torres Strait Islander peoples. Ninety per cent of the papers referenced factors that influenced this theme, including those related to impacts on daily living (39), trauma informed care (31), lived experience (38), and awareness (29) (Ariotti, 1999; Armstrong, Coffin, et al., 2021; Armstrong et al., 2019; Armstrong et al., 2015; Armstrong et al., 2012; Armstrong, McCoy, et al., 2021; Blackburn, 2016; Cockram et al., 2007; Dew et al., 2020; Dew et al., 2019; DiGiacomo et al., 2017; Elder, 2013; M. Fitts et al., 2019; M. S. Fitts et al., 2019; Fitts & Soldatic, 2020, 2022; Gibbs et al., 2004; Gibson et al., 2021; Gilroy et al., 2021; Graham et al., 2022; Grant et al., 2017; Green et al., 2018; Green et al., 2016; Greenstein et al., 2016a; 2016b; S. Hamilton et al., 2020; S. L. Hamilton et al., 2020; Higgins et al., 2013; Jeffries-Stokes et al., 2004; Jobling et al., 2016; Kake et al., 2016; Lambert et al., 2021; Lilley et al., 2020; McGruer et al., 2019; McInerney-Leo et al., 2022; McRae et al., 2019; Sanders et al., 2011; Shen et al., 2018; Smiler & McKee, 2007; Soldatic, 2018a, 2018b; Soldatic et al., 2017; Spurling et al., 2021; Spurway & Soldatic, 2016; Townsend et al., 2019). We have seen how it is crucial to use lived experience when doing research with Indigenous people. Our criteria in looking at the research was hearing the voices from Indigenous people living with a disability or caring for an Indigenous person with a disability. Informed perspectives scored extremely high throughout the papers, making it important to have these when researching Indigenous people.

11.3.8 Stigma, stereotypes, and prejudice

The research papers have reported on the ongoing impact of stigma, stereotypes, and prejudice faced by Aboriginal and Torres Strait Islander and Māori peoples. All of the 47 research papers reported on these issues, noting that discrimination is highly prevalent for all Indigenous people with disability. Stereotypes are inaccurate generalisations about a group of people, often based on their identity. They can be used to justify discrimination and prejudice by unfair assumptions about disabled Aboriginal and Torres Strait Islander or Māori persons, which was mentioned in six papers (Dew et al., 2020; Gilroy et al., 2021; Green et al., 2018; Green et al., 2016; McInerney-Leo et al., 2022; Soldatic, 2018a). The operation of stereotypes within society can have mental impacts, leaving Aboriginal and Torres Strait Islander or Māori peoples feeling isolated and alone. Prejudice as a preconceived opinion was also highlighted in several papers, especially Aboriginal and Torres Strait Islander or Māori peoples, and how society acts towards their disability in a way that is not based on reason or evidence, but rather on false or incomplete information (Ariotti, 1999; Armstrong, Coffin, et al., 2021; Armstrong et al., 2019; Armstrong, McCoy, et al., 2021; Cockram et al., 2007; Dew et al., 2020; Dew et al., 2019; Fitts & Soldatic, 2020, 2022; Gibbs et al., 2004; Grant et al., 2017; Green et al., 2016; S. Hamilton et al., 2020; Sanders et al., 2011; Shen et al., 2018).

Nine papers highlighted workforce themes. Specifically, the difficulties in obtaining a job and career growth (Armstrong, Coffin, et al., 2021; Armstrong et al., 2012; Fitts et al., 2019; Fitts & Soldatic, 2020; Gibson et al., 2021; Gilroy et al., 2021; Green et al., 2018; Green et al., 2016; Greenstein et al., 2016a), even where there were policies in place not to exclude people with a physical, sensory, or mental impairment. Working in the workforce when impaired with a disability rated high in the papers as this affects an individual's ability to perform tasks or activities, and often makes it difficult or impossible for them to participate in various aspects of work or keep a job (Blackburn, 2016; Cockram et al., 2007; Elder, 2013; Graham et al., 2022; Lambert et al., 2021). Eleven of 47 papers touched on matters of homelessness and housing (Gilroy et al., 2021; Green et al., 2018; Greenstein et al., 2016b; S. Hamilton et al., 2020; Jobling et al., 2016; Lilley et al., 2020; Soldatic, 2018a, 2018b; Spurway & Soldatic, 2016), primarily identifying the needs of housing modifications and equipment such as ramps and accessible needs.

11.3.9 Access to services

All the papers reported on access barriers to services by Māori, Aboriginal and Torres Strait Islander peoples with disabilities. In this theme we merged topics on the social determinants and social economic status to create the access to services theme. Identifying and addressing the social determinants of health is essential to tackle inequalities and inequities between Indigenous and non-Indigenous peoples in accessing services. Of the 47 papers, we saw that six papers spoke about education (Armstrong et al., 2012; Dew et al., 2020; Elder, 2013; Gibson et al., 2021; Grant et al., 2017; McRae et al., 2019). Specifically, these papers discussed the services that are available in education and the support needs of students.

Access to health services, resources, and specialist services remains the highest explored areas throughout the literature, with 33 papers reporting on this topic (Ariotti, 1999; Armstrong, Coffin, et al., 2021; Armstrong et al., 2019; Armstrong et al., 2012; Armstrong, McCoy, et al., 2021; Blackburn, 2016; Dew et al., 2020; Dew et al., 2019; DiGiacomo et al., 2017; Elder, 2013; M. Fitts et al., 2019; Fitts & Soldatic, 2020, 2022; Gibbs et al., 2004; Gibson et al., 2021; Gilroy et al., 2021; Grant et al., 2017; Green et al., 2018; Greenstein et al., 2016a; 2016b; Hamilton et al., 2020; Jeffries-Stokes et al., 2004; Lambert et al., 2021; Lilley et al., 2020; McGruer et al., 2019; McInerney-Leo et al., 2022; McRae et al., 2019; Shen et al., 2018; Soldatic, 2018a, 2018b; Spurling et al., 2021; Spurway & Soldatic, 2016). The papers reported that Indigenous people living closer to major cities were able to access services but felt culturally unsafe, while people living further away in remote or regional areas lack support to access services that were understanding of or culturally safe for their disability needs.

Services and facilities are not accessible to Indigenous peoples with disabilities, particularly those living in rural or remote areas (Gibson et al., 2021; Lambert et al., 2021; McGruer et al., 2019). This can be due to a lack of infrastructure, transportation, and technology. Long wait times to see doctors in larger towns can be overwhelming, causing undue stress and anxiety for individuals with disabilities and their caregivers. Navigating the healthcare system can be a daunting task, resulting in a negative impact on both the individual's well-being and that of their caregiver.

The challenges in accessing healthcare are multifaceted, including lengthy travel times, inaccessible facilities, and a lack of specialised services. For Indigenous people who have barriers in accessing services this can have consequences on their health, such as delayed diagnosis, inadequate treatment, and a decreased quality of life.

Indigenous peoples with disabilities may face stereotyping and stigma from service providers, which can affect their ability to access services and feel valued as individuals (Ariotti, 1999; Armstrong, Coffin, et al., 2021; Armstrong et al., 2019; Cockram et al., 2007; Gibson et al., 2021; Graham et al., 2022; Soldatic et al., 2017; Townsend et al., 2019).

11.4 Discussion

Globally, Indigenous peoples with disabilities are not properly included in the decision-making process about the services that affect them. Our study, together with Gilroy's (2010) historical study and Gilroy et al.'s (2023) and Veli-Gold et al.'s (2023) recent literature reviews on the Australian NDIS, has shown that this is true for the research process since the early 1980s. This can lead to a lack of understanding of Indigenous people's needs and experiences when research is transferred to disability legislation and policy. This *pattern of exclusion* has further ramifications for the distribution of taxpayer funds to the Australia Aboriginal Community Health Controlled Health Services and Māori-managed health organisations for people with disability. These agencies are usually overbooked, have poor access rates due to staff challenges, and require transport in order to access them.

Our study has also highlighted the poor participation of Aboriginal and Torres Strait Islander peoples in research relating to the Disability Support Pension (DSP) and the NDIS. The DSP is a government personal income support programme to assist with living costs for people with a disability who cannot engage in full-time paid employment. Following the recent COVID-19 pandemic, the cost of living has risen in Australia, which places a greater burden on a person with a disability who often requires additional expenses, such as mobility aids, assistive technology, and medical treatments. These costs can be particularly high for Aboriginal and Torres Strait Islander peoples, where access to healthcare services and accessibility infrastructure may be limited and challenging due to a lack of disability support workers, advocacy services, or rehabilitation programmes. New Zealand and Australia have financial income support programmes for people with disability. These are a key source of income that is often inadequate to cover the costs of living with a disability, particularly in remote areas where costs are higher. Additionally, the DSP is subject to income and assets tests, which can be restrictive. However additional support using the National Disability Insurance Scheme (NDIS), an Australian government-funded scheme which provides individualised support and services to people with disability, has been designed with limited involvement of Aboriginal and Torres Strait Islander peoples involved in the research phase. It is designed to give people with disabilities the freedom to make choices about their own lives, and to support them in achieving their goals. But the scheme is also challenging and problematic for people to access, with long wait times and no comprehension or multiple barriers completing the paperwork to be literate or skills to manage their finances effectively, which can lead to debt, financial stress, and reliance. This is an example of a policy that has not been made with a clear understanding of the experiences of Aboriginal and Torres Strait Islander peoples with disability.

The World Health Organization reports that Indigenous peoples experience high rates of discrimination (United Nations, 2007). Our study has shown that discrimination and cultural safety are among the highest challenges for Aboriginal and Torres Strait Islander peoples and Māori people with disabilities. Physical and attitudinal barriers can limit access to education, employment, healthcare, and other essential disability services. There is a heightened need to further advance the cultural safety of disability services and communities generally through policy and its effective implementation. Stigma leads to social exclusion, discrimination, and marginalisation. Racial stigmas aim to disempower or marginalise people as the 'other' or 'inferior'. When experiencing mental illness, people are labelled as 'crazy' or 'fragile', which in most cases is considered a crippling mental disability. A person with an impairment or physical disability is seen as 'broken' or 'incompetent'. These experiences are historical and are a direct legacy of colonialism. In the Western research academy, Gilroy has shown that these European racialised ideals are embedded in the disability research sciences (Gilroy et al., 2013; Gilroy, 2009; Schofield & Gilroy, 2015).

Furthermore, Māori communities and some Aboriginal and Torres Strait Islander peoples may not speak English as their first language. This barrier compounds the existing challenges of living with disability, which can create communication barriers in the research and policy development spaces.

Now more than ever these challenges have accelerated in Australia since the 2023 Australian Indigenous Voice referendum. The core function of the Voice was to introduce a government body that could make government and parliament representations on issues relevant to Aboriginal and Torres Strait Islander peoples that would have constitutional protection and thereby make policy more effective (Appleby & Synot, 2023). This referendum, however, was ultimately rejected by Australian voters. The impacts of this national policy outcome on Aboriginal and Torres Strait Islander peoples are still being felt today – it brought a lot of stigma, stereotypes, and prejudice. Nonetheless, the Voice campaign has raised awareness about the ongoing struggles faced by Indigenous Australians. Also, many of the initiatives launched during the campaign are continuing to drive change and progress, which are the results of new relationships between governments and Indigenous Australians, including increased collaboration and consultation that could lead to more effective policy development and implementation, acknowledging ongoing disparities faced. It is essential that research knowledge led by the interests of Aboriginal and Torres Strait Islander peoples with disability leads into the development of policy to address these disparities.

11.4.1 Limitations

A limitation of our study is the boundary line in defining mental illness/health and disability. As such, our disability inclusion criteria are that the mental illness must be chronic and life-long and that it impacts on activities of daily living, requiring some level of support for independence and social inclusion.

11.5 Conclusion: Indigenous informed future disability research and policy directions

While historically scientists and government agencies have developed health tools, techniques, and services that suit able-bodied people, much of this work has not properly involved Aboriginal and Torres Strait Islander and Māori peoples. This also reflects social stigma and the way healthcare is provided to the population (Sherwood, 2013). This can change with the inclusion of lived experience in research to make our policy more relevant and inclusive. Our lived experience-led research shows some immediate areas where policy needs to be improved by including the lived experiences of these groups. For example, our findings revealed that not enough Indigenous peoples have the qualifications to deliver culturally safe practices within healthcare, thus showing a need for policy to enable more training and mentoring when engaging with Indigenous populations. Also highlighting a persisting gap in the co-design and co-development of knowledge, the voices of the Indigenous people living with a disability are not being captured enough within research about disability services. There is a vital role for governments in health and other disability service areas to be ethical in the consideration and genuine inclusion of Indigenous people in research in this area, so that the disability services that governments fund are relevant to the people they serve.

Indigenous populations should be involved in the co-development and management of research and policy that impacts their lives. Their voices should be heard and actioned to improve the needs of people living with a disability or for a carer who is supporting an Indigenous person with a disability. Our systematic review showed that a lot of the data was written from the clinical perspective of what should be improved rather than from consultation with people with disability. It showed that these two Indigenous populations suffered from similar experiences of racism and disablism in the research process when it came to Indigenous cultures. Leading on from this it showed how important culture is to Indigenous people, and how this culture needs to be consistently respected in disability research and policymaking activities.

More research needs to be conducted to include Indigenous people with a lived experience of disabilities, to understand the struggles they are facing in accessing disability services and in other areas. This co-designed research could investigate pressing disability topics such as: (1) finding evidence-based ways to better include Indigenous peoples in the design, development, and implementation of disability services; (2) advising how to increase the representation of Indigenous peoples with disability among disability service staff; and (3) revealing measures to redress the racism and ableism that collectively stops the development of inclusive disability services, research, and policymaking spaces. It is essential that this research is linked to training and awareness programmes to change researcher behaviour when working with Indigenous peoples so that knowledge is collected in partnership and in culturally relevant ways. Such research programmes must be led by universities and government agencies that have carriage over research ethics and practice and can adequately consider whether research is culturally respectful and ethical.

References

Alatas, S. F. (2003). Academic dependency and the global division of labour in the social sciences. *Current Sociology, 51*(6), 599–613.

Appleby, G. & Synot, E. (2023). The Voice: What is it, where did it come from, and what can it achieve? https://theconversation.com/the-voice-what-is-it-where-did-it-come-from-and-what-can-it-achieve-202138#:~:text=The%20key%20function%20of%20the,litigation)%20to%20follow%20these%20representations

Ariotti, L. (1999). Social construction of an Angu disability. *Australian Journal of Rural Health, 7*(4), 216–222.

Armstrong, E., Coffin, J., Hersh, D., Katzenellenbogen, J. M., Thompson, S. C., Ciccone, N., Flicker, L., Woods, D., Hayward, C., & Dowell, C. (2021). 'You felt like a prisoner in your own self, trapped': The experiences of Aboriginal people with acquired communication disorders. *Disability and Rehabilitation*, *43*(13), 1903–1916.

Armstrong, E., Coffin, J., McAllister, M., Hersh, D., Katzenellenbogen, J. M., Thompson, S. C., Ciccone, N., Flicker, L., Cross, N., & Arabi, L. (2019). 'I've got to row the boat on my own, more or less': Aboriginal Australian experiences of traumatic brain injury. *Brain Impairment*, *20*(2), 120–136.

Armstrong, E., Hersh, D., Hayward, C., & Fraser, J. (2015). Communication disorders after stroke in Aboriginal Australians. *Disability and Rehabilitation*, *37*(16), 1462–1469.

Armstrong, E., Hersh, D., Hayward, C., Fraser, J., & Brown, M. (2012). Living with aphasia: Three Indigenous Australian stories. *International Journal of Speech-Language Pathology*, *14*(3), 271–280.

Armstrong, E., McCoy, K., Clinch, R., Merritt, M., Speedy, R., McAllister, M., Heine, K., Ciccone, N., Robinson, M., & Coffin, J. (2021). The development of aboriginal brain injury coordinator positions: A culturally secure rehabilitation service initiative as part of a clinical trial. *Primary Health Care Research & Development*, *22*, e49.

Battiste, M. (2013). *Decolonizing Education. Nourishing the Learning Spirit*. Purich Publishing Ltd.

Blackburn, C. (2016). Relationship-based early intervention services for children with complex needs: Lessons from New Zealand. *Journal of Children's Services*, *11*(4), 330–344.

Centre for Disability Research and Policy. (2014). *Report of Audit of Disability Research in Australia* [Internet]. Centre for Disability Research and Policy. http://sydney.edu.au/health-sciences/cdrp/projects/auditresearch.shtml

Cockram, J., Hancock, P., & Jarvis, J. (2007). Supporting older carers of people with a disability: An evaluation of a respite care program in Western Australia. *Asia Pacific Journal of Health Management*, *2*(2), 58–62.

Dew, A., Barton, R., Gilroy, J., Ryall, L., Lincoln, M., Jensen, H., Flood, V., Taylor, K., & McCrae, K. (2020). Importance of land, family and culture for a good life: Remote Aboriginal people with disability and carers. *Australian Journal of Social Issues*, *55*(4), 418–438.

Dew, A., Vaughan, P., McEntyre, E., & Dowse, L. (2019). 'Our ways to planning': Preparing organisations to plan with Aboriginal and Torres Strait Islander people with disability. *Australian Aboriginal Studies*, (2), 3–18.

DiGiacomo, M., Green, A., Delaney, P., Delaney, J., Patradoon-Ho, P., Davidson, P. M., & Abbott, P. (2017). Experiences and needs of carers of Aboriginal children with a disability: A qualitative study. *BMC Family Practice*, *18*, 1–11.

Elder, H. (2013). Indigenous theory building for Māori children and adolescents with traumatic brain injury and their extended family. *Brain Impairment*, *14*(3), 406–414.

Fitts, M., Bird, K., Fleming, J., Gilroy, J., Clough, A., Esterman, A., Maruff, P., & Potter, M. (2019). The potential of a narrative and creative arts approach to enhance transition outcomes for Indigenous Australians following traumatic brain injury. *Brain Impairment*, *20*(2), 160–170.

Fitts, M. S., Bird, K., Gilroy, J., Fleming, J., Clough, A. R., Esterman, A., Maruff, P., & Fatima, Y. (2019). A qualitative study on the transition support needs of Indigenous Australians following traumatic brain injury. *Brain Impairment*, *20*(2), 137–159.

Fitts, M. S. & Soldatic, K. (2020). Why extended time on Newstart is unsuitable for Aboriginal and Torres Strait Islander Australians living with a disability. *Australian Social Work*, *73*(2), 191–203.

Fitts, M. S. & Soldatic, K. (2022). Who's caring for whom? Disabled Indigenous carers' experiences of Australia's infrastructures of social protection. *Journal of Family Studies*, *28*(2), 477–492.

Gibbs, A., Dawson, J., Forsyth, H., Mullen, R., & Tanga, T. O. T. (2004). Maori experience of community treatment orders in Otago, New Zealand. *Australian & New Zealand Journal of Psychiatry, 38*(10), 830–835.

Gibson, C., Chatfeild, K., O'Neill-Baker, B., Newman, T., & Steele, A. (2021). Gulburra (to understand): Aboriginal Ability Linker's person-centred care approach. *Disability and Rehabilitation, 43*(19), 2713–2719.

Gilroy, J. (2009). The theory of the cultural interface and Indigenous people with disabilities in New South Wales. *Balayi: Culture, Law and Colonialism, 10*(November), 44–59.

Gilroy, J. (2010). History of Aboriginal people with disability in NSW: How are Aboriginal people with disability positioned and represented in the NSW disability services sector? *Interaction: Special Edition on Aboriginal People with Disability, 24*, 6–29.

Gilroy, J. (2012). The participation of aboriginal persons with disability in disability services in New South Wales, Australia [unpublished doctoral thesis on the internet]. University of Sydney. http://sydney.edu.au/education_social_work/doctoral_studies/completed_theses/2013/Gilroy.shtml

Gilroy, J., Colmar, S., Donelly, M., & Parmenter, T. (2013). Conceptual framework for policy and research development with Indigenous persons with disability. *Journal of Australian Aboriginal Studies, 2*, 42–58.

Gilroy, J., Dew, A., Barton, R., Ryall, L., Lincoln, M., Taylor, K., Jensen, H., Flood, V., & McRae, K. (2021). Environmental and systemic challenges to delivering services for Aboriginal adults with a disability in Central Australia. *Disability and Rehabilitation, 43*(20), 2919–2929.

Gilroy, J. & Donelly, M. (2016). Australian Indigenous people with disability: Ethics and standpoint theory. In S. Grech & K. Soldatic (Eds.), *Disability in the Global South: The Critical Handbook* (p. 545). Springer International Publishing.

Gilroy, J., Lincoln, M., Taylor, K., Flood, V., Dew, A., Jensen, H., Barton, R., Ryall, L., & McRae, K. (2018). *Walykumunu Nyinaratjaku: To Live a Good Life*. Ngaanyatjarra Pitjantjatjara Yankunytjatjara Women's Council Aboriginal Corporation.

Gilroy, J., Ragen, J., & Meekosh, H. (2018). Decolonizing the dynamics of media power and media representation between 1830 and 1930: Australian Indigenous peoples with disability. In K. Ellis, G. Goggin, & B. Haller (Eds.), *Routledge Companion to Disability and Media*. Routledge.

Gilroy, J., Uttjek, M., Gibson, C., & Smiler, K. (2018). Yuin, Kamilaroi, Sámi, and Maori peoples' reflections on experiences as 'Indigenous scholars' in disability studies and decolonisation. *Disability and the Global South, 5*(2), 1344–1364.

Gilroy, J., Veli-Gold, S., Wright, W., Dew, A., Jensen, H., Bulkeley, K., & Lincoln, M. (2023). Disability workforce and the NDIS planning process in regional, rural and remote regions of Australia: Scoping review. *Australian Journal of Rural Health, 31*(5), 839–854. https://doi.org/10.1111/ajr.13020

Graham, F., Boland, P., Jones, B., Wallace, S., Taylor, W., Desha, L., Maggo, J., McKerchar, C., & Grainger, R. (2022). Stakeholder perspectives of the sociotechnical requirements of a telehealth wheelchair assessment service in Aotearoa/New Zealand: A qualitative analysis. *Australian Occupational Therapy Journal, 69*(3), 279–289.

Grant, E., Zillante, G., Srivastava, A., Tually, S., & Chong, A. (2017). Lived experiences of housing and community infrastructure among Indigenous people with disability. Australian Housing and Urban Research Institute.

Grech, S. & Soldatic, K. (2016). *Disability in the Global South*. Cham: Springer.

Green, A., Abbott, P., Davidson, P. M., Delaney, P., Delaney, J., Patradoon-Ho, P., & DiGiacomo, M. (2018). Interacting with providers: An intersectional exploration of the experiences of carers of Aboriginal children with a disability. *Qualitative Health Research, 28*(12), 1923–1932.

Green, A., Abbott, P., Delaney, P., Patradoon-Ho, P., Delaney, J., Davidson, P. M., & DiGiacomo, M. (2016). Navigating the journey of Aboriginal childhood disability: A qualitative study of carers' interface with services. *BMC Health Services Research*, *16*, 1–11.

Greenstein, C., Lowell, A., & Thomas, D. (2016a). Communication and context are important to Indigenous children with physical disability and their carers at a community-based physiotherapy service: A qualitative study. *Journal of Physiotherapy*, *62*(1), 42–47.

Greenstein, C., Lowell, A., & Thomas, D. P. (2016b). Improving physiotherapy services to Indigenous children with physical disability: Are client perspectives missed in the continuous quality improvement approach? *Australian Journal of Rural Health*, *24*(3), 176–181.

Hamilton, S., Reibel, T., Maslen, S., Watkins, R., Jacinta, F., Passmore, H., Mutch, R., O'Donnell, M., Braithwaite, V., & Bower, C. (2020). Disability 'in-justice': The benefits and challenges of 'yarning' with young people undergoing diagnostic assessment for fetal alcohol spectrum disorder in a youth detention center. *Qualitative Health Research*, *30*(2), 314–327.

Hamilton, S. L., Maslen, S., Watkins, R., Conigrave, K., Freeman, J., O'Donnell, M., Mutch, R. C., & Bower, C. (2020). 'That thing in his head': Aboriginal and non-Aboriginal Australian caregiver responses to neurodevelopmental disability diagnoses. *Sociology of Health & Illness*, *42*(7), 1581–1596.

Higgins, N., Phillips, H., & Cowan, C. (2013). Eighty years of growing up kāpo (blind) Māori: What can we learn about inclusive education in New Zealand? *International Journal of Inclusive Education*, *17*(8), 812–826.

Hong, Q. N., Fàbregues, S., Bartlett, G., Boardman, F., Cargo, M. & Dagenais P. (2018). The Mixed Methods Appraisal Tool (MMAT) version 2018 for information professionals and researchers. *Education for Information*, *34*(4), 285–91.

Jeffries-Stokes, C., Lehmann, D., Johnston, J., Mason, A., Evans, J., Elsbury, D., & Wood, K. (2004). Aboriginal perspective on middle ear disease in the arid zone of Western Australia. *Journal of Paediatrics and Child Health*, *40*(5–6), 258–264.

Jobling, K., Lau, P., Kerr, D., Higgins, R. O., Worcester, M. U., Angus, L., Jackson, A. C., & Murphy, B. M. (2016). Bundap Marram Durn Durn: Engagement with Aboriginal women experiencing comorbid chronic physical and mental health conditions. *Australian and New Zealand Journal of Public Health*, *40*, S30–S35.

Kake, T. R., Garrett, N., & Te Aonui, M. (2016). Cognitive neuropsychological functioning in New Zealand Māori diagnosed with schizophrenia. *Australian & New Zealand Journal of Psychiatry*, *50*(6), 566–576.

Kaomea, J. (2001). Dilemmas of an Indigenous academic: A Native Hawaiian story. *Contemporary Issues in Early Childhood*, *2*(1), 67–82. https://doi.org/10.2304/ciec.2001.2.1.9

Lambert, M., Wyeth, E. H., Brausch, S., Harwood, M. L., Anselm, D., Wright-Tawha, T., Metzger, B., Ellison, P., & Derrett, S. (2021). 'I couldn't even do normal chores': A qualitative study of the impacts of injury for Māori. *Disability and Rehabilitation*, *43*(17), 2424–2430.

Lilley, R., Sedgwick, M., & Pellicano, E. (2020). Inclusion, acceptance, shame and isolation: Attitudes to autism in Aboriginal and Torres Strait Islander communities in Australia. *Autism*, *24*(7), 1860–1873.

McGruer, N., Baldwin, J. N., Ruakere, B. T., & Larmer, P. J. (2019). Māori lived experience of osteoarthritis: A qualitative study guided by Kaupapa Māori principles. *Journal of Primary Health Care*, *11*(2), 128–137.

McInerney-Leo, A. M., West, J., Meiser, B., West, M., Toombs, M. R., Brown, M. A., & Duncan, E. L. (2022). The impact of Marfan syndrome on an Aboriginal Australian family: 'I don't like it as much as I don't like cancer'. *Journal of Genetic Counseling*, *31*(3), 620–630.

McRae, T., Adams, E., Clifton, E., Fitzpatrick, J., Bruce, K., Councillor, J., Pearson, G., & Walker, R. (2019). Overcoming the challenges of caring for a child with foetal alcohol spectrum disorder: A Pilbara community perspective. *Rural and Remote Health*, *19*(4), 1–12.

Moreton-Robinson, A. (2000). *Talkin' Up to the White Woman: Aboriginal Women and Feminism*. University of Queensland Press.

Nakata, M. (2007). *Disciplining the Savages: Savaging the Disciplines*. Aboriginal Studies Press.

Pace, R., Pluye, P., Bartlett G., Macaulay, A. C., Salsberg J., & Jagosh J. (2012). Testing the reliability and efficiency of the pilot Mixed Methods Appraisal Tool (MMAT) for systematic mixed studies review. *International Journal of Nursing Studies*, *49*(1), 47–53.

Pluye, P., Gagnon, M.-P., Griffiths, F., & Johnson-Lafleur, J. (2009). A scoring system for appraising mixed methods research, and concomitantly appraising qualitative, quantitative and mixed methods primary studies in mixed studies reviews. *International Journal of Nursing Studies*. *46*(4), 529–546.

Ravindran, S., Brentnall, J., & Gilroy, J. (2017). Conceptualising disability: A critical comparison between Indigenous people in Australia and New South Wales disability service agencies. *Australian Journal of Social Issues*, *52*(4), 367–387. https://doi.org/10.1002/ajs4.25

Sanders, D., Kydd, R., Morunga, E., & Broadbent, E. (2011). Differences in patients' perceptions of schizophrenia between Māori and New Zealand Europeans. *Australian & New Zealand Journal of Psychiatry*, *45*(6), 483–488.

Schofield, T. & Gilroy, J. (2015). Indigeniety and health. In T. Schofield (Ed.), *A Sociological Approach to Health Determinants* (pp. 99–122). Cambridge University Press.

Shen, Y.-T., Radford, K., Daylight, G., Cumming, R., Broe, T. G., & Draper, B. (2018). Depression, suicidal behaviour, and mental disorders in older Aboriginal Australians. *International Journal of Environmental Research and Public Health*, *15*(3), 447.

Sherwood, J. (2013). Colonisation – it's bad for your health: The context of Aboriginal health. *Contemporary Nurse*, *46*(1), 28–40. https://doi.org/10.5172/conu.2013.46.1.28

Smiler, K. & McKee, R. L. (2007). Perceptions of Māori deaf identity in New Zealand. *Journal of Deaf Studies and Deaf Education*, *12*(1), 93–111.

Soldatic, K. (2018a). Disability poverty and ageing in regional Australia: The impact of disability income reforms for indigenous Australians. *Australian Journal of Social Issues*, *53*(3), 223–238. https://doi.org/10.1002/ajs4.51

Soldatic, K. (2018b). Indigenous mothering and disabled children in regional Australia: 15A narrative study. In *Disability, Gender and Violence over the Life Course* (pp. 14–29). Routledge.

Soldatic, K., Somers, K., Spurway, K., & van Toorn, G. (2017). Emplacing Indigeneity and rurality in neoliberal disability welfare reform: The lived experience of Aboriginal people with disabilities in the West Kimberley, Australia. *Environment and Planning A*, *49*(10), 2342–2361.

Spurling, G. K., Askew, D., & Reath, J. (2021). Mixed-methods evaluation of screening for hearing loss using the hearScreen™ mobile health application in Aboriginal and Torres Strait Islander children presenting to an urban primary healthcare service. *Australian Journal of Primary Health*, *27*(5), 371–376.

Spurway, K. & Soldatic, K. (2016). 'Life just keeps throwing lemons': The lived experience of food insecurity among Aboriginal people with disabilities in the West Kimberley. *Local Environment*, *21*(9), 1118–1131.

Townsend, C., McIntyre, M., Wright, C. J., Lakhani, A., White, P., & Cullen, J. (2019). Exploring the experiences and needs of homeless aboriginal and Torres Strait Islander peoples with neurocognitive disability. *Brain Impairment*, *20*(2), 180–196.

Tuhiwai Smith, L. (2012). *Decolonizing Methodologies: Research and Indigenous Peoples* (2nd edn.). Zed Books.

United Nations. (2007). *Declaration on the Rights of Indigenous Peoples*. United Nations. https://www.un.org/development/desa/indigenouspeoples/wp-content/uploads/sites/19/2018/11/UNDRIP_E_web.pdf

United Nations. (2009). *State of the World's Indigenous Peoples*. United Nations.

Veli-Gold, S., Gilroy, J., Wright, W., Bulkeley, K., Jensen, H., Dew, A., & Lincoln, M. (2023). The experiences of people with disability and their families/carers navigating the NDIS planning process in regional, rural and remote regions of Australia: scoping review. *Australian Journal of Rural Health*, *31*(4), 631–647. https://doi.org/https://doi.org/10.1111/ajr.13011

12 The good, the bad and the ugly: Accommodations for Indigenous Canadian civil servants with disabilities

John T. Ward, Kevin P. Morgan, Lexi (Giizhigokwe) Nahwegiizhic and Elder Annie Smith St-Georges

12.1 Introduction

This chapter reflects the perspectives of the authors, who are Indigenous public servants, including retired (Annie Smith St-Georges), with disabilities, and who work in various departments and agencies for the Canadian federal government, on the challenges they face on many levels. These public servants include senior policy advisors, executives, and others. One of them, who is retired from the government yet provides a wealth of knowledge as an Elder, is Annie Smith St-Georges, who is an Algonquian from Kitigàn-Zibi. All of the author team, and other consulted past and present Indigenous federal workers with disability, have shared their unique lived experiences in this chapter. They have shared information about their experiences of Indigenous disabilities and knowledge systems at various locations within the government such as agencies, departments, and networks. In applying an Indigenous lens to these challenges, one must first account for whether a person has disabilities or is Indigenous, or both. Various organizations and key individuals are promoting a diverse government work environment that caters to Indigenous people with disabilities. This chapter bridges the intersectionality of Indigeneity and disability with the context of the government of Canada's public servants.

12.2 Indigenous Canadians with disability

Many Indigenous peoples and groups living in Canada and possibly around the world do not have a word for disability in their languages (Ward, 2024a). This knowledge provides a wealth of insight into why Indigenous people do not understand disabilities and learning disabilities the way settlers do. The settlers, on the other hand, also do not understand the challenges faced by Indigenous people working within the same environ as themselves. Elder Annie Smith St-Georges points to the conflicts that remain while working with white-settler employees such as the lingering effects of the

Indian Residential Schools (1950s to present day) which contributed to many mental, physical, sexual, and spiritual disabilities, and diagnostic assessments that victimized Indigenous people. All this generational trauma, when passed down, further contributes to the challenges of government employee recruitment, retention, and engagement with Indigenous peoples and communities, who have all suffered as a result of school abuse. Indigenous people must reclaim their disability as being a different way of learning, which is not the same way as settlers, so it is labelled as different – disabled. Elder Annie Smith St-Georges goes on to say that "disability labels as a colonial process limit and control people and their potential". This difference, based on a socio-cultural perspective, can have a major impact not only on how Indigenous people perceive disabilities but also on how it can bring about policy changes within the government. Indigenous knowledge believes that those with a disability are seen as 'sacred' and often 'gifted by the Creator' (Ward, 2023). Many other cultures around the world think the same way. The Public Service of Canada (the Civil Service of Canada before 1967) is the civilian workforce of the Government of Canada's departments, agencies, and other public bodies. It is from this national organization that Canadians are guided, advised, funded, and governed by the laws of Canada. It is meant to serve all Canadians including, Indigenous peoples. Indigenous people in Canada are often seen as forgotten and as third-class people concerning funding and support due to the continuous colonialism that has impacted their ability to thrive in a settler system that continues to victimize them. Changes are slowly moving forward; yet more is needed.

If one applies an Indigenous lens to the challenges Indigenous people with disabilities face in the Canadian government, one sees that the federal government's primary focus is to 'level the playing field'. Indigenous people with a disability are twice, if not three times, more affected by many social issues due to racism and other challenges (Cotter, 2022; Statistics Canada, 2024). By reflecting Indigenous differences, the 'playing field' can be levelled to include Indigenous perspectives to become more inclusive. Non-Indigenous teachers, politicians, and federal policy advisors are unaware of the social, economic, and political divide that Indigenous people live daily. This type of challenge can negatively impact Indigenous civil servants when interacting with non-Indigenous management due to a divide in cultural understanding, ways of processing knowledge (information), and even certain social attributes that could lead to miscommunication and even contribute to traumatization and termination. To do this, people need to be included in the public services; however, often they are not. However, by assessing the gifts, talents, and even cultural ways of learning by an individual, human resources or managers are able to understand a potential Indigenous employee better and are able to move beyond negative standpoints that so many Indigenous people (students and federal workers) have endured in the public service. Many Indigenous people do not have an undergraduate degree, which is essential for many jobs within the Canadian government. Traditional Indigenous knowledge is rarely given equivalence to educational expertise. This educational divide has furthered cultural barriers. An Indigenous employee's 'gifts' should best be applied to what they are good at to optimize their contribution fully. This would improve the public service in its duty to serve and reflect all Canadians and Indigenous people whom the government serves.

Indigenous people with disability face many challenges and barriers while working as a Canadian government public servant. However, many have not experienced any major changes to federal government processes, nor have been provided with tools that would help them fulfil their tasks and use their abilities to perform to the best of their abilities. It is by no means an easy task to get the right accommodations. Examples of challenges include telling managers multiple times over that one is blind and that this will not get better; asking someone to drive, who is legally blind, and having to explain it all again to senior officials. This is more than just offensive: it is just plain ignorance. For someone who has a guide dog or is in a wheelchair it is just as offensive to ask whether they still need the dog or wheelchair. Kevin Morgan has faced many such intrusive yet offensive comments about his blindness and has been constantly asked to provide proof of blindness. Therefore, he says "improvements in this area in the government are needed". These improvements will not only improve the situation for Indigenous workers with disability but also the quality of the work produced, because by including lived experience government decision-making is more relevant.

12.3 Indigenous Canadian federal government members with a disability

This section looks at the different protective measures taken by the Canadian federal government that are aimed at including an Indigenous perspective related to disabilities in relation to accessing accommodations through legal representation and internal governmental implementation. Bahner (2022) explains that the disability saying 'Nothing About Us Without Us' speaks to this sentiment and must be extended to deciding what people with disability use as methods of accommodation. This is an important step towards disability rights that allows for social justice to be achieved.

Some changes within the Canadian federal government are happening. The only intergovernmental federal group that applies an Indigenous-specific lens in Canada is the Knowledge Circle for Indigenous Inclusion (KCII). At a KCII gathering of Indigenous federal members with a disability, a collective understanding is formed through a network on Indigenous disability. This Canadian federal public service initiative was based on *Many Voices One Mind: A Pathway to Reconciliation*, which was to support Indigenous federal public servants and provide culturally appropriate support towards their development. The KCII organization decided that "the biggest needs are funding and political will to support Indigenous federal employees with disabilities" (KCII, 2024, p. 11). A KCII Elder stated, "We have suffered loss of culture and language which is a form of cultural disability due to colonization and the Indian Act" (KCII, 2024, p. 5). To address this through the public service, KCII provides a detailed list of actions required for culturally appropriate workplace accommodation based on a national survey of Indigenous federal employees with disabilities:

- Timely accommodations and supports without long wait times.

- 40% of employees report being dissatisfied with their employment. This needs to be addressed.
- Indigenous federal employees with disAbilities do not feel valued in the federal government. Change is required.
- Integration of Indigenous worldviews is needed including Elders, healers, mentors, and peers, as well as greater disability awareness.
- Elimination of attitudes and prejudices, myths, misconceptions, and stigmas towards Indigenous employees with disAbilities is needed.
- Reconciliation and access to Traditional Knowledge Holders is needed.
- Language and official language requirements are a barrier. This needs to be acknowledged and addressed.
- Essential accommodations, flexible working hours, etc., are often overlooked or ignored. Action is required.
- Policies and practices of the government are challenges to inclusiveness and hiring practices; recruiting especially, which needs to be enhanced.
- A better understanding of intersectionality is needed, such as social class, income, poverty, education, age, ethnicity, etc.
- Improvements to address barriers to accessibility such as recruiting targets, response time for requests for accommodation, computer technology, funding, built environment, etc., are needed.
- A vision shift from being a 'problem' to being seen as integral members of the Public Service is required for Indigenous Federal Employees with disAbilities (IFED) (pp. 8–10).

There may be other committees, groups, or networks, but the intersectionality of Indigenous and disability is not yet a common thread of thought in colonial organizations. Indeed, within settler-colonial academic literature, journals, and publications there is little to no intersectionality from a global Indigenous perspective, even less within Canada (Gilroy et al., 2021). The Canadian Human Rights Commission paper 'What is the Duty to Accommodate?' reveals that: "Employers and service providers must adjust rules, policies, or practices to enable them to participate fully. It applies to needs that are related to the grounds of discrimination." The Duty to Accommodate is about removing discriminatory barriers that are prohibited by the Canadian Human Rights Act. Managers should take a positive approach to accommodating people with disabilities, and do it promptly and with the support needed, such as providing tools, software, and specialized equipment that would enable the employee to fully participate in the workplace. For example, asking all job applicants to pass a written test may not be fair to a person with a visual disability. Therefore, the Duty to Accommodate requires that alternative arrangements be made to ensure that a person or group can fully participate. KCII, right now, is the only organization (federal network) that provides an Indigenous-specific lens regarding Duty to Accommodate issues for Indigenous federal public servants.

12.4 Gifted ones' perspectives on disabilities

Many Indigenous people, like the lead author of this chapter, have immersed themselves in their culture to become increasingly aware of Indigenous perspectives on disabilities such as being known as 'gifted ones', and seeing how communities embrace these gifts and help people flourish based on their gifts. Indigenous peoples and 'gifted ones' perspectives on disabilities translate into our lived experiences within the federal government. Understanding the socio-cultural belief systems of Indigenous peoples is a core part of who they are and aligns with their internal viewpoint of how disabilities are understood as a 'true disability'. This presents a challenge for obtaining the disability proof that they need in order to receive accommodations for work. Those who view disabilities as a 'gift' from the Creator do not consider them as a disability, but unfortunately, because of government rules, they may have to struggle before they get accommodations (Morgan, 2024). Thus, how they see these different cultural attributes can change the narrative of how disabilities are seen and understood from an Indigenous perspective. Once accommodated in the government, over time employers would try to understand their employees and acknowledge certain gifts or talents of their workers and begin to see the gift instead of the disability. Thus, a dialogue of understanding would take place between the employer and employee to better situate the employee. The accommodations need to be in place for this to happen.

This can be illustrated by an Indigenous person who struggles with reading and writing yet excels at oral skills – they might be best suited to giving presentations instead of writing reviews. If a candidate is nervous at public events, they might be suited for research by being behind the scenes. There is one example given by Elder Annie where a blind supervisor was perfect for the position of fire warden because, with the heavy dark smoke that blinds people, he was already well familiar with the surroundings, as he had to walk and touch his way around the office, and he could feel temperature change, and smell chemical odors and had a heightened sense of awareness to fire and smoke. The use of sign language can also be an asset in communicating with deaf employees or when giving a presentation on accessibility.

Some have the gift of orality, as Indigenous people are often gifted with great skills in oral communication along with storytelling. Another positive characteristic is a superior visual-spatial ability when one can visualize themselves walking through a building by looking at blueprints, as part of their superior 3D thinking, or even doing cartography by navigating waterways without the use of maps (Ward, 2023). Another good example of these talents was used long ago by Algonquin Elder William Commanda (1913–2011), who developed cybercartography as a natural learning ability for Indigenous people due to their superior visual-spatial talents when mapping waterways as they navigated (Thumbadoo & Fraser Taylor, 2019). Taylor (2003) defines cybercartography as "the organization, presentation, analysis, and communication of spatially referenced information on a wide variety of topics of interest and use to society in an interactive, dynamic, multimedia, multisensory, and multidisciplinary format" (p. 406). This talent of mapping out land surroundings could explain why North America is known by many Indigenous people in Canada and the USA as Turtle Island (see Figure 12.1). (How were the Indigenous people able to visualize North America as 'a turtle' without any technology or satellites?)

These hidden gifts are like a 'superpower' that can change the current colonial way of conducting research, design a human-centred approach human resources (HR) programme, or develop a new way of conducting engagement. This approach,

Source: Created by John T. Ward, 21 June 2023.

Figure 12.1 Map of Turtle Island

acknowledged by leadership/management, could provide an additional character skill – being able to assess candidates beyond their cognitive abilities. Therefore, there are other ways of assessing talent beyond the typical settler-colonial written and oral competency skills.

12.5 Managerial support for Indigenous employees with disabilities

The role of managers in supporting Indigenous employees with disabilities is an ever-changing landscape, which becomes challenging if the manager or supervisor is not Indigenous as this could contribute to misunderstandings. How Indigenous people understand 'disabilities' as actual learning differences can change inclusive and adaptive policies. It moves beyond the traditional viewpoint of acceptance to an approach of following the 'Duty to Accommodate' by acknowledging the right fit of the employee and employer, when assigning tasks and duties that not only align with the employee when performing their responsibilities but also complement their manager's role. Thus, it becomes a team effort or partner role. However, organizations should take a more culturally appropriate approach to accommodations; after all, it is not only Indigenous people who believe that those with disabilities are 'the gifted ones' (Norris, 2014; Ward, 2024b). An employee impacted may be better suited to apply their gifts elsewhere in the organization, so the employee's special talents could be tapped rather than just trying to level the playing field by assigning them the position and roles that would best utilize their natural gifts and talents.

Allies may be managers who are not Indigenous yet support those who are and actively work to promote a positive working environment. This type of encouragement can offset negative actions and avoid any traumatization and victimization of Indigenous employees, and may even lead to Indigenous clients and partners that further improve policy work. This type of developmental action towards leadership of character enables managerial supports for Indigenous peoples with disabilities and learning disabilities. It can make the biggest impact on their respective teams and ultimately the entire organization just by this act of reconcilAction, which can go far towards improving the working relationship between employer and employee.

12.6 Indigenous managerial challenges

Working in the government as an Indigenous manager with a disability, one has many day-to-day challenges, but one also develops skills, knowledge, abilities, behaviours, competencies, and various types of perspectives. In a managerial position, one starts to delegate, which doesn't mean allowing others to do your work but does mean using the position to oversee responses, which can be influenced by one's unique perspective and lived experience. The challenges of accommodations for disabled people are still as real and relevant in this context; being a manager means managing one's responsibilities and following directives from above, which could also include learning a second language as in the case of Canada.[1] One is not promoted to management if one hasn't obtained second language test results, or has not done the work in a timely fashion (even where it is because of a lack of access to accommodations). Sometimes, one waits 5–20 years for accommodations. This may mean that one may be stifled or neglected in a position, which does not provide for a good work ethic, and nor does the abuse or trauma endured by some government workers. Managers must understand that employees must be able to access the necessary accommodations to do their work and progress to manager roles themselves. Failure to adequately equip a worker with disability limits their productivity and makes them feel more disabled.

On a holistic scale the federal government is trying very hard to progress accommodations and has an easy-to-access, understandable, and seamless Duty to Accommodate process. Occasionally, an employee may also work with a director, who wants to understand the challenges and opportunities from an Indigenous perspective, even though they are not Indigenous. So, a manager, on their own, might make an effort to better understand Indigenous perspectives on a variety of issues, including disabilities and accommodations. These holistic and individual actions are necessary for advancing Indigenous disability inclusion.

12.7 Impact of Indigenous disability on the Canadian government's accommodation process

The lived experiences shared by Indigenous people with disability haven't had much impact or influence on the Canadian government's disability or accommodation strategy. Yet, they can sometimes influence or change the disability work policy enough to impact the implementation of the disability strategy. They can, for example, influence a change in the environment to suit the needs of the employee, to become inclusive of Indigenous knowledge and belief systems. Challenges concerning disability generally are the same whether one is Indigenous or not, and often the biggest challenge is being able to talk about one's challenges and how to optimize one's true gifts. Therefore, building dialogue with management can provide necessary information about the employee's talents, challenges, and other sorts of information that, if not communicated, could contribute to miscommunication, confusion, and even a feeling of isolation that can lead to poor performance reviews followed by termination due to an inability to meet working objectives.

Presentations, workshops, seminars, and various other types of training are often inaccessible to those who have hearing and vision impairments and who cannot fully participate in these work events. These should be provided via alternative methods so that all members of a team can fully contribute, and co-workers can even learn a

---

1 Managers and executives within the Canadian government must be bilingual (English and French) to keep their positions or advance in their careers. This does not apply to unilingual jobs.

new skill. A clearly laid out accommodation process includes working with a manager, a director, an Early Intervention and Return to Work (EIRTW) representative, or a Labour Relations advisor, who are well versed in the Indigenous disability field. It can also be somebody who, on their own, is making sincere efforts to bridge that knowledge gap. However, the accommodation process should be applied consistently to all who participate, regardless of their being Indigenous or having other equity-deserving status.

In the government, various networks are available such as the Indigenous Employee Network, the Person with Disabilities Network, and the Infinity Network.[2,3,4] These networks may have a different perspective than an Indigenous person with a disability, but the government is progressing in offering them. Such networks provide support for members who can share their struggles, in activities engaging in self-wellness, by being in a safe space group that can provide informative suggestions, as well as a place to present on topics that often are not always evident, such as Indigenous and disability, by merging the interests of both networks towards cooperation for inclusion. The government is thus making efforts to treat Indigenous people better, with more accessible accommodations.

12.7.1 Challenges: Speaking up and the medical model

Other than the new KCII there are only a few people who speak up about the needs of Indigenous with disability. Those who do include Kevin Morgan, who has worked for the Government of Canada for over 25 years and is a 1960s Scoop survivor[5] of Oji-Cree and French descent, from Red River Manitoba and Chippewa of North Dakota. John Ward also considers himself as someone who speaks up. He is a Métis and Non-Status Indian from the Algonquin territory of Kitchisibi, with dyslexia, attention deficit hyperactivity disorder (ADHD), and light sensitivity, who has worked within disability, learning disabilities, and dyslexia among Indigenous people in Canada, and in the Government of Canada. As Indigenous with a disability, the authors of this chapter

---

2 The Indigenous Employee Network provides support for Indigenous employees and their colleagues within the CRA and fosters awareness and inclusion of Indigenous Peoples and their cultures.

3 The CRA Person with Disabilities Network provides support for employees with disabilities, their colleagues, and managers within the Agency and promotes awareness of the importance of accessibility and the reality experienced by people with disabilities and their inclusion.

4 Infinity is a professional network made by and for neurodivergent public servants that strives to connect, empower, and drive personal and professional growth among current and aspiring public servants, who identify as neurodivergent.

5 The Sixties Scoop, sometimes referred to as The Scoop, was a period between the 1960s and 1980s when the Government of Canada, through its child welfare, authorized authorities to take, or ‘scoop up’, Indigenous children from their families and communities for placement in foster homes or to be adopted by white families to purge their Indigenous identity. Some of these children were sent as far away as New Zealand or to the USA as free child labour.

are not always vocal but are not silent as they know that their voices, stories, histories, and lived experiences pave the way for change and new understandings of how disabilities are understood and what direction to take. Kevin says that to "share about my disability and my lived experiences up … has an impact on people's knowledge, but this hasn't translated into process changes ... Procedural changes are wanted at the end of the day and an Indigenized 'Duty to Accommodate' process … That's what they want to see".

Alexis (Lexi) Giizhigokwe (Little Sky Woman) Nahwegiizhic, is a two-spirit, Ojibwe woman living with several neurodiverse medical conditions, including ADHD and dyslexia. She is from Sheguiandah First Nation in Ontario and works for the government as she has a background in neuroscience, Indigenous teachings, and mental health. She said:

> I have shared my perspective on disability, (and) individualistic differences to managers and employees using cultural teachings in my branch (and showed) my colleagues that the medical model of disability is not the only way to view disability ... my differences (do not) make me unable to do something ... My gifts being tied to an abnormality creates an awkward appreciation of my efforts. (And) the stigma in my culture/community does not use the same medical diagnostic tools and language that the western world uses, (which) creates a separate identity for who I am as an Indigenous person and who I am in society.

Medical models of disability have been used to justify, classify, and even medicate people with disabilities and learning disabilities. They are used because the diagnoses, treatments, and an assortment of therapies used for learning disabilities such as dyslexia and ADHD, etc., fall under the medical field (Runswick-Cole, 2008). However, that model of assessment can contribute to a false diagnosis of Indigenous people (Ward, 2024b), who are already over-represented in having disabilities. Kevin highlights that: "the supervisor asked me in the early days, (to) provide him with my medical documentation again as being legally blind. After (being asked) twice it becomes offensive because I am legally blind." Therefore, not using the medical model to assess disabilities would deter potential internal strife among employees and enable the lived experiences of Indigenous peoples with disabilities to influence a change to any disability policy.

12.8 Duty to accommodate disabilities

The 'Duty to Accommodate' benefits the way policy is made by increasing the diversity of knowledge available to develop policy within the Canadian public service. This is facilitated by providing specialized accommodation, but one of the many challenges that arise in actually making accommodations is the cost of such accommodation and the technical support necessary. People are challenged again and again by systems that do not work for them. It is these barriers that ultimately are the biggest challenges for moving forward for an inclusive public service. Kevin seems to have suffered the most for the longest time trying to get proper accommodations. He mentioned that the government's technical systems must always interface with a disabled staff member's adaptive software, but it is updated very frequently, including security status, so every time they make a major system change, technical issues bring a great deal of stress to the people with disability using them. If they are not fully compatible, then one's adaptive technology does not function optimally, or function at all. As Kevin explains:

> I can end up in a situation where for a period or even (longer), I am unable to perform my work duties ... My adaptive software does not function optimally, or, in some cases, I've been without it for weeks. The inability to acquire the necessary adaptive tools even after sending in multiple requests, adds to an already stressful work environment, by making a disability a real technical disability makes one become (re)disabled. (It is a) highly detrimental concern. As an employee, (I) want to give my best day after day … when I can't do that, I'm upset with the organization. I become frustrated because I try to figure out how I can do things without this.

Many public servants wonder why their departments and/or agencies do not take a more culturally specific approach, or at least a culturally nuanced approach, to the accommodations process. The employer has a responsibility to provide accommodations, but often chooses minimal supports – large print for the visual challenge of less than 25% – versus auto-read text that would more appropriately provide for needs while being able to work in a non-traumatic way.

Others sometimes confuse accommodations for special treatment. For example, one person was moved to another job at the same group and level, not a promotion, because that was where his talents were. Other people saw the sudden move as preferential treatment so someone complained about it. This process was not just levelling the playing field, but getting the most out of his talents. He could be his best and be happy and productive at the end of the day in that environment. Thus, potential conflicts can arise from coworkers and other employees; public outcry begins about whether the person competed for the job. So, there are bridges to cross for the public service as a whole to get to 'Duty to Accommodate'. This opens many doors to consider things other than just levelling the playing field. Providing reasonable accommodations, whatever they may be, allows for an employee struggling to be able to work and have a new opportunity.

Many haven't been accommodated to the best of their ability because, sometimes, the organization demonstrates an incapacity to accommodate certain disabilities as well as they accommodate others. Kevin says: "By opening our eyes to the possibilities, it's not discrimination, but it's a very myopic approach ... I think widening it for everybody is very beneficial. Many people have a disability. Many more are inviable and others may not be aware that they have a disability; yet, making excuses is their common defense, but no defense is needed because accommodations are a human right." Kevin also revealed that:

> Not a great deal (has changed) with the disability policy over the years. (However) I think those working here are more culturally competent than years ago … some more than others bring this into the standardized Duty to Accommodation process ... Every time I needed an accommodation, I am no longer asked for medical certification. So, we have progressed. We (now) have databases (where) we keep people's records intact (so they don't have to jump) through the same (hoop) … A lot has changed as the process has become faster ... people in this are more culturally competent and seek to understand so ask for shared lived experiences. This makes all the difference when a supervisor can understand your specific needs and requirements.

These changes allow for a safe work environment – a change from one that historically has been rooted in trauma, abuse, and removal from work due to mishandling and misinformation regarding accommodation as a cost-effective management approach (Cardinal, 2022).

EIRTW has been challenged over the years due to its inability to fully provide reasonable accommodations, which has caused overwhelming mental and physical trauma in some of those who are supported by this measure. The details of the process aren't working as effectively as they should; however, the overall process does, which has resulted in a streamlined approach. Kevin says,

> This process hasn't integrated an Indigenous perspective, but for those who are trying to do so … on their own, they are changing the process one person at a time ... my Return-to-Work advisor demonstrated a real desire to want to take a culturally competent, informed and lived experience, and even trauma-informed approach to grasp the challenges I face, as a blind disability Indigenous person …; the Human Resources people building our policies need to actually integrate it into their policies, otherwise, it will be people on the periphery. It will be people on the front lines that are doing it because some people want to be able to become great, while others just want to work. Those people can contribute to kinks in the production line and lead to delays in services.

Duty to Accommodate does not always consider the culture and ethnicity of a person. One's ability to be accommodated often lies with the human resource officers – the gatekeepers of this service. They are only as effective as the information received, so often managers want to help but are limited to what is listed on an employee's accessibility profile. Additional assessments regarding services needed by an employee must be discussed with an advisor, who delegates this request. A good manager asks what types of accessibility services are needed. Then, they may provide an in-person assessment advisor who may go to one's home. One person received this extra help, so within six months he received an adjustable electric desk, ergonomic chair, ergonomic mouse, ergonomic keyboard, and large mouse pad. His assistant director worked in accessibility, which was an invaluable resource when obtaining the accommodations. However, within the People with Disability and Infinity networks, some people have been waiting over 16 years for their accommodations. Additionally, a policy advisor had to work longer each day to catch up on his work schedule because he was not properly accommodated. If he had told his manager, he could have been reprimanded for working too much as it can lead to burnout. Twenty-five years later he is still working a 60-plus-hour work week because he does not have the proper accommodations in place. Processes with the front-line people need to be more culturally appropriate and congruent in all cases. The wrong front-line person will just say: "Look ... You're telling me about your Indigenous perspective on things, but ... I need to follow the policy. Here's what it says I need to do and the policy right now ... ."

Another employee shared that he has had to work 16-hour days for the last 22 years not because he wanted to, but to hide his disability. If he worked a standard 7.5-hour day, he would have been fired years ago because he had never received any sort of accommodations due to funding. However, a manager commented that "people with disabilities cost more money than normal people", so he had to work longer hours to overcome his challenges. A woman shared that because of her dyslexia, her manager excluded her from meetings and did not provide any form of accommodations, which resulted in her dismissal due to her inability to perform her full duties. Her manager was promoted to director because of his careful money management. Yet, the woman went to another federal department and within one year she received an excellence award. Two different managers with two different outcomes. Saving money should not be a reason to fire a woman who has disabilities (Cardinal, 2022).

Another employee spoke of the challenge of accessing accommodations at the higher levels of the public service and pointed to a director general, who waited over six months to obtain specialized computer programs to do his job because of being blind. Thus, even at that level, challenges still occur. If these issues of providing accommodations are not addressed promptly how can a federal leader be able to lead his team if he struggles with an accessibility issue while still performing his supervisorial responsibilities? Leading by example is a challenge in this setting. Au (2022) reveals that the Canadian federal government has implemented a national strategy to "hire 5,000 people with disabilities by 2025" (p. 15). Is it ready? Only time will tell and once we have access to the full data and hiring information from 2025 we can review it and make this judgement. However, initial data shows that the objective to hire 5000 new employees with disabilities has been exceeded with 6921 by the end of 2024 (Hunt, 2025). One of the most significant results of this hiring objective is retention – and we must support new staff with disabilities so that the 5,000 new positions will not be in vain. However, like many jobs the fluctuation reflects changes in times, which have significantly impacted the most vulnerable Indigenous and disabled - even worse amongst them are those who are both Indigenous with disabitites - due to economic changes in government that have removed part-time, fixed term, and acting positions as many of these were filled by those who were Indigenous.

12.9 Making changes in a broken system: Learning steps for HR and management

The current process in the federal government towards disability policy shows that there are many hiring managers across the public service who do not understand the prevalence of disabilities among Indigenous populations (Burlock, 2017), which in Canada is higher compared to the non-Indigenous population. The first step is education, involving specialized training for hiring managers so that they recognize different types of disabilities and learning disabilities to better understand both 'dis' and 'abilities' (Beaton, 2024). For example, someone with autism could excel at interviews, language examinations, detailed analyses, and statistical data, whereas a person with dyslexia would struggle in interviews, language examinations, and giving information without going off-topic. Yet, both dyslexia and autism have their strengths and weaknesses, which need to be acknowledged by hiring managers to properly assess each one.

This same approach needs to be applied in the workplace to combat any negative effects from disability that may significantly impact the learning and working ability of the employee. 'Training the trainers' was developed in the 1990s as a core component of Training Within Industry. The model is a framework for preparing practitioners to pass these methods and expertise on to others, who may then become trainers themselves. The initial training is typically facilitated by an outside consultant or Master Trainer. This can be used in the context of the Canadian public servant at spreading knowledge about the lived experiences of Indigenous disability needs and accommodations. This process allows for a greater realization that Indigenous people with disabilities often struggle with these differences due to the colonial restrictions placed on them, which result in indoctrination (D'Souza et al., 2023; Hairston, 2011). Thus, the need exists to decolonize from these settler-colonial learning approaches with a cultural training approach that would Indigenize the learning process for HR and hiring managers and enable a greater learning capacity within the federal government that would benefit the Canadian population that the public servants work for.

A disability or learning difference can become 'a superpower' or a way to benefit one's current lived experience. Most Indigenous people would not call it a superpower, as they are still on a learning journey to help them better understand and apply their 'gifts'. They are continuously developing their ability to share a common vision of the future. Kevin said: "Even though I am legally blind, those closest to me suggest that 'while I cannot see, I have great vision.'" Alexia responded: "Everyone is unique. My skills and talents are the results of my lived experience as an Indigenous person with disabilities. I am simply in a perfect job for my unique characteristics. Rather than having power, I have balance – stability." From what has been shared, government policy or HR should reshape themselves to better focus on the 'gifts' approach to disability that would inspire change beyond the general recommendations that are often presented within the 'Duty to Accommodation' policy. These should go further to allow for the talents and positive characteristics of Indigenous people, who struggle with their disabilities/differences to be able to fully embrace their unique learning styles as a way to excel, rather than struggle, in their work environment.

Many different types of accommodations can be obtained that can help alleviate the work. One blind employee, for instance, was able to receive various forms of accommodation and equipment that allowed him to fulfil his learning needs. These included:

- Handheld magnifiers
- Large font prints
- Large screen
- Adaptive software (ZoomText)
- Additional time for testing during competitive processes
- Full-time working from home exception

One of the major accommodations noted by this employee was being able to work from home during the COVID-19 pandemic. During this pandemic, there was a time when everyone was accommodated as they worked from home. One positive factor in working from home resulted in uplifting morale as many people worked effectively within their comfort zones (and lessened the environmental factors of gas consumption, traffic, accidents, and parking). One of the drawbacks was less human interaction – no networking and connecting with colleagues or people. Then the government later required that we follow a two-day return-to-office (RTO) back-to-work schedule. Regardless of how the RTO schedule impacted employees, those who learn and have mobility concerns are often more impacted, having their ability to succeed in the workplace impeded again by this decision. This two-day RTO schedule ignited a national strike as people with disabilities were overlooked as it systemically impacted the needs of all those who required specialized equipment such as ergo chairs, distraction of movement, and even the use of private rooms. The challenge to equip accessibility concerns at home and in the office was costly, so those who needed accommodations had to choose where to use their accessibility equipment. Moving equipment back and forth is prohibitive. Some people and groups were thus exempt from returning to onsite office work, which required a case-by-case review. Group exceptions and extensions have now come to an end. Thus, starting 9 September 2024, over one year, employees in this situation were required to gradually return to an onsite presence. This must consider real property constraints. Additional data on how the three-day RTO can work is required. However, if requirements for accommodations and accessibility are not met in the workplace, then people will fall through the cracks, which contributes to the anxiety, stress, and trauma of being a disabled federal public servant.

The biggest changes the government is starting to see generally are that regardless of Duty to Accommodate or service to Canadians, the organization is incrementally and increasingly becoming culturally competent. This goes beyond accommodations. The Canada Revenue Agency (CRA), for example, excels in working with Indigenous with disabilities as they offer training, information sessions, and consultations with Indigenous and equity groups. This influences policy, as this diversity breeds innovation, creativity, and a better service to Canadians. Recognition of Indigenous people with disabilities should be further embedded in policies and procedures, ultimately to encourage those who are less inclined to act, so that the whole public service moves in a direction to benefit even those struggling to reach out due to past inaction and discrimination. However, this depends on management. There is a long way to go but things have changed, with the federal government making significant advancements, such as the Indigenous Language Act,[6] Accessible Canada Act, and the Plain Language Act, along with many other policies aimed at combating barriers to employment.

The CRA cares about culture, so is much more culturally competent than before. Thus, Indigenous perspectives increase year after year. They created a 'decolonizing of our language' as a form of reconciliation to settler-colonial terms, expressions, and language in work ethic documents, and developed sharing circles as an Indigenous method for understanding sensitive topics such as trauma, workplace trauma, employment recruitment challenges, etc. These sharing circles are similar to yarning circles. Both place a situation or topic in the middle for discussion. These lead in turn to national Indigenous disability circles to help those who have struggled and become victimized due to their disabilities. The government is already incorporating circle pedagogy and its many Indigenous approaches to learning, which can benefit all parties by better incorporating Indigenous knowledge into government policymaking. Working from within can be the most challenging process in achieving accessibility, as well as respect beyond appearance and learning differences. Yet, our differences make us who we are, and we can provide our unique characteristics by serving the Canadian population and, above all, reflecting our differences to make better policy. In September 2025 a joint program between the Ministries of Employment and Social Development of Canadaand Indigenous Services Canada offered a sharing circle for Indigenous people with a disability for non-executives we and executives as the first of its kind and as a participating member the raw emotions, traumas, and confusion couldfinally be shared and brought to light, knowing that senior Indigenous members at the highest level were there for them beyond a political gesture as true supports in this time of great need

12.10 Recommendations for improving the inclusion of the public service

There are specialized accessibility services and accommodations that hiring managers can utilize. However, detailed training to support specific characteristics such as those related to dyslexia, ADHD, autism, and even light sensitivity would increase the hiring capacity as interviews pose a significant challenge for certain neurodiverse people. Specific HR training could lead to processes that work to avoid having certain people such as dyslexics fail interviews, written tests, struggle with demand speech, and go off-topic. One important measure to providing effective accommodations

6 The basis for the Indigenous Language Act was to support "the efforts of Indigenous Peoples to reclaim, revitalize, maintain and strengthen Indigenous languages" as not learning or using a language has disabled many Indigenous people, and learning a colonial language (English or French) has recolonized and retraumatized Indigenous federal workers. Ward (2024a) explains that the need to use a traditional language supports their development as some Indigenous people process information by following the syntax of their language, which for a non-speaker has been referred to as dyslexia – learning disabilities.

from one agency/department to another would be to implement a protocol that could benefit all government areas. This could be conducted by HR advisors, who could deliver national directives which would cover all federal public service employees. These directives would ensure that, if people moved around the country, they could access the service. This would go hand and hand with the Accessibility Act, which enables a national initiative that follows the employee to fully embrace the disability slogan of 'Nothing About Us Without Us'. These two federal initiatives would enable a gradual acceptance by the government that would ensure employers can support and manage accessible services from HR and managerial support, which would then support their employees.

The current government disability policy, generally, could be optimized by the government by including various perspectives of equity-seeking groups and Indigenous people with disabilities alongside that of networks. This merger could provide an overall response to accessibility and accommodations that would include the socio-cultural perspectives of federal public servants with disabilities who work to serve the public. From an Indigenous perspective, a need exists to create a learning product such as how to engage in culturally appropriate discussions on accommodations, and best job fit, which could be used across the federal public service. Eady and Keen (2021) reveal that traditional Indigenous learning methods such as yarning circles generate insightful information as to what has occurred, what is missing, and what needs focus. Presentations from outside organizations or by other agencies/departments on what they have implemented can provide additional insight into the design of learning products. This would help hiring managers and others involved in accommodations to better understand why disabilities are so prevalent among Indigenous people and the Indigenous people's perspectives on disabilities.

An ombudsperson is usually tasked with handling complaints and mediates as a spokesperson for the rights of a particular person or group, so would be trusted to advocate on behalf of Indigenous peoples with disabilities, and possibly for Indigenous peoples more broadly. A disability ombudsperson or an ombudsperson for accessibility in the compacity of each organization within the federal public service would help matters a great deal. For example, if someone felt that their accommodation process was not flowing exactly how it should, the ombudsperson would have the ability to make real changes by officially advocating for these changes through their position (Farrell, 2013). However, not every federal department or agency has an ombudesperson which means that disability organizations as well as Indigenous peoples are often without an ombudsperson, further contributing to anxiety and trauma because of the inability to resolve conflict or trauma. Thus, an ombudsperson could do more than just ensure the public service accommodates people. From an Indigenous perspective, the concerns raised earlier in this chapter warrant considering this. Knowing that change would eventually occur is one solution. Real change must begin with support from a whole organization stance. One employee said that he had pitched this idea in years past and was told that it was actually "a very good idea", but it was thought that "if Indigenous people have one, then other networks and groups would have to have one too". It could bring changes to the government, but it is not viewed as a cost-effective response.

When a hiring manager and an employee have taken a culturally appropriate and innovative approach to the accommodations process, a mechanism is needed where one is allowed to share success stories, which would empower others to do more, to seek out help, and to address areas of concern. It would thus breed more success. Stories are a powerful tool that Indigenous people have used since time immemorial. Another employee suggested that they should: "stop seeing accommodations as a service for some people and view them as a customization process for others to build their ideal work environment. The (government) should (also) eliminate having to identify with a disability to access productivity/accessibility tools."

The Treasury Board of Canada (2023) did a survey, which revealed that:

- 39% of survey respondents identified employment as the most important area in which to improve accessibility
- 14% of respondents suggested that the government raise awareness and change attitudes about accessibility by:
- Leading by example, and
- Having more people with disabilities in government
- 15.6% of the Canadian workforce (aged 25 to 64) is made up of people with a disability.
- between 2017 and 2018 "only 5.3% of public servants self-identified as a person with a disability [while] 2.9% identified as a person with a disability, when applying for a position".

Therefore, the government needs to build on this knowledge by engaging external experts to seek ways to Indigenize the current Duty to Accommodate process and make real change in the workplace. The British Colombia Aboriginal Network on Disability Society or the Deaf First Nation of Ontario can both provide insight and direction on engagement, including providing accessibility to Indigenous members. Other internal experts can provide advice on how to accommodate Indigenous people; we're the ones that can help them achieve their goals and expectations. These experts could help alleviate much of the lack of action surrounding the intersectionality of Indigeneity and disability, which is an area that is not well-supported (Ward, 2023) and not well-researched (Gilroy et al., 2021). Including various Indigenous partners in the conversation and drawing on research, such as examples of workplace situations, and ways of providing supports through sharing circles and wellness programmes, could contribute to the overall success of addressing disabilities for Indigenous people within the federal government.

The CRA is much further ahead when it comes to Indigenous peoples, as it offers access to Elders, KCII networks, and various other supports, which include an Indigenous service division; but when it comes to Indigenous plus disability, it is more problematic. The CRA also offers sharing/yarning circles as a way of cleansing the mind, which has led to it being a leader in offering Indigenous circles for National Reconciliation Day (30 September). As they are not practitioners in this field, there are no experts who can help in the training. More work is needed as this is an ever-changing landscape with new challenges arising. With the hiring of more Indigenous people and Indigenous senior executives, changes will come into effect. Kevin Morgan (2024) reveals that "at times, it feels that within the federal public service there are so many Indigenous people with disabilities, and we have so much experience that we could just work it all out ourselves (within the government) …". Kevin provides insightful information as a senior Indigenous blind advisor about his accessibility challenges. The federal government cannot be accused of not making any effort – it is – but the services it offers are limited. The question arises: How can federal public servants serve the public, if we struggle with our own challenges? More needs to change and we hope that, through this publication, a direction can emerge towards reconciliation of inclusion, which would become a reconcilAction by doing through leading.

12.11 Conclusion

How can public servants help the people they are tasked to help if they are struggling with their internal strife? A driving force for change at the time of writing was a person who advocated and connected with many – including the lead author of this chapter – Yazmine Laroche, Deputy Minister of Public Service Accessibility (2023) who said: "One of my first goals has been what can I do to make a difference, to make sure that I won't ever be the only visible disabled Deputy Minister in the public service in Canada? We have a way to go."

Through dialogue, presentations, workshops, and various support networks the *minibimaadiziwin* (the good life – as this Ojibway meaning would suggest) could contribute to a best practice for Indigenous employees and, indeed, for all federal public servants who have disabilities, to show them that they are not alone and that there are solutions. In terms of this volume further, inclusive research, led by Indigenous with disabilities, is essential for improving practices. Let the voices and experiences included here be the jumping-off point for future research in all of these areas, to enable better inclusion of lived experiences in the Canadian public service and thus the policies that it produces.

This chapter has shared the wisdom and lived experiences of several Indigenous peoples with disabilities within the federal government of Canada, and this is a good way to start as we need to see better approaches to accessibility among federal public organizations. It should help facilitate an ease of transition both for employees with disability and those Indigenous people with disabilities. By making these changes, real change can begin, which can influence policy within the government. Still, strides are to be made with all the diversity that reflects the Canadian population and the federal organization, which should be the leader in this area. Leading by example allows the federal government to step up to discrimination by supporting those who need help, and not just giving assurances that things will change.

References

Au, K. (2022). Call for the Federal Public Service to create an initiative to recruit and hire employees with Autism: How they can become more diverse, agile, and higher performing while improving staff retention rates and reducing staffing/training costs. *Canadian Journal of Autism Equity*, *2*(1), 11–17.

Bahner, J. (2022). Nothing about us without ... Who? Disability Rights organisations, representation and collaborative governance. *The International Journal of Disability and Social Justice*, *2*(2), 40–64.

Beaton, T. (2024). *Specialized Training for HR and/or Managers – Disabilities*. Kitchener, ON: Disability Inclusion Learning Solutions that Work.

Burlock, A. (2017). *Women with Disabilities*. Ottawa, ON: Statistics Canada.

Cardinal, M.-L. (2022). Understanding the challenges of obtaining accessibility in the government. Interviewed by John T. Ward on 1 July 2022.

Cotter, A. (2022). Experiences of discrimination among the Black and Indigenous populations in Canada, 2019. *Juristat: Canadian Centre for Justice Statistics*, 1–14.

D'Souza, P., Nayak, B., Bhumika, T. V., Dickson, K., & Oliver, S. (2023). Indigenising systematic reviews with a collaborative model of 'training the trainers'. *Nurse Researcher*, *31*(4), 14–20.

Eady, M. J. & Keen, J. (2021). Employability readiness for Aboriginal and Torres Strait Islander students: Yarning circles as a methodological approach to illuminate student voice. *Journal of Teaching and Learning for Graduate Employability*, *12*(2), 1–18.

Farrell, N. J. (2013). *The Canadian Ombuds/man/person: Impartial and Independent Aspirational, Achievable or Impossible?* York University, Toronto: PhD in Law.

Gilroy, J., Uttjek., M., Lovern, L., & Ward, J. (2021). Indigenous people with disability: Intersectionality of identity from the experience of Indigenous people in Australia, Sweden, Canada, and USA. *Disability and the Global South*, *8*(2), 2017–2093.

Hairston, P. G. (2011). *The Power to Promote Justice: A Train-the-Trainer Model for the Development of Culturally Competent Teaching Practices Among Secondary Educators*. Wright State University: PhD Dissertation.

Knowledge Circle for Indigenous Inclusion. (2024). *Indigenous Federal Employees with disAbilities (IFED) Survey Summary Report Equal Access – Equally*. Ottawa, Ontario: Indigenous Cultures, Protocols and Accessibility Resource Centre.

Knowledge Circle for Indigenous Inclusion. (2024). *Indigenous Federal Employees with disAbilities (IFED) Survey Summary Report Equal Access – Equally*. Ottawa, Ontario: Indigenous Cultures, Protocols and Accessibility Resource Centre.

Morgan, K. P. (2024). To see or not to see: Am I blind or is that just another colonial label. In *Indigenous Disability Studies* (pp. 71-82). Routledge.

Norris, H. (2014). Colonialism and the rupturing of Indigenous worldviews of impairment and relational interdependence: A beginning dialogue towards reclamation and social transformation. *Critical Disability Discourse*, *6*, 53–79.

Runswick-Cole, K. (2008). Between a rock and a hard place: Parents' attitudes to the inclusion of children with special educational needs in mainstream and special schools. *British Journal of Special Education*, *35*(3), 173–180.

Statistics Canada. (2024). Half of racialized people have experienced discrimination or unfair treatment in the past five years. https://www150.statcan.gc.ca/n1/en/daily-quotidien/240516/dq240516b-eng.pdf?st=uoECcw5J

Taylor, D. R. F. (2003). The concept of cybercartography. In M. P. Peterson (Ed.), *Maps and the Internet*. Amsterdam: Elsevier, pp. 405–420.

Taylor, D. R. F., Anonby, E., & Murasugi, E. (2019). Further developments in the theory and practice of cybercartography: International dimensions and language mapping (3rd edn.).

Cambridge, MA: Elsevier. (Chapter 15: Storytelling and cybercartography: The William Commanda story. *Modern Cartography Series*, 9, 247–278.)

Treasury Board of Canada Secretariat. (2023). Employment: Accessibility strategy for the Public Service of Canada. https://www.canada.ca/en/government/publicservice/wellness-inclusion-diversity-public-service/diversity-inclusion-public-service/accessibility-public-service/accessibility-strategy-public-service-toc/accessibility-strategy-public-service-employment.html

Ward, J. T. (2023). *Nòswàhanà-n Wìsakedjàk of Indigenous Elders' Knowledge of Disabilities, Learning Disabilities, and Dyslexia through the Lens of Indigenous Disability Methodologies.* Ottawa, ON, University of Ottawa Press: PhD Thesis.

Ward, J. T. (Ed.). (2024a). *Indigenous Disability Studies*. Taylor & Francis.

Ward, J. T. (2024b). How colonialism contributed to the racialized history of Indigenous People by unethical diagnostic implementations of categories and classifications – overlooking exceptionalities. *Roeper Review*, *46*(2), 160–169.

13 Radical disability disclosure: How to encourage an invisible community to engage in disability policymaking

Téa Rundback

13.1 Introduction

I acknowledge the Wodi Wodi people as the Traditional Owners of the land upon which this chapter was written and I pay respects to Elders past, present, and emerging.

My name is Téa Rundback and I am a proud neurodivergent, disabled woman currently living in New South Wales, Australia. I am writing this chapter because doing so aligns with what I currently choose to do with my life, which is applying my lived experience, skills, and education to create a positive impact on the lives of others with invisible disabilities and neurodivergence. I am a disability activist, business owner, consultant, lived experience researcher, speaker, emcee, and entrepreneur. My research interests include the topics of invisible disabilities, neurodivergence, and disability employment. I am Autistic and have attention deficit hyperactivity disorder (ADHD). I also have multiple autoimmune syndrome, which basically means I collect autoimmune diseases like Pokémon at this point (I really don't want to catch them all). I have a Bachelor of Commerce with Distinction majoring in Human Resource Management, and I am a trained psychosocial recovery coach. My goal is to help others, particularly those with similar lived experiences to attain and maintain employment. I have pursued this goal with tenacity and in a variety of ways, such as supporting my client to pursue higher education and navigate their journey to finding employment and speaking about my employment journey at an event for invisible disabilities. I hope one day to have the opportunity to experience pursuing my overarching goal while being employed.

In this chapter I propose a lived experience-informed concept called Radical Disability Disclosure (RDD) with the aims of helping to overcome barriers to safely disclosing disability in the workplace, encouraging the engagement of people from the invisible disability community in disability policymaking, and exploring what RDD might mean for disability employment policy in general. Next, I will introduce and critically discuss the concept of Radical Disclosure of an invisible disability in the workplace, and in particular its related barriers, enablers and potential outcomes. Thereafter, I will bring in a case study where I will talk about my practical experiences of RDD and link these experiences to the relevant policy context – i.e., Australian disability employment-related policy. Finally, I will discuss what RDD might mean for Australian disability employment policy and future research directions.

13.2 What is radical disclosure of an invisible disability?

For me, being a young woman living with invisible disabilities has been quite lonely. It feels like I am part of this invisible community that I can only access if I disclose my disability. Invisible disabilities are not immediately apparent, except under unusual circumstances, and include conditions like chronic illnesses, mental ill-health, and learning disabilities (Norstedt, 2019; Santuzzi et al., 2014). People with invisible disabilities have the privilege and burden of choice – the choice of whether to disclose their disability. The disclosure of disability, especially invisible disabilities, involves individuals revealing their disabilities to others, such as employers or colleagues (Dalgin & Gilbride, 2003). Disclosure can lead to receiving necessary accommodations but also carries risks of stigma and discrimination (Toth & Dewa, 2014).

While disclosure of disability in the workplace is described in the academic literature as noted above, to my knowledge I am not aware of the availability of any formal definition of RDD. Radical is defined as "very different from the usual or traditional" (Merriam-Webster, n.d.). What follows are my ideas around why RDD is 'radical' as per this definition.

Disability is part of being human (World Health Organization, 2023). But what happens when you are scared that revealing your lived experiences of invisible disability in the workplace will result in negative consequences (e.g., discrimination)? I was raised in a home where a strong work ethic was role-modelled and employment was viewed as a vital part of maturing into an adult. When I was a child, I wanted to be a veterinarian because I always felt a better connection to and understanding of animals in contrast to the people around me. However, when I realised that lifting heavy animals all day would take a negative toll on my disabled body, I decided that I wanted to work in a corporate environment like my Mum did. I wanted to be employed in meaningful work (passion), have water cooler conversations with colleagues who I got along well with (connection and belonging), and earn a comfortable amount of money that would support my independence as well as having my pets of choice (security). I thought that I would take the path of finishing high school, graduating from university, and then starting work in my field of choice. As I grew up, I realised that my journey towards this picture-perfect life was not going to be typical and was going to require a level of flexibility and adaptability.

When I was a teenager, my Mum told me that in order to be successful at work I must never disclose my disabilities. This is a common narrative for people who can go through life 'passing' as non-disabled. This is evidenced by Dolan (2023, p. 691) when they described the experience of recognising similar ADHD characteristics in another academic and asked "You have ADHD, don't you?", and being met with the response, "Indeed, I do have ADHD. But if you ever tell anyone, I'll deny we ever met." I know my Mum had the best of intentions as a woman who also lived with invisible disabilities (i.e., multiple sclerosis) and she wanted to protect me and my future career/job prospects. This worry and fear that my mother projected onto me with this message was not unfounded. Disclosing disabilities such as multiple sclerosis can lead to the need for workplace accommodations, which may not always be positively received by employers (Frndak et al., 2015).

So, what is the 'radical' part of Radical Disability Disclosure? Disclosing invisible disabilities in the workplace can lead to both positive outcomes, such as receiving necessary accommodations, and negative outcomes, like experiencing stigma (Lindsay et al., 2019). Recognising that a lot of people, for valid reasons, won't disclose in the workplace is what makes proudly and confidently disclosing invisible disabilities 'radical' in a sense.

13.3 Radical disclosure of an invisible disability in the workplace and its barriers, enablers, and potential outcomes

There are wide-ranging barriers that stand in the way of RDD in the workplace. Starting with ableism, this barrier involves the fear of discrimination, stigma, and prejudice as well as worries about the accommodations received as a result of disclosure being perceived as unfair by work colleagues, who may view them as getting 'special treatment' (Santuzzi et al., 2014). Another barrier occurs when a person tells someone to not disclose their invisible disability, which usually results in that person sharing the same advice with others. This in turn produces silence, and saneism, stigma, and discrimination, as all thrive in such silence (Procknow, 2017).

RDD involves not being silent. However, RDD demands safety. In order for people to disclose their invisible disabilities they need to feel psychologically safe (Haque, Stein, & Marvit, 2021). To increase psychological safety, it will be vital that people, including workplace leaders in positions of influence, be role models by engaging in RDD. An example of engaging in RDD could include managers being open and speaking about their invisible disabilities and sharing about their access needs, which could encourage others to speak up or to start learning about their own accessibility requirements. The more people who are seen to disclose their invisible disability in safe work environments, the more likely that others with invisible disabilities will be encouraged to disclose (Norstedt, 2019). The more who disclose, the greater the opportunities for contact with people with invisible disabilities in the workplace, which, in addition to education, can help to address ableism (Santuzzi et al., 2014).

Workplaces with a strong positive corporate culture and climate are more likely to support successful employment outcomes for people with disabilities, with these workplaces implementing best practices like diversity training, affinity groups, and corporate diversity councils to enhance the inclusion of individuals with disabilities (Schur et al., 2005; Schur et al., 2009; Madera, 2013). Therefore, another way to overcome or at least reduce ableism-related RDD barriers might involve creating a Disability Employee Network (DEN) within the workplace, being an employee-led group with voluntary participation (Australian Human Rights Commission, n.d.). A key role of a DEN involves building awareness about disability within the workplace. By providing a platform for employees to share their experiences and discuss the challenges they face, DENs could facilitate greater understanding and acceptance of disabilities, particularly invisible ones, among all employees (Madera, 2013). The act of participating in a DEN at your workplace is a way of engaging in RDD, as it openly acknowledges and validates the existence of disabilities, thereby normalising them in professional settings. Moreover, DENs could provide a support network for individuals who may be contemplating whether to disclose their invisible disabilities. Seeing others actively participating in a DEN and sharing their experiences may inspire those who have yet to disclose to consider doing so. The visible presence of a supportive community that acknowledges and values disability could potentially reduce the perceived risks associated with disclosure, making it more likely for individuals to engage in RDD. By fostering an environment where disability is openly discussed and embraced, DENs can empower employees to disclose their disabilities confidently, leading to positive changes in workplace culture and disability employment policy (Kulkarni, 2016). In this way, DENs not only support individual members but also contribute to the broader movement towards inclusivity and acceptance of disabilities as a normal part of workplace diversity.

I envision that RDD has the potential to drive awareness of how prevalent invisible disabilities are in society, while also supporting experiences of empowerment among this cohort in the workplace. Positive and empowering outcomes of RDD could also include not having to conceal a potentially stigmatising identity, saving cognitive resources and energy from not having to mask, reducing feelings of isolation, and facilitating social support connections with other people with disability (Santuzzi et al., 2014). I see the ultimate goal of RDD being to facilitate movement from awareness to acceptance of invisible disability as a normal part of being human in workplaces and elsewhere.

13.4 My experience of radical disability disclosure

Now, my ideal career path involves using my lived experience of disability and neurodivergence, education, and skills to help people with disability attain and maintain employment. In Australia, however, there is a significant gap in employment rates between people with disability and people without disability, with lived experience of disability currently undervalued in Australian disability services (Mellifont, Smith-Merry, & Bulkeley, 2023; Davies & Butler, 2023). So, as a disabled woman living in Australia who would potentially like to work in Australian disability services, it's not looking good! It is for this exact reason that I have chosen to engage in and write about RDD as a radically different approach to what I was told to do while growing up.

I am not saying that engaging in RDD isn't hard or scary. There have been two instances thus far where I have taken the opportunity to wield the power of a microphone and had an audience to influence, which provided me with a platform to engage in RDD. My first engagement in RDD was during my speech at the 'Sunflower and a Smile High Tea' event hosted by the City of Sydney and SSI, where I spoke about my lived experience and employment journey during the weeks surrounding International Day of People with Disability 2023 (City of Sydney, 2023). I originally called the host to enquire about attending the event but was told that the tickets had sold out. However, during the call, they casually mentioned that they were still looking for a few speakers. I jumped on the opportunity to be a speaker, despite never having done it before. I spent a lot of time and energy writing my speech. I also sought advice from friends and family; one of whom raised the question of whether I should be making the speech in the first place, since it was voluntary and it could have negative consequences for my career, such as making securing employment more difficult. The night before I was meant to present my speech, I had the overwhelming realisation of: "Oh my god, I'm about to tell a bunch of people that I'm Autistic." I have only been diagnosed with Autism as an adult within the last few years and I am still learning what it means for me today. This reaction is a reflection of the internalised ableism I felt, and my fear of the stigma and how I would be perceived due to the lack of education surrounding Autism that exists (Baldwin, Costley, & Warren, 2014). Even though I was nervous, I felt very strongly about delivering my speech and engaging in RDD (which I mentioned during my speech) as I believed that it would help others by normalising disability. I was also strongly motivated by my overarching goal of helping people to attain and maintain employment.

The most recent event, and by recent I mean that it actually occurred a few days ago from the time that I am writing this sentence, was when I had the opportunity to be the emcee for the National Disability Service's Disability at Work 2024 conference in Sydney. I was once again in a position of embarking on a new venture, having never been an emcee before. However, this time the stakes were significantly higher. At the previous event where I presented my speech, there were about 50 people in the audience who were from a variety of walks of life. In contrast, there were approximately 300 people at the 2024 National Disability Services conference, approximately 90% of whom I believe were in positions that could have an impact on the future of my career; whether that be good or bad. Right before I was about to walk onto the stage to introduce myself as the emcee, I had the same "Holy shit, am I about to tell everyone here that I'm disabled and Autistic?!" thoughts running through my head, just as I did when I first engaged in RDD for my speech about my lived experience and employment journey. I am proud that, despite the raised stakes, I continued to choose to engage in RDD, and I hope that by doing so I was able to have a positive impact on my community by normalising discussions surrounding health and disability. I also had a fun ongoing joke, which was not really a joke, that I am currently open to flexible part-time employment and/or other paid opportunities, because I want to move out of my parent's house. By engaging in RDD at the start of the event, I feel reassured that any opportunities that arise will be offered knowing that I am a proudly disabled and neurodivergent woman. I received overwhelmingly positive feedback from the event attendees and look forward to continuing to engage in RDD in the Disability Employment sector.

13.5 What could RDD mean for Australian disability employment policy and future research?

The perspective of people with lived experience of disability is critical to disability policymaking and will benefit all Australians (Gauntlett, 2020). About 4.4 million people in Australia have disability (Australian Institute of Health and Welfare, 2022). There is limited data on the prevalence of invisible disabilities; however, a statistic commonly referred to in digital media states that approximately 90% of the 4.4 million people with disabilities in Australia live with an invisible disability (Advanced Personnel Management, 2023; Australia Wide First Aid, 2023; University of Sydney, 2021). The Australian government is required by the United Nation's Convention on the Rights of Persons with Disabilities to engage people with disabilities in the design of policies relevant to their lives (Quilliam et al., 2022). Therefore, the high numbers of people living with invisible disabilities in Australia reported in the media, as mentioned above, highlights the importance of encouraging the inclusion of their lived experience and expertise in co-developing disability policymaking. Furthermore, if RDD occurs in the workplaces of Australian policymakers it could encourage Australian policymakers to disclose their invisible disabilities and support the employment goals of existing policies; see for example the Australian Public Service Disability Employment Strategy 2020–2025 (Australian Public Service, 2020).

With my major in Human Resource Management, the first thought that came to my mind when considering what RDD could mean from a human resources policy perspective was: "Okay, let's consider the possibility that more people with invisible disabilities start radically disclosing their disabilities in the workplace after reading this super great chapter. Now what?" I anticipate that there will be an increased demand for co-designed workplace disability employment policies and procedures relating to disclosure and reasonable accommodations within the Australian Public Service and beyond. I also foresee an increased demand for workplace education and disability confidence training. Additionally, I hope that RDD will result in changes to higher educational courses like Human Resource Management in the form of disability being considered as an integral topic to be included and valued, rather than the afterthought that it seemed to be back when I completed my degree.

Research topics that I hope once addressed will help to advance greater knowledge about RDD and its practical implications for people with invisible disabilities in the workplace include research to investigate: competing constructions of RDD as informed by people with invisible disabilities; RDD related barriers, enablers, and outcomes that extend beyond those discussed in this chapter; the prevalence of RDD of invisible disabilities across Australian workplaces; and whether RDD occurs more frequently in Australian public or private organisations. These research topics will assist in addressing the policy issue of people with invisible disabilities not feeling safe to disclose and will provide a much broader picture of what RDD can be and the context around it.

13.6 Conclusion

In conclusion, RDD offers a transformative approach to addressing the barriers that individuals with invisible disabilities face in the workplace. By fostering an environment of psychological safety and encouraging open discussions about disabilities, RDD holds the potential to significantly reduce stigma and promote acceptance. This chapter has highlighted the importance of creating supportive workplace networks, such as Disability Employee Networks, and engaging role models in leadership positions to normalise disability disclosure. Through personal anecdotes, research insights, and future research opportunities, it is appropriate to recognise the prospects of RDD to support societal change and support more inclusive disability employment policies in Australia. However, further research is needed to explore RDD's implications and to inform the co-development of national disability employment and workplace policies that embrace the unique experiences of those with invisible disabilities. Ultimately, the goal of RDD is to move from awareness to a broader acceptance of invisible disabilities, recognising them as an integral part of human diversity in both workplaces and society. To achieve this, policy has a vital role in shifting from compliance-based approaches to creating cultures of psychological safety, where disclosure is enabled and valued as a driver of inclusion.

References

Advanced Personnel Management. (2023). Invisible disabilities: What are they, and how can we support them? APM. https://apm.net.au/job-seekers/resources/invisible-disabilities-what-are-they,-and-how-can

Australia Wide First Aid. (2023). Understanding invisible disabilities: A comprehensive guide. https://www.australiawidefirstaid.com.au/resources/understanding-invisible-disabilities

Australian Human Rights Commission. (n.d.). Advocating for disability employment. Australian Human Rights Commission. https://humanrights.gov.au/our-work/disability-rights/establishing-disability-employee-network

Australian Institute of Health and Welfare. (2022). People with disability in Australia 2022. AIHW. https://www.aihw.gov.au/getmedia/3bf8f692-dbe7-4c98-94e0-03c6ada72749/aihw-dis-72-people-with-disability-in-australia-2022.pdf?v=20230605172353&inline=true

Australian Public Service. (2020). Australian Public Service Disability Employment Strategy 2020–2025. https://www.apsc.gov.au/sites/default/files/2020-12/apsc_-_disability_strategy.pdf

Baldwin, S., Costley, D., & Warren, A. (2014). Employment activities and experiences of adults with high-functioning autism and Asperger's disorder. *Journal of Autism and Developmental Disorders*, *44*(10), 2440–2449.

City of Sydney. (2023). Sunflower and a Smile High Tea. City of Sydney.

Dalgin, R. S. & Gilbride, D. (2003). Perspectives of people with psychiatric disabilities on employment disclosure. *Psychiatric Rehabilitation Journal*, *26*(3), 306.

Davies, K. & Butler, K. (2023). (Under) valuing lived experience in the disability workforce: A snapshot of Australian job recruitment. *Australian Journal of Social Issues*, *58*(2), 425–440.

Dolan, V. L. (2023). '… but if you tell anyone, I'll deny we ever met': The experiences of academics with invisible disabilities in the neoliberal university. *International Journal of Qualitative Studies in Education*, *36*(4), 689–706.

Frndak, S. E., Kordovski, V. M., Cookfair, D., Rodgers, J. D., Weinstock-Guttman, B., & Benedict, R. H. (2015). Disclosure of disease status among employed multiple sclerosis patients: Association with negative work events and accommodations. *Multiple Sclerosis Journal*, *21*(2), 225–234.

Gauntlett, B. (2020). Good disability policy benefits everyone. Australian Human Rights Commission. https://humanrights.gov.au/about/news/good-disability-policy-benefits-everyone

Haque, O. S., Stein, M. A., & Marvit, A. (2021). Physician, heal thy double stigma – doctors with mental illness and structural barriers to disclosure. *New England Journal of Medicine*, *384*(10), 888–891.

Kulkarni, M. (2016). Organizational career development initiatives for employees with a disability. *International Journal of Human Resource Management*, *27*(14), 1662–1679.

Lindsay, S., Cagliostro, E., Leck, J., Shen, W., & Stinson, J. (2019). Disability disclosure and workplace accommodations among youth with disabilities. *Disability and Rehabilitation*, *41*(16), 1914–1924.

Madera, J. M. (2013). Best practices in diversity management in customer service organizations: An investigation of top companies cited by Diversity Inc. *Cornell Hospitality Quarterly*, *54*(2), 124–135.

Mellifont, D., Smith-Merry, J., & Bulkeley, K. (2023). The employment of people with lived experience of disability in Australian disability services. *Social Policy & Administration*, *57*(5), 642–655.

Merriam-Webster. (n.d.). Radical. Merriam-Webster. https://www.merriam-webster.com/dictionary/radical

Norstedt, M. (2019). Work and invisible disabilities: Practices, experiences, and understandings of nondisclosure. *Scandinavian Journal of Disability Research*, *21*(1), 14–24.

Procknow, G. (2017). Silence or sanism: A review of the dearth of discussions on mental illness in adult education. *New Horizons in Adult Education & Human Resource Development*, *29*(2), 4–24.

Quilliam, C., O'Shea, A., Holgate, N., Alston, L. (2022). Starting with us: Imagining relational, co-designed policy approaches to improve healthcare access for rural people with disability. *Australian Journal of Rural Health*, *30*(6), 809–815.

Santuzzi, A. M., Waltz, P. R., Finkelstein, L. M., & Rupp, D. E. (2014). Invisible disabilities: Unique challenges for employees and organizations. *Industrial and Organizational Psychology*, *7*(2), 204–219.

Schur, L., Kruse, D., & Blanck, P. (2005). Corporate culture and the employment of persons with disabilities. *Behavioral Sciences & the Law*, *23*(1), 3–20.

Schur, L., Kruse, D., Blasi, J., et al. (2009). Is disability disabling in all workplaces? Workplace disparities and corporate culture. *Industrial Relations: A Journal of Economy and Society*, *48*, 381–410.

Toth, K. E. & Dewa, C. S. (2014). Employee decision-making about disclosure of a mental disorder at work. *Journal of Occupational Rehabilitation*, *24*, 732–746.

University of Sydney. (2021). Invisible disabilities: They are more common than you think. https://www.sydney.edu.au/study/student-life/student-news/2021/09/14/invisible-disabilities--they-are-more-common-than-you-think.html
World Health Organization. (2023). *Disability and Health*. WHO. https://www.who.int/news-room/fact-sheets/detail/disability-and-health

14 Co-producing knowledge to inform policy: A disabled person's reflections on processes, learnings, strengths, and challenges

Susan Wadsworth and Rachelle A. Martin

Glossary

Aotearoa:	Māori name for New Zealand.
Kāinga:	Māori term encapsulating aspects of house and home – including a sense of place and community, where one's collective identity is lived out.
Māori:	The Indigenous people of Aotearoa, New Zealand.
Te Reo Māori:	The Indigenous language of Aotearoa, New Zealand.
Te Tiriti o Waitangi:	Aotearoa New Zealand's founding document, a partnership agreement between Māori and the British Crown, signed in 1840.
Tāngata whaikaha:	Māori term for 'disabled people'; literally translated as 'people in the pursuit of empowerment'.
Whānau:	Family; can include extended family and friends who may not have kinship relationships but who are like family.

14.1 Introduction

It is critical that disabled people[1] are included in formulating comprehensive, cross-sector policies and programmes, given the impact of these policies and programmes on their health and well-being (Bhattarai et al., 2020; Frier et al., 2018; Greenhalgh et al., 2019; Jull et al., 2017; Magnusson et al., 2019; Saran et al., 2020). However,

[1] In this chapter we have chosen to use identity-first language (disabled person) or language acknowledging the Social Model of Disability ('people experiencing disability'), thereby emphasising individuals' capacities and strengths and the ways in which society disables and disempowers them.

despite the development of guidelines in Aotearoa New Zealand to support community engagement with disabled people (New Zealand Ministry of Health, n.d.), the disabled community continues to experience a lack of meaningful inclusion in policy development (Baker, 2020; New Zealand Disability Network, 2020; Tilley, 2020), with rhetoric failing to materialise into sustained action and political success (Head, 2016; Kuchenmüller et al., 2022; WHO Commission on Social Determinants of Health & World Health Organization, 2008). Additionally, disabled people have anecdotally reported that it is difficult to engage in unaccommodating policy development processes, further contributing to underrepresentation – and policymakers report challenges in achieving a broad representation of the diverse disability experiences and in synthesising their insights into a cohesive and usable form. Furthermore, there is a substantial critique of the levels of participation and partnership within these consultation processes (Crompton, 2019; Ní Shé et al., 2020; Oliver et al., 2019; Rose & Kalathil, 2019; Williams et al., 2020), which is problematic as the degree of power-sharing appears to substantially impact outcomes and authenticity of participation and contribution (Chung & Lounsbury, 2006; Goodyear-Smith et al., 2015; Jagosh et al., 2015).

To ensure tāngata whaikaha Māori[2] and disabled people in Aotearoa New Zealand achieve equitable health outcomes, their experiences, needs, and aspirations must be included in ways that can be accessed, understood, and utilised meaningfully by policy advisors at both national and local government levels. In 2013, approximately 24% of individuals in New Zealand reported disability (Statistics New Zealand, 2013), with projections indicating an increase to 27% by 2038 (Mcintosh & Leah, 2017a). Māori experience higher age-adjusted disability rates (32%) compared to non-Māori (24%) (Statistics New Zealand, 2013). There is substantial evidence of disparities in outcomes, unmet needs, and challenges in accessing health-enhancing systems and services for disabled individuals (Mccoll et al., 2010; Murray, 2019), especially tāngata whaikaha Māori within Aotearoa New Zealand (Came et al., 2016; Graham & Masters-Awatere, 2020; King, 2019; Palmer et al., 2019; Wyeth et al., 2019).

Employing participatory co-production methods in policy and programme development is argued to lead to more responsive and effective planning and service design, thereby enhancing health, well-being, and equity outcomes (Micsinszki et al., 2021; Mulvale et al., 2021; Smith et al., 2022). Co-production methods that enhance social capital and citizenship and create spaces for dialogue (Harrison et al., 2019; Ottmann et al., 2009) have the potential to improve the quality and responsiveness of health-related policies and programmes (Gelech et al., 2017; Langley et al., 2018). There is also a growing consensus on the importance of empowering individuals to co-produce meaning as a vital mechanism for ensuring that research findings translate into practical applications (Graham et al., 2018; Greenhalgh et al., 2016; Lamont et al., 2020). Therefore, to optimise equitable health outcomes for disabled people, we argue there is

2 'Tāngata Whaikaha Māori' (literally 'people in pursuit of empowerment') is a term used by disabled Indigenous people of Aotearoa New Zealand, to identify themselves.

a need to develop participatory partnership approaches supporting the creation, synthesis, and articulation of their knowledge and experiences for use by health-related policy planners (Langley et al., 2018, 2022; Micsinszki et al., 2021). However, despite the widespread adoption of participatory methodologies, research aimed at co-producing new knowledge is frequently limited in scope and impact, with the 'co' aspects constrained in intent and process and the 'production' aspects not contributing to meaningful outputs being generated (Phillips et al., 2022).

Housing is a specific health-related topic that dominates disabled people's concerns within Aotearoa New Zealand (Mcintosh & Leah, 2017b). Disabled people report difficulties accessing and maintaining kāinga, housing and home, that meets their needs and aspirations and allows them to thrive rather than just survive (Boulton et al., 2022). They want homes that meet their physical and social needs, allow full involvement with their whānau family and friends, and promote full inclusion and participation in their communities. Furthermore, inadequate housing for disabled people negatively impacts social and economic participation, and access to housing is also recognised as a key determinant of health more broadly (Maclachlan et al., 2018). However, a United Nations Monitoring Report conducted in 2018–2020 on the housing rights of disabled people under Article 33.3 of the United Nations Convention on the Rights of Persons with Disabilities found that disabled people in Aotearoa New Zealand face challenges and human rights violations when accessing adequate housing and experience a lack of control over their living situations (Donald Beasley Institute, 2022).

In the following sections, we will firstly describe the Aotearoa New Zealand disability policy context before providing an overview of the Flourishing Together research project. Next, we will describe the first author's (Susan's) involvement with this project as a disabled person while also offering some critical reflections on her participation. Finally, we will discuss implications from these critical reflections for co-designed disability research and policy that is inclusive of disabled voices.

14.2 Aotearoa New Zealand disability policy context

14.2.1 Obligations and responsibilities

Several strategies and action plans guide government agencies on disability issues, outlining obligations and providing decision-making support on issues that are important to disabled people. First, the United Nations Convention on the Rights of Persons with Disabilities (UNCRPD) (2006) was ratified by Aotearoa New Zealand in 2008 – thereby agreeing to reform laws and establish policies and processes to ensure that the rights of disabled people are protected. For example, Article 19 (Living independently and being included in the community) states: 'Persons with disabilities have the opportunity to choose their place of residence and where and with whom they live on an equal basis with others and are not obliged to live in a particular living arrangement.'

A second responsibility relates to Māori, the Indigenous people of Aotearoa New Zealand. In 1840, representatives of the Crown (represented by the Government of New Zealand) and Māori entered into an agreement, Te Tiriti o Waitangi (The Treaty of Waitangi, 1840). The Treaty provides a framework for the ongoing relationship of partnership between the Crown and Māori, protecting Māori interests, ensuring that each party has a voice in how the relationship is managed, and actively protecting Māori in the use of their lands, fisheries, forests, and other treasured possessions, both tangible and intangible. In 2018, 'Whāia Te Ao Mārama 2018 to 2022: The Māori Disability Action Plan' (Ministry of Health, 2018) was developed to support tāngata whaikaha to achieve their aspirations and to reduce the barriers they face in culturally anchored ways. 'Whāia Te Ao Mārama' builds on the promise the Crown made to Māori when signing Te Tiriti o Waitangi and recognises that everyone must work together to achieve the vision – tāngata whaikaha pursuing a good life with support.

14.2.2 Disability systems

Over the past decade, the 'Enabling Good Lives' (Ministry of Social Development, n.d.) movement – including a foundational framework, a vision, and eight principles – has guided positive change within the disability sector. Enabling Good Lives was co-designed by leaders of the disability community in 2011. They developed the transformational systems approach, hoping to increase choice and control for disabled people and their whānau (families). The eight principles include Self-determination, Beginning Early, Person-Centred, Ordinary Life Outcomes, Mainstream First, Easy to Use, Mana Enhancing, and Relationship Building; all of which are based on trusting and respecting the disabled person and their families to be decision-makers in their own life and to govern the resources used for their support. Enabling Good Lives asserts that people can bring positive change in their own lives when they are invested in, have control over resources, have access to independent allies, and build leadership within the community. The intent is to shift power and authority from the government to disabled people and their families. It is a social movement in response to the oppression of disabled people.

One of the government's responses to the UNCRPD, Enabling Good Lives, and disability community advocacy was to form a new centralised government ministry in 2022. The aim was that 'Whaikaha: Ministry of Disabled People' (www.whaikaha.govt.nz/) would partner with the community, Māori, and government to transform the current disability system in line with Enabling Good Lives principles and to create a better, more independent future for disabled people and their whānau in Aotearoa New Zealand. Guided by the voices of disabled people and working in partnership across agencies, Whaikaha strives to create systems that are easier to access and provide more choice and control over how funding is used. At the time of writing, the current government has mandated significant changes within Whaikaha: Ministry of Disabled People, moving responsibility for managing disability funding to another Ministry – the Ministry for Social Development (www.msd.govt.nz/). It is currently not clear what ongoing role Whaikaha: Ministry of Disabled People will play in disability-related policy development.

In Aotearoa New Zealand disabled people can access funding via two streams. Accident Compensation Corporation (ACC; www.acc.co.nz/) provides support and funding to those who acquire their short- or long-term impairment via an accident. The Ministries for Social Development and/or Health (www.health.govt.nz/) fund disabled people whose disability is not accident-related (i.e., from birth and acquired because of medical events). These two funding streams offer significantly different funding and support levels to disabled people, with people eligible for ACC funding receiving significantly higher entitlements, including access to housing modifications. While both are based on needs, differences in the allocation of funds, availability of equipment and modifications, and choice and control over services that can be accessed contribute to inequitable disability-related supports for disabled people.

14.3 Overview of the flourishing together project

To develop methods and tools empowering disabled people to co-produce and articulate knowledge informing equitable policy development, the Flourishing Together research project is partnering with both Māori and non-Māori tāngata whaikaha and disabled people to, as an exemplar, co-produce advice for policymakers related to kāinga, housing and home (Martin et al., 2022). We are doing this by developing a deeper understanding of how disabled people access and maintain kāinga, housing and home in ways that meet their needs and aspirations. Along the way, the project is co-designing and co-developing novel processes and methods to include whaikaha disabled persons' perspectives more effectively in future health-related policy development spaces. As detailed in Figure 14.1, the research has two primary objectives:

1. Develop co-production methods and tools supporting disabled people to contribute their knowledge and experiences to policy spaces.
2. Develop and share co-produced knowledge about kāinga, housing and home in ways that can support policy decision-making processes.

The research is structured into four phases: (1) co-developing the scope and focus of the policy question, (2) co-designing a qualitative data survey collection tool to gather nationwide data from disabled people, (3) co-designing and piloting a process to incorporate disabled people's experiences and expertise into a literature review, and (4) co-producing materials that disseminate the knowledge gained throughout the research, including co-production methods, tools, and housing policy recommendations. Phases 2 and 3 were completed mid-2025, with the dissemination phase occuring in 2025 and 2026.

14.3.1 Involvement of the co-production team

All four research phases are conducted in partnership with disabled people, called the 'co-production team' (CPT). Within a nationwide recruitment strategy, anyone who self-identified as experiencing disability was invited to participate in the CPT. One of the research team contacted each person expressing an interest, and they were asked to share their reasons for wanting to contribute and about any accessibility needs,

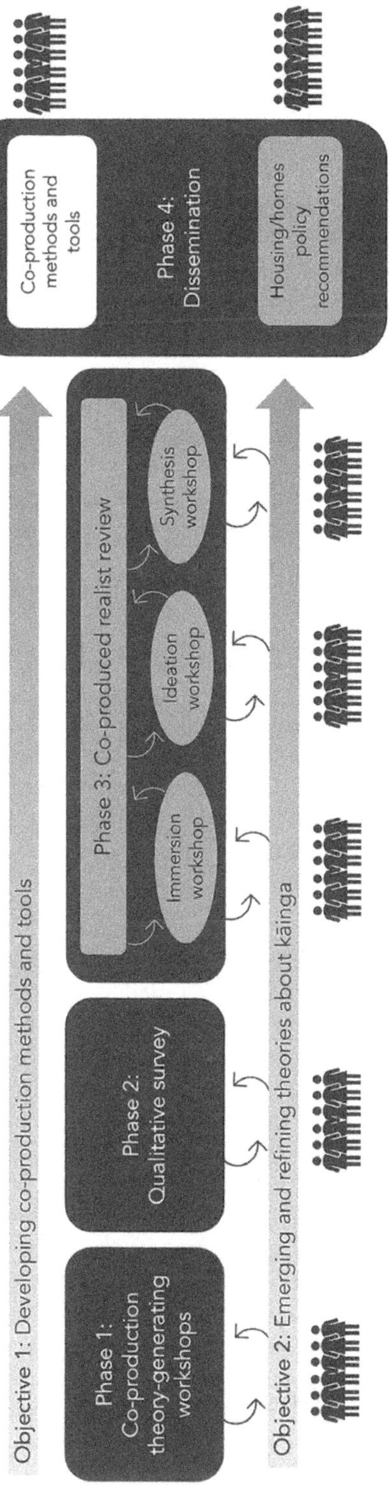

Source: Authors.

Figure 14.1 Overview of research objectives and phases

accommodation requirements, or preferences they might have in contributing to the research. The CPT has varied in number and people across the various phases; however, we have had around 15 people actively involved at any one time. To date, around 40 disabled people have contributed to this project. They come with varied disability experiences (e.g., physical impairments, sensory impairments, neurodivergence) and ages (range 20–78 years). They live in different (but mainly urban) parts of New Zealand and are predominantly female (70%).

In terms of contribution, the CPT has been involved in diverse ways, as overviewed in Table 14.1. Instead of viewing the CPT as a stable group that produced knowledge in a synchronous, linear way, we have moved to think about co-production in terms of a 'sushi train'. Instead of offering a single co-production activity that suits everyone, we provide a variety of options to the people sitting around the 'train' at any given time, and they choose what they can manage or prefer (one small tray versus a whole banquet). Of course, sushi trains only work if people engage with what is on offer – otherwise, the 'content' gets stale or loses the ability to engage potential recipients. So, the co-production process is an interdependent, iterative process, and is often a-synchronous in nature.

14.4 Susan's involvement in the flourishing together project

The following sections describe Susan's involvement in the Flourishing Together project as a disabled person and her reflections on the process. She reflects on her learnings, the tensions and challenges inherent in a co-production project, how policy development processes could be more accommodating, and the ways in which disabled voices could contribute to policy development more meaningfully.

14.4.1 Susan's involvement

I saw the Flourishing Together project advertisement and signed up as a participant. Having lived experience of disability, I was interested in the research. This was mainly because I was trying to create a home where my disability was accommodated in a way that worked for me and my family. My hope was, and is, to have a modified house that I could call home – where I would be able to live, socialise, and thrive, with my disability needs met. My challenges were mainly due to a lack of funding and resources, as well as complicated policies, regulations, and procedures. This concerned me as I was good at figuring things out and could articulate my needs, and yet it became challenging to navigate all of this while also living with a disability that causes constant pain and fatigue. I wondered how others with different disability experiences might have their needs met within this system. This sparked my interest in improving the accessibility to the systems at both central and local government levels and within the wider community. I was certain one of the most important changes required was ensuring that the people making the decisions needed to understand and be more in touch with the needs of the disabled community. I believe that this can only be attained through engagement with disabled people and hearing people's stories, not

Table 14.1 Overview of disabled people's involvement across the Flourishing Together research project

-	Aims of phase	CPT tasks	Resources offered by CPT	Modes
Phase 1: Co-production theory-generating workshops	Co-develop the scope and focus of policy question under consideration	Gathering ideas about what kāinga, house and home means to people, and what is needed to support ideal outcomes. Generating a focused research question for ongoing exploration.	Personal housing and disability experiences. Knowledge of disability support systems. Expertise related to advocacy for policy change, and from paid work roles.	1:1 meetings. Online interactive workshops. Emails. Online interactive board. Website forum.
Phase 2: Qualitative survey	Co-design a qualitative data survey collection tool to gather nationwide data from disabled people	Co-design of survey questions. Co-design of the survey, including piloting. Supporting recruitment. Analysis of survey responses. Generation of recommendations.	Phase 1 data from CPT informed survey questions. Offering personal stories to be added to the survey to facilitate responses from participants (e.g., written, video, audio files) Interpretation of demographic and qualitative data.	Online interactive workshops. Emails. Personal completion of survey - with suggestions for ongoing development. 1:1 meetings and video recording sessions. Online interactive board.

-	Aims of phase	CPT tasks	Resources offered by CPT	Modes
Phase 3: Co-produced realist review	Co-design process for including disabled people's experiences and expertise in a literature review and then test the process	Co-design of literature review process. Data screening support alongside the research team. Reading, synthesising, and feeding back on literature. Participation in interactive workshops. Generation of recommendations.	Personal housing and disability experiences. Knowledge of disability support systems. Expertise related to advocacy for policy change, and from paid work roles. Discussion and shared interpretations, additional considerations, and gaps within current evidence.	Online interactive workshops. Emails. Social media messaging tools (e.g., WhatsApp and Facebook groups).
Phase 4: Dissemination	Co-produce materials to share knowledge with policy stakeholders – both co-production of knowledge methods and tools, and housing policy recommendations.	Participation in interactive workshops to synthesise Phase 2 and 3 findings. Generation of recommendations in partnership with the research team. Review of final recommendations, including policy report.	Personal housing and disability experiences. Knowledge of disability support systems. Expertise related to advocacy for policy change, and from paid work roles.	Online interactive workshops. 1:1 meetings. Emails.

Source: Authors.

just looking at figures and graphs created from the minimal data available and collected here in Aotearoa New Zealand.

Soon after my first interview and starting my involvement in the group activities, Rachelle approached me and asked if I would like to become a paid research team member. Alongside my personal lived experience of disability, I thought I could assist with different areas of the project, utilising my networking skills, connecting, and getting people to talk to add value to conversations. I had no experience in research, but I was keen to help as the Flourishing Together project was very much in line with my values and goals for ensuring the opportunity to understand and improve outcomes for disabled people in the housing area.

Since acquiring my spinal cord injury in 2017, I have embedded myself into the disability community of Aotearoa New Zealand. I have been happy to provide information and ideas for others seeking guidance and understanding in areas I have in-depth knowledge of, including income benefits, disability funding systems, housing modifications, and social housing options. My work history, including working in government agencies, has allowed me to understand legislation and policy and how these can influence decisions made about the needs of people. My ability to get people talking, interacting with other participants and asking follow-up questions has helped to connect people within the co-production team.

14.4.2 Susan's reflections about being involved in the process

Being part of the co-production team and then moving into a paid research assistant role has been challenging and fascinating, from learning the behind-the-scenes of research papers to coordinating group sessions and working with varying needs and requirements. While there are many areas that I could comment on, in this chapter I will focus on how the processes that co-produce policy recommendations need to consider the needs of disabled people.

Firstly, disabled people are time-poor, and flexibility is required. I have noticed that on top of the commitments that everyone has (i.e., work, family, pets, and household management), disabled people also have additional commitments and daily challenges, including an increased number of healthcare appointments, times when pain and fatigue or other health issues hinder participation, and support workers not turning up. They can also have less discretionary time due to many activities taking much longer because of adapted ways of doing them. All of this contributes to the complexity of committing to set days and times for group or one-on-one catch-ups. This makes me wonder if this adds to the reasons that disabled people are not always called upon to participate or why only some disabilities are represented in results (i.e., as seen in the literature review). Health was and is always going to be something to mitigate when working with disabled people. I always say that I have 'add-ons' to my disability, health issues that can and do pop up, life that gets in the way, fatigue that causes delays, etc. Understanding this and allowing the co-production team members to pop in and out of the process as needed was an important part of our process. Working in a time-poor environment with a co-production team needing extra time has encouraged us to be creative and provide as many participation options as possible. Having a range of different ways for the co-production team to engage with us was really important. While online group discussions offered at multiple times were appreciated by most, some preferred 1:1 sessions, and a few just wanted to send in their notes or thoughts and leave it at that.

Secondly, the need to ensure inclusion and accessibility for all – hearing all voices – was underscored. One of the biggest learnings related to the accessible qualitative survey we co-designed with the co-production team using the Accessible Survey platform (https://accessiblesurveys.com). The platform already provided accessibility features such as larger print, and screen reader friendliness with alternate colour palettes. However, we took extra time and provided additional resources to make easy-to-understand English, Te Reo (Māori language), and NZ Sign Language available in video, audio, and written versions. In terms of data collection, we also worked with the Accessible Surveys team to develop the ability for respondents to add audio data input options (i.e., voice memos) in addition to the existing audio and video file upload options. Nevertheless, the intellectual disability community still found the survey inaccessible. To make sure their voices were heard, research team members travelled to community group meetings to gather the data in their environment via conversations based around the survey questions and recording their responses for inclusion in the findings. The specific participation needs of those with intellectual disabilities left me wondering which other groups were missing and how we could have connected with them to ensure all networks, groups, organisations, and individuals in the disabled community are aware of and have a chance to have their voices heard in the project. It seemed particularly challenging to facilitate collaboration and full engagement across the range of organisations representing disabled people. Reflecting on this, it has been difficult to understand how and why the disabled community has become so segregated or siloed. I wonder how society will learn to become inclusive if our own disabled community is not fully inclusive and collaborative in how it supports people?

Thirdly, I became increasingly aware of internalised ableism within the co-production team. Self-criticism and self-doubt were frequently expressed by co-production team members, stopping them in their tracks when giving feedback or sharing their experiences and knowledge. I heard repeatedly, 'I am sorry I didn't or couldn't do more', 'I am not sure I understand that', or 'It was a bit too technical for me'. However, I also noticed that when the co-production team members were further encouraged to explore what they didn't understand, amazing gems of wisdom would emerge. At times, I wondered if the self-doubting was perhaps the feeling that we, as disabled people, are not an important part of anything; but, as people saw the value of their contributions, their confidence grew.

The previous point is linked to the fourth, concerning the resourcefulness of disabled people. When working with the co-production team, I was frequently reminded of the underestimated creativity, and untapped potential, in the disabled community. Disabled people frequently demonstrate resourcefulness in finding accommodations that work for them, are cost-effective, and result in quality solutions. Throughout the project, I noticed that questions and discussion points raised by the co-production team often left the wider research team wondering about possible solutions. To see seasoned researchers stumped about how to work through a solution was, as a disabled person, quite funny to watch. Comments often just made sense, such as, 'At one time in our life we will find ourselves being mobilised on a set of wheels – a stroller as a child, or a wheelchair or walker as we age', which provided a poignant moment in reinforcing the concept of entry-level access as a universal design requirement. Realising that disabled people often have the solutions and reasoning behind why things should be done in specific ways created a pivotal learning moment for me – a moment when I more fully considered the much bigger issue of how we get disabled people's stories, solutions, and ideas to the right people.

Fifthly, through the project, I have become increasingly aware of the required stance of researchers as learners. Researchers can gain valuable and significant insights when genuinely working with disabled people in ways that allow them to share their experiences and knowledge meaningfully. The differing perspectives – the what ifs and the whys discussed with the co-production team performing the literature review – have opened up a whole new research environment. Previous research findings were questioned for reasons our experienced researchers had never considered. For example, as a co-production team, we questioned whether research exploring the impact of housing modifications on community participation had been completed during summer or winter. While the season may not necessarily matter for non-disabled people, for disabled people it matters a lot! People who use wheelchairs for mobility find it harder to get out and about in wet, muddy seasons. Various factors also impact community participation, including illness, hospital stays, and other disability-related issues. Therefore, we argued the need to consider many factors when designing, delivering, and measuring the outcomes of programmes and policies impacting the disabled community.

Finally, due to my role in facilitating connections between the co-production team and the research team, I was very aware of the need to maintain engagement in the co-production processes, especially as timelines extended. Most projects have timelines, and there is always some flexibility required due to hold-ups or delays – and the Flourishing Together project was no different. We had long periods of little engagement with the co-production team while waiting for the project's next phase to happen. Overall, this meant there seemed to be insufficient time for the co-production team to complete their activities when asked to do so. My suggestion for future co-production work would be to build in more time to engage with the co-production team since this would lead to more insights, further understanding, and a greater overall picture of how kāinga, housing and home outcomes could be improved.

14.4.3 The importance of lived experience voices in policy spaces

Throughout my participation, I have become increasingly aware that there is a need to confront and challenge the status quo if lived experience-led and co-produced research can inform evidence-based disability policy measures. Developing more inclusive and accommodating policy processes for disabled people requires researchers and policymakers to re-look at their perceptions of what is normal, what can be done, and even how things *should* be done.

Creating policies and procedures without consulting stakeholders often results in inequitable or unrealistic outcomes. It is, therefore, essential to involve disabled people in co-designing processes to co-produce knowledge – and then co-develop policies about what will work best for the diverse needs and preferences of the disabled community. For example, in the literature review (Phase 3), we asked individuals with lived experience to read and comment on research papers and articles we could find relating to kāinga, housing and home. The co-production team found many gaps resulting from researchers not fully understanding the diversity of disability lived experience. Anyone experiencing disability will have different needs and abilities; therefore, having people who understand the diverse communities' needs is critical. However, even though each disabled person's needs differ, frequently common issues can be identified, and solutions can be created that meet the majority of needs. Therefore, there is a need for disabled voices to be included in policy development to counteract and offer alternative perspectives.

One reason why researchers and society may not fully understand the lived experiences of disabled people is because disabled people have been, and continue to be, less visible. A higher number of disabled people live on low incomes due to issues around lack of accessibility to suitable employment, societal attitudes, unconscious bias, and unaccommodating environments. Also, the individual's capacity to work while also living with disability may be constrained by ableism and unaccommodating or inaccessible environments that are designed for non-disabled people in society to flourish. These factors can lead to a reduced ability to participate fully in the community due to a lack of discretionary funds available to socialise and be involved in a full range of activities and roles, leading to society having a general lack of understanding of disabled people and their capabilities. Disabled people's ongoing challenges with navigating unaccommodating environments and participating fully, therefore, contribute to a lack of understanding of the policies needed to support positive change.

However, disabled people are often creative and excellent at problem-solving. They frequently can offer solutions to complex problems. In contrast, non-disabled people may have fixed ideas of what would work or a perception of what a person who is disabled can do. An individual who desires to participate in an activity will frequently find a way to make that happen; it may not look pretty, and it will often fall outside of the typical way of doing something, but the outcome of participation in the activity will be the same. It is about what works for an individual, but the end goal is the same, no matter how the task is completed. Therefore, disabled people frequently have an existing set of skills that support the development of creative, innovative, and often pragmatic policy solutions.

14.4.4 Reflections on co-designed disability research and co-produced policy development that is inclusive of disabled voices

Including disabled people in policymaking is crucial for creating equitable and effective policies. Disabled people have first-hand experience of the barriers they face in everyday life, and their insights are essential for crafting policies that address these challenges. Unless disabled and non-disabled people get together around a table, there is no chance for people to learn from each other, challenge their perceptions, and change their thought processes, as people do not know what they don't know! I also believe that the participation of disabled people in policymaking promotes a sense of ownership and empowerment within the disabled community. When disabled people are involved in shaping the policies that affect them, they are more likely to be invested in their success. This can lead to more effective implementation and better outcomes for everyone.

When I started, I was super green to research. When I was asked to join the team as a research assistant, I laughed, as I honestly thought it was a joke – I knew very little and felt I had nothing to bring to the table. However, I have learned so much from those around me – I now have insights into co-production methods, literature reviews, and writing. I still do not think of myself as a research assistant, but I am also proud of what I have been able to contribute and what has been achieved so far. My key learnings from this process are that you have to roll with it, adapt as needed, make tweaks to the process as things crop up, and have some fun with it.

Watching other disabled people engage in this process has been so valuable in learning what is and isn't helpful when co-producing with disabled people. Over the last year, I have witnessed a group of individuals who are now more connected, confident, and empowered. Giving disabled people a chance to be a part of a research project, to know that their voice was being heard and that they were appreciated for it, was an 'add-on' that was most welcomed.

There is no magic to what we created – we simply asked the disabled community to trust us, join us, and allow us to work out how we can involve disabled people more in co-creating policies that impact them. One thing to remember when working with a group of disabled people is that nothing will ever be 100% inclusive or 100% accessible, and definitely not 100% pretty. But I can assure you that you will learn a lot, have a lot of fun and laughter, and be encouraged by the new friends you have created during the process.

14.5 Implications for research and policy development that is inclusive of disabled voices

There are several key implications for the development of inclusive research and policy processes. First, relationships are fundamental, and relationship building takes time.

Secondly, disability experiences impact people in complex ways and, therefore, it is important to intentionally build flexibility into the processes from the outset. Thirdly, working alongside disabled people over time leads to tangible changes in their self-identified confidence and capability to share their knowledge and expertise. Fourthly, when co-producing knowledge to inform inclusive policies, careful thought should be given to *who* should be involved to ensure that power dynamics are fully considered. In this project, the disabled people have been the experts in housing experiences, and the research team had limited expertise, which was very helpful in equalising the power dynamic in terms of knowledge. Maybe policy experts are not the best at facilitating the co-production of knowledge alongside disabled people.

There are also several possible directions for ongoing policy development and/or research. Firstly, we would like to explore how policymakers interact with the housing and home knowledge co-produced by the co-production team. Specifically, is the knowledge synthesised in a way that is useful for policy formulation? We are also interested in the role of individual responses to help policymakers contextualise the co-produced recommendations in lived experience. Secondly, we would like to better understand if and how a group similar to the co-production team could function alongside a policy team in an ongoing way. Thirdly, we would like to research online tools for gathering disabled people's perspectives and allowing them to interact to develop more nuanced ideas and priorities. One possible tool is https://pol.is/home, a real-time system for gathering, analysing, and understanding what large groups of people think in their own words, enabled by advanced statistics and machine learning.

14.6 Conclusion

The Flourishing Together project has reinforced the importance of integrating disabled people's experiences into research and policy development and has supported a deeper understanding of and practical ideas for how policymaking should continue incorporating these experiences. However, as articulated by Susan, it is the role of non-disabled people to value what disabled people can contribute, and then be willing to enact co-production principles in the complexity of the everyday.

> I think a lot of researchers and policy advisors are too scared to get their hands dirty in this area. You know, they'll put in a disability advisor or something like that. But they won't actually do co-production or co-design or whatever words you want to use. They won't. They won't bring people on board. Basically, they don't know how to do it. I think we need to push how beneficial the ideas coming from the conversations are and highlight that there is untapped potential in the disability community. (Susan)

References

Baker, G. (2020, 19 June). Does the health and disability system review deliver for Māori. *The Spinoff.* https://thespinoff.co.nz/atea/19-06-2020/does-the-health-and-disability-system-review-report-deliver-for-maori/#:~:text=There%20are%20marked%2C%20persistent%2C%20inequities,and%20District%20Health%20Board%20data.&text=The%20health%20and%20disability%20system%20review%20panel%20has%20not%20shied,not%20meet%20its%20Treaty%20obligations

Bhattarai, J. J., Bentley, J., Morean, W., Wegener, S. T., & Pollack Porter, K. M. (2020). Promoting equity at the population level: Putting the foundational principles into practice through disability advocacy. *Rehabilitation Psychology.* https://doi.org/10.1037/rep0000321

Boulton, A., Allport, T., Kaiwai, H., Harker, R., & Potaka Osborne, G. (2022). Māori perceptions of 'home': Māori housing needs, wellbeing and policy. *Kotuitui, 17*(1), 44–55. https://doi.org/10.1080/1177083X.2021.1920984

Came, H., Mccreanor, T., Doole, C., & Rawson, E. (2016). The New Zealand Health Strategy 2016: Whither health equity? *NZMJ, 129*, 1447.

Chung, K. & Lounsbury, D. W. (2006). The role of power, process, and relationships in participatory research for statewide HIV/AIDS programming. *Social Science and Medicine*, 63(8), 2129–2140. https://doi.org/10.1016/j.socscimed.2006.04.035

Crompton, A. (2019). Inside co-production: Stakeholder meaning and situated practice. *Social Policy and Administration*, 53(2), 219–232. https://doi.org/10.1111/spol.12466

Donald Beasley Institute. (2022). My experiences, my rights: A monitoring report on disabled people's experiences of health and wellbeing in Aotearoa New Zealand. (Monitoring Long Report). New Zealand Disabled People's Organisations Coalition. https://www.donaldbeasley.org.nz/assets/publication-file/My-Experiences-My-Rights-A-Monitoring-Report-on-Disabled-Persons-Experience-of-Housing-in-Aotearoa-New-Zealand.pdf

Frier, A., Barnett, F., Devine, S., & Barker, R. (2018). Understanding disability and the 'social determinants of health': How does disability affect people's social determinants of health? *Disability and Rehabilitation, 40*(5), 538–547. https://doi.org/10.1080/09638288.2016.1258090

Gelech, J., Desjardins, M., Matthews, E., & Graumans, R. (2017). Why do working relationships not change? The need for a new approach to disability partnership research and social change. *Disability and Society, 32*(2), 176–192. https://doi.org/10.1080/09687599.2017.1281104

Goodyear-Smith, F., Jackson, C., & Greenhalgh, T. (2015). Co-design and implementation research: Challenges and solutions for ethics committees. In *BMC Medical Ethics, 16*(1). BioMed Central. https://doi.org/10.1186/s12910-015-0072-2

Graham, I. D., Kothari, A., McCutcheon, C., Alvarez, G., Banner, D., Botti, M., Bucknall, T., Botting, I., Considine, J., Duke, M., Dunn, S., Dunning, T., Gagliardi, A., Gainforth, H., Gifford, W., Harlos, K., Horsley, T., Hutchinson, A., Kastner, M., … & Tetroe, J. (2018). Moving knowledge into action for more effective practice, programmes and policy: Protocol for a research programme on integrated knowledge translation. *Implementation Science, 13*(1). https://doi.org/10.1186/s13012-017-0700-y

Graham, R. & Masters-Awatere, B. (2020). Experiences of Māori of Aotearoa New Zealand's public health system: A systematic review of two decades of published qualitative research. *Australian and New Zealand Journal of Public Health, 44*(3), 193–200. https://doi.org/10.1111/1753-6405.12971

Greenhalgh, T., Hinton, L., Finlay, T., Macfarlane, A., Fahy, N., Clyde, B., & Chant, A. (2019). Frameworks for supporting patient and public involvement in research: Systematic review and co-design pilot. *Health Expectations, 22*(4), 785–801. https://doi.org/10.1111/hex.12888

Greenhalgh, T., Jackson, C., Shaw, S., & Janamian, T. (2016). Achieving research impact through co-creation in community-based health services: Literature review and case study. *Milbank Quarterly*, *94*(2). https://doi.org/10.1111/1468-0009.12197

Harrison, J. D., Auerbach, A. D., Anderson, W., Fagan, M., Carnie, M., Hanson, C., Banta, J., Symczak, G., Robinson, E., Schnipper, J., Wong, C., & Weiss, R. (2019). Patient stakeholder engagement in research: A narrative review to describe foundational principles and best practice activities. In *Health Expectations*, *22*(3), 307–316. Blackwell Publishing Ltd. https://doi.org/10.1111/hex.12873

Head, B. W. (2016). Toward more 'evidence-informed' policy making? *Public Administration Review*, *76*(3), 472–484. https://doi.org/10.1111/puar.12475

Jagosh, J., Bush, P. L., Salsberg, J., Macaulay, A. C., Greenhalgh, T., Wong, G., Cargo, M., Green, L. W., Herbert, C. P., & Pluye, P. (2015). A realist evaluation of community-based participatory research: Partnership synergy, trust building and related ripple effects. *BMC Public Health*, *15*(1). https://doi.org/10.1186/s12889-015-1949-1

Jull, J., Giles, A., & Graham, I. D. (2017). Community-based participatory research and integrated knowledge translation: Advancing the co-creation of knowledge. *Implementation Science*, *12*(1). https://doi.org/10.1186/s13012-017-0696-3

King, P. T. (2019). WAI 2575, #B22. Māori With Lived Experience of Disability Part I, Wellington: Waitangi Tribunal. https://forms.justice.govt.nz/search/Documents/WT/wt_DOC_150437272/Wai%202575%2C%20B022.pdf

Kuchenmüller, T., Boeira, L., Oliver, S., Moat, K., El-Jardali, F., Barreto, J., & Lavis, J. (2022). Domains and processes for institutionalizing evidence-informed health policy-making: A critical interpretive synthesis. In *Health Research Policy and Systems*, *20*(1). BioMed Central Ltd. https://doi.org/10.1186/s12961-022-00820-7

Lamont, R., Fishman, T., Sanders, P. F., 'ofanoa, M., & Goodyear-Smith, F. (2020). View from the canoe: Co-designing research pacific style. *Annals of Family Medicine*, *18*(2), 172–175. https://doi.org/10.1370/afm.2497

Langley, J., Kayes, N., Gwilt, I., Snelgrove-Clarke, E., Smith, S., & Craig, C. (2022). Exploring the value and role of creative practices in research co-production. *Evidence & Policy*, 1–13. https://doi.org/10.1332/174426421x16478821515272

Langley, J., Wolstenholme, D., & Cooke, J. (2018). 'Collective making' as knowledge mobilisation: The contribution of participatory design in the co-creation of knowledge in healthcare. In *BMC Health Services Research*, *18*(1). BioMed Central Ltd. https://doi.org/10.1186/s12913-018-3397-y

MacLachlan, M., Young Cho, H., Clarke, M., Mannan, H., Kayabu, B., Ludolph, R., & McAuliffe, E. Web. (2018). Annex F: Report of the systematic review on potential benefits of accessible home environments for people with functional impairments. In *WHO Housing and Health Guidelines*. World Health Organization, Geneva, Switzerland. https://www.ncbi.nlm.nih.gov/books/NBK535292/

Magnusson, D., Eisenhart, M., Gorman, I., Kennedy, V., & Todd, E. (2019). Adopting population health frameworks in physical therapist practice, research, and education: The urgency of now. *Physical Therapy*, *99*(8), 1039–1047. https://academic.oup.com/ptj/article-abstract/99/8/1039/5420521

Martin, R. A., Baker, A. P., Smiler, K., Middleton, L., Hay-Smith, J., Kayes, N., Grace, C., Apiata, T. A. M., Nunnerley, J. L., & Brown, A. E. (2022). Flourishing together: Research protocol for developing methods to better include disabled people's knowledge in health policy development. *BMC Health Services Research*, *22*(1). https://doi.org/10.1186/s12913-022-08655-2

Mccoll, M. A., Jarzynowska, A., & Shortt, S. E. D. (2010). Unmet health care needs of people with disabilities: Population level evidence. *Disability and Society*, *25*(2), 205–218. https://doi.org/10.1080/09687590903537406

Mcintosh, J. & Leah, A. (2017). Mapping housing for the disabled in New Zealand. *NZMJ*, *16*, 1457. https://www.msd.govt.nz/about-msd-and-our-work/work-programmes/disability-system-transformation/enabling-good-lives.html

Micsinszki, S. K., Buettgen, A., Mulvale, G., Moll, S., Wyndham-West, M., Bruce, E., Rogerson, K., Murray-Leung, L., Fleisig, R., Park, S., & Phoenix, M. (2021). Creative processes in co-designing a co-design hub: Towards system change in health and social services in collaboration with structurally vulnerable populations. *Evidence & Policy*, 1–20. https://doi.org/10.1332/174426421x16366319768599

Ministry of Health. (2018). Whāia Te Ao Mārama 2018 to 2022: The Māori Disability Action Plan. Wellington: Ministry of Health. https://www.health.govt.nz/publications/whaia-te-ao-marama-2018-to-2022-the-maori-disability-action-plan

Ministry of Social Development. (n.d.). Enabling Good Lives (EGL). https://www.msd.govt.nz/about-msd-and-our-work/work-programmes/disability-system-transformation/enabling-good-lives.html

Mulvale, G., Miatello, A., Green, J., Tran, M., Roussakis, C., & Mulvale, A. (2021). A COMPASS for navigating relationships in co-production processes involving vulnerable populations. *International Journal of Public Administration*, *44*(9), 790–802. https://doi.org/10.1080/01900692.2021.1903500

Murray, S. (2019). *The State of Wellbeing and Equality for Disabled People, their Families, and Whānau*. https://www.ccsdisabilityaction.org.nz/news/state-of-wellbeing-2021

New Zealand Disability Network. (2020). *Enabling Good Lives Sooner Rather Than Later. Where To From Here? A Sector Briefing*. https://nzdsn.org.nz/wp-content/uploads/2020/06/NZDSN-2020-Sector-Briefing-Final-19-11-2019-1.pdf

New Zealand. Ministry of Health. (n.d.). *A Guide to Community Engagement with People with Disabilities*. https://www.health.govt.nz/publications/a-guide-to-community-engagement-with-people-with-disabilities

New Zealand. Statistics New Zealand. (2013). *Disability Survey, 2013*. https://www.stats.govt.nz/information-releases/disability-survey-2013/

Ní Shé, É., Cassidy, J., Davies, C., de Brún, A., Donnelly, S., Dorris, E., Dunne, N., Egan, K., Foley, M., Galvin, M., Harkin, M., Killilea, M., Kroll, T., Lacey, V., Lambert, V., McLoughlin, S., Mitchell, D., Murphy, E., Mwendwa, P., … & O'Philbin, L. (2020). Minding the gap: Identifying values to enable public and patient involvement at the pre-commencement stage of research projects. *Research Involvement and Engagement*, *6*(1). https://doi.org/10.1186/s40900-020-00220-7

Oliver, K., Kothari, A., & Mays, N. (2019). The dark side of coproduction: Do the costs outweigh the benefits for health research? In *Health Research Policy and Systems*, *17*(1). BioMed Central Ltd. https://doi.org/10.1186/s12961-019-0432-3

Ottmann, G., Laragy, C., & Damonze, G. (2009). Consumer participation in designing community based consumer-directed disability care: Lessons from a participatory action research-inspired project. *Systemic Practice and Action Research*, *22*(1), 31–44. https://doi.org/10.1007/s11213-008-9110-z

Palmer, S. C., Gray, H., Huria, T., Lacey, C., Beckert, L., & Pitama, S. G. (2019). Reported Māori consumer experiences of health systems and programs in qualitative research: A systematic review with meta-synthesis. *International Journal for Equity in Health*, *18*(1). https://doi.org/10.1186/s12939-019-1057-4

Phillips, L., Christensen-Strynø, M. B., & Frølunde, L. (2022). Arts-based co-production in participatory research: Harnessing creativity in the tension between process and product. *Evidence & Policy, 18*(2), 391–411. https://doi.org/10.1332/174426421X16445103995426

Rose, D. & Kalathil, J. (2019). Power, privilege and knowledge: The untenable promise of co-production in mental 'health'. *Frontiers in Sociology, 4*. https://doi.org/10.3389/fsoc.2019.00057

Saran, A., White, H., & Kuper, H. (2020). Evidence and gap map of studies assessing the effectiveness of interventions for people with disabilities in low- and middle-income countries. *Campbell Systematic Reviews, 16*(1), e1070. https://doi.org/10.1002/cl2.1070

Smith, B., Williams, O., Bone, L., & Collective, the M. S. W. C. Production. (2022). Co-production: A resource to guide co-producing research in the sport, exercise, and health sciences. In *Qualitative Research in Sport, Exercise and Health*. Routledge. https://doi.org/10.1080/2159676X.2022.2052946

Te Tiriti o Waitangi [Māori version], 6 February 1840.

Tilley, E. (2020, 28 June). Opinion: Health is health, disability support is disability support. *RNZ*. https://www.rnz.co.nz/news/on-the-inside/420009/opinion-health-is-health-disability-support-is-disability-support

United Nations. (2006). Convention on the Rights of Persons with Disabilities. United Nations Treaty Series. https://social.desa.un.org/issues/disability/crpd/convention-on-the-rights-of-persons-with-disabilities-crpd

WHO Commission on Social Determinants of Health, & World Health Organization. (2008). *Closing the Gap in a Generation: Health Equity through Action on the Social Determinants of Health*. World Health Organization, Commission on Social Determinants of Health. https://iris.who.int/bitstream/handle/10665/43943/9789241563703_eng.pdf

Williams, O., Sarre, S., Papoulias, S. C., Knowles, S., Robert, G., Beresford, P., Rose, D., Carr, S., Kaur, M., & Palmer, V. J. (2020). Lost in the shadows: Reflections on the dark side of co-production. In *Health Research Policy and Systems, 18*(1). BioMed Central Ltd. https://doi.org/10.1186/s12961-020-00558-0

Wyeth, E. H., Samaranayaka, A., Lambert, M., Tapsell, M., Anselm, D., Ellison, P., Harwood, M., Metzger, B., Wright-Tawha, T., & Derrett, S. (2019). Understanding longer-term disability outcomes for Māori and non-Māori after hospitalisation for injury: Results from a longitudinal cohort study. *Public Health, 176*, 118–127. https://doi.org/10.1016/j.puhe.2018.08.014

Index